# Cultural Moves

AMERICAN CROSSROADS

Edited by Earl Lewis, George Lipsitz, Peggy Pascoe, George Sánchez, and Dana Takagi

# Cultural Moves

*African Americans and the Politics
of Representation*

Herman S. Gray

UNIVERSITY OF CALIFORNIA PRESS
*Berkeley · Los Angeles · London*

Chapter 1 appeared as "The New Conditions of Black Cultural Production, Or Prefiguring of a Black Cultural Formation," in *Between Law and Culture: Relocating Legal Studies*, ed. L.C. Bower, D.T. Goldberg, and M. Musheno (University of Minnesota Press, 2001). Chapter 2 appeared as "Jazz Tradition, Institutional Formation, and Cultural Practice: The Canon and the Street as Frameworks for Oppositional Black Cultural Politics," in *From Sociology to Cultural Studies*, ed. Elizabeth Long (Blackwell, 1997). Chapter 4 appeared as "Black Representation in the Post Network, Post Civil Rights World of Global Media," in *Race, Racism, and the Mass Media*, ed. Simon Cottle (Open University Press, 2001). Parts of chapter 6 appeared as "A Different Dream of Difference" in *Critical Studies in Mass Communication* (December 1999). Chapter 7 appeared as "Cultural Politics as Outrage(ous)" in *Renaissance Noire*, vol. 2, no. 1 (2000).

University of California Press
Berkeley and Los Angeles, California

University of California Press, Ltd.
London, England

Library of Congress Cataloging-in-Publication Data

Gray, Herman, 1950–
    Cultural moves : African Americans and the politics of representation / Herman S. Gray.
        p. cm.—(American crossroads ; 15)
Summary: "Examines the importance of culture in the push for black political power and social recognition and argues the key black cultural practices have been notable in reconfiguring the shape and texture of social and cultural life in the U.S. Drawing on examples from jazz, television, and academia, Gray highlights cultural strategies for inclusion in the dominant culture as well as cultural tactics that move beyond the quest for mere recognition by challenging, disrupting, and unsettling dominant cultural representations and institutions. In the end, Gray challenges the conventional wisdom about the centrality of representation and politics in black cultural production."—Provided by publisher.
    Includes bibliographical references and index.
    ISBN 0-520-23374-3 (cloth : alk. paper).—ISBN 0-520-24144-4 (pbk. : alk. paper)
    1. African Americans on television.   2. African Americans—Songs and music—History and criticism.   I. Title. II. Series.

PN1992.8.A34G68  2005
791.45′652996073—dc22

                                                                              2004022297

Manufactured in the United States of America
14   13   12   11   10   09   08   07   06   05
10   9   8   7   6   5   4   3   2   1

Printed on Ecobook 50 containing a minimum 50% post-consumer waste, processed chlorine free. The balance contains virgin pulp, including 25% Forest Stewardship Council Certified for no old growth tree cutting, processed either TCF or ECF. The sheet is acid-free and meets the minimum requirements of ANSI/NISO Z39.48-1992 (R 1997) (Permanence of Paper).

# Contents

# Acknowledgments

Work on this book was supported through the generosity of the Rockefeller Foundation and the Bellagio Conference and Study Center; the University of California Humanities Research Institute at University of California, Irvine; and the Division of Social Science at the University of California, Santa Cruz.

Many generous and amazing people contributed in large and small ways to the realization of this book. For their wise counsel, critical insight, sustaining friendship, and so many "bright moments" over the years, a thousand thanks to Earl Lewis, George Lipsitz, Peggy Pascoe, George Sánchez, and Dana Takagi, editors at University of California Press for the American Crossroads series; Barbara Abrash, Charles Amerkanian, Daphane Brooks, Cheryl Brown, Leonard Brown, John T. Caldwell, Richard Campbell, John Brown Childs, Jim Clifford, Steve Coleman, Jon Cruz, Michael Curtin, Angela Davis, Gina Dent, Manthia Diawara, David Eason, Harry Elam, Steven Feld, Raul Fernandez, Andrew Frisardi, David T. Goldberg, Robert Goldman, Jennifer Gonzales, Gayatri Gopinath, Larry Gross, Ed Guererro, Jocelyn Guilbault, Beth Haas, Michelle Habel-Pallen, Bambi Haggins, Craig Haney, Michael Hansen, John Hartley, Randy Heyman, Melessa Hemler, Darnell Hunt, Aida Hurtado, Robin D. G. Kelley, L. S. Kim, Valerie Kuletz, Josh Kun, George Lewis, Elizabeth Long, Chip Lord, Tommy L. Lott, James Lull, Anthony Macias, Toby Miller, David Morley, Monica McCormick, Jim Neumann, the Oakland Museum of California, Michael Omi, Kent

Ono, Other Minds, Lesleigh Owen, Armando Pena, Rene Tajima-Pena, Eric Porter, Lourdes Portillo, B. Ruby Rich, Art Sato, Mary Severance, Lynn Spigel, Clyde Taylor, Sasha Torres, Gayle Wald, Mary Helen Washington, David Wellman, Clark White, Richard Yarborough, and Pamela Z.

At the invitation of many generous colleagues, I presented papers, gave talks, and exchanged ideas about cultural politics in many places, near and far to home. Thanks to colleagues and students at the following institutions for a warm welcome and critical engagement with my work: the Graduate Program in American Studies at Indiana University; African American Studies at University of California, Irvine; School of Mass Communication at Middle Tennessee State University; California College of Arts and Crafts; Chicano Latino Research Center at UCSC; American Studies Program, Canterbury University, Christchurch, New Zealand; Center for Media, Culture, and History, New York University; Institute for the Study of Social Change, UC Berkeley; Department of English Pamona College; UCLA School of Theater, Film and Television; Casa de America, Madrid; Institute for Future Studies and the Critical Studies Program, School of Cinema, University of Southern California; Center for 21st Century Studies, University of Wisconsin, Milwaukee; Ethnic Studies Department, University of California, San Diego; Center for Advanced Studies, Stanford University; School of Justice Studies, Arizona State University.

The influences of present and former students with whom I've worked over the years are evident in this work in ways that I hope they will recognize. My thanks to Barbara Barnes, Delia Douglas, Jennifer Eichstedt, Michelle Erai, Kevin Fellez, Lynn Fujiwara, Sarita Gaytan, Macarena Gómez-Barris, April Henderson, Needra James, Cindy Lui, Dacia Mitchell, Sudarat Musikawong, Akiko Naono, Celine Pascale, Tammy Ko Robinson, Russell Rodriguez, Rebecca Scott, Aaron Selverston, Inger Stark, Robert Thompson, Deborah Vargas, Eddie Yuen.

Finally, thanks to my parents for their commitment to social justice. Thank you, Xochi, for your courage, Jas for your joy, Sergio for your determination, and Rosa Linda for your love and example.

*Herman Gray*
*Oakland, California*
*September 2003*

# Introduction

*Strategies, Tactics, Moves*

In Norman Lear's hit television show from the 1970s, *All in the Family,* there is a memorable moment when Edith—wife of the show's lead character, Archie Bunker—quips that blacks certainly have "come a long way, on television." Edith, and Norman Lear, may have been prescient. Twenty years later, in another televisual moment, Regina, the black woman who works as the maid of a prominent Southern family, a leading character in the dramatic series *I'll Fly Away,* talks intensely with one of the family's sons about his apparent inability to see her. After the boy has apologized to Regina for being brash and insensitive, Regina responds with a polite but firm "reading" of the young white man: she tells the youngster, in effect, that he doesn't know her, that he can't know her—in other words, that *she* is *invisible* to *him.* (The scene implies that a source of Regina's invisibility is the son's constellation of privileges: middle-class, white, and male.)

In relationship to Edith's claims about black televisual progress, I want to call attention to the fact that the exchange itself is emblematic of the distance traveled by black representation on television. In other words, in a dramatic liberal gesture, to acknowledge black invisibility on a television show whose topic is the struggle of blacks for visibility— ostensibly the Southern phase of the American civil rights movement— is to acknowledge the *presence* of blackness in the national imagination.

If one takes even a cursory tour through America's commercial image culture—television, cable, cinema, advertising, the Internet, music, news, sports, politics, intellectual discourse—one can easily find African American representations (the quality and types of representations is a separate question). The distance between *All in the Family*'s attention to black progress on television and *I'll Fly Away*'s concern with black invisibility is notable.

At first glance (and for conservatives who claim we've achieved a color-blind America, this is more than a passing point), it might seem that representations of African Americans are everywhere. So a scene that could play thirty years ago on *All in the Family*, as a recognizable joke and a trenchant critique of television and media for their dismal record when it comes to black presence and visibility, might not be recognizable to today's television audiences. Given the international visibility of African Americans in commercial arenas like hip-hop and sports, Regina's admonition to the young white Southerner seems dated, and Edith Bunker's observation about black televisual progress seems, well, like something we can take for granted.

And yet, media activists and cultural critics continue to monitor, boycott, and occasionally negotiate with arbiters and image makers about black visibility and representation. What gives? How do we make sense of the proliferation of black images and representation in American commercial and popular culture, and the continued dissatisfaction with and calls for more images of black people in media and popular culture? Is the problem the images themselves or the racism of the cultural producers? And what of this desire for more images? More images of what, exactly? Of what we now have? More images that more positively and satisfyingly represent blackness? More realistic representation? Perhaps the problem is less with specific images than with the investment in a conception of cultural politics that continues to privilege representation itself as the primary site of hope and critique.

*Cultural Moves* questions conventional assumptions about recognition and visibility, and, especially, assumptions about African American investment in representation as a route to African American membership in national culture. In this book, I focus on the assumptions, social contexts, and conditions of possibility that produced the desire for visibility and representation (and the political moves they engender). I ask whether such conditions still hold in the new century. I use art exhibits, television shows, debates about the jazz canon, the cultural practices of musical collectives, and discourses about technology and identity to survey, monitor, and search for disturbances, even rejections of conventional assumptions, goals, and approaches to questions of representation and black presence in mainstream media, culture, and politics.[1] This book is an investigation into the shape, shifts, and effects of black struggles over identity, recognition, and representation. I illustrate as amply as I can, and appraise as critically as possible, enduring black investments in political (the civil rights movement) and cultural (canonical) projects that continue powerfully to allure black collective imagination, at the heart of which are deep investments in the politics of representation. Above all, I try to show that projects, which result in the successful assertion, accumulation, and defense of cultural representations by African Americans, while occasionally myopic and exclusive, are also crucial political moves against racism and white supremacy, sexism, and class inequality. At the same time, I remain watchful for and critical of stubborn forms of ethnic absolutism, racial nationalism, sexism, and homophobia that may still enjoy wide appeal at the level of culture and representation.

Inasmuch as my quest in *Cultural Moves* is to identify and examine cultural strategies that emphasize struggles for black recognition, I also discuss cultural tactics and organizations that move beyond mere recognition to challenge, disrupt, and unsettle dominant cultural representations and institutions.[2] I do this by asking how and where different and sometimes unsettling alternative visions, practices, and forms of organization operate, and with what cultural and political effect. I explore black self-representation and collective self-fashioning in music, visual arts, broadcast television, and new information technologies in search of leads into how particular cultural maneuvers and practices move beyond cultural politics preoccupied solely with inclusion, representation, and identity.

In short, the book's chapters move widely across different black cultural forms and practices to grasp how *culture matters politically and how politics matter culturally*. I am especially critical of traditionalism, fundamentalism, nationalism, and, most especially, romantic cultural politics offered in the name of a marginal and beleaguered blackness. Such narrow political and cultural ideas about blackness (born of cultural maneuver in the latter quarter of the twentieth century) are, I argue, too often organized by myopic (and often self-righteous) conceptions of what does and doesn't count as black culture, black representation, and (in some cases) black people.

*Cultural Moves* is concerned, as well, with media, commodification, and technology as social forces and circumstances structuring the conditions of possibility within which black cultural politics are enacted, constrained, and mediated.[3] (Commodified) representations of American blackness circulate widely via mass media and popular culture, achieving in the process some measure of global visibility, influence, admiration, imitation, or scorn. From New Zealand to Sweden, from Japan to Mexico, black popular music and culture exerts a recognizable influence on visions (and, in some cases, practices) of different cultural, social, and political selves and communities. The cultural politics that enable these visions of possibility are what specifically interest me about how blackness is commodified and circulates, disrupting and threatening, domesticating and reorganizing social and cultural relations, as it touches down, is taken up, disarticulated, and redeployed in different locations.[4]

## CULTURAL MANEUVER AND INSTITUTIONAL FORMATION

I take the strategic interventions by composer and trumpeter Wynton Marsalis at the Lincoln Center as a starting point for exploring some of the cultural politics involved in mobilizing race, organizational networks, and aesthetics as strategic resources with which to "actively construct" jazz as a discursive object of serious institutional attention and investment. The highly prized recognition and legitimacy that drive the search for such institutional investment, of course, yield certain social, cultural, and economic gains. It is this very yield, this social, cultural, and economic capital, that has forced me to expand my notion of cultural politics, to dwell more seriously on institutional relations of power and culture. In my estimation, Marsalis and his supporters understood the political importance of establishing institutional recognition and legitimacy, if jazz were to be taken seriously as a cultural object with a permanent institutional status and resources. Marsalis's cultural move at Lincoln Center is significant because it demonstrates a different and more sophisticated level of cultural understanding and politics than simply rehearsing old debates about musical style, positive representations, or whether or not jazz should be showcased at one of American's premier cultural institutions. My contention is that the cultural and political struggle for the institutional recognition of jazz at Lincoln Center is, above all, a strategic maneuver, one defined as much by the terrain of culture as by organizational and economic issues and stakes.

The political and cultural rearticulation of dominant cultural spaces like Lincoln Center is by no means the only significant cultural move (even if it has been one of the most visible and widely covered in the press) in black cultural politics since the 1990s. To take the example of jazz once again, a different group of cultural workers is also engaged in significant cultural practices, in this case at specifically local levels— music teachers, marching band directors, high school choir leaders, and performers in local venues that include dances, churches, and civic organizations. At these levels of cultural practice, black artists and cultural workers of all sorts are involved in the less glamorous but certainly no less consequential work of struggling for resources, training a new generation of musicians, exposing new audiences to black music, and thereby enacting and reproducing the jazz tradition. Following clarinetist and composer Don Byron, I call this model of local cultural practice, and the politics that enable it, *the jazz left*.

I use the concept of the jazz left in two ways: (1) to describe jazz styles and approaches that remain to the left (and therefore often on the margins) of the mainstream; (2) to designate those practices that operate outside of and beyond the institutional and aesthetic orbit of dominant cultural centers of power and authority like the Lincoln Center, PBS, and the *New York Times*. The concept of the jazz left then serves as an alternative point of entry for exploring the cultural politics surrounding the practice, recognition, and reproduction of jazz; different, that is, from the cultural politics and social practices enacted at recognized mainstream cultural organizations and institutions. The issues that I address in my elaboration of the jazz left are, in many respects, similar to those that frame my analysis of the cultural moves at Lincoln Center: How do musicians associated with this formation define their practice? What is their conception of the jazz tradition, and what is the role of that tradition in relationship to their own practices and struggles for recognition and legitimacy?[5] What kind of networks and forms of social organization do they generate to effectively sustain their practice as musicians and their aesthetic and political visions? What sorts of maneuvers for resources, recognition, and legitimacy do these cultural producers practice?

Rather than trying to make a case for such black cultural moves as the expression of some predetermined resistance whose politics are always already finished, I try to make sense of these internal tensions, to understand what they mean for cultural struggle. I argue for approaching cultural politics in terms of the fits and starts, the indeterminacy, and unanticipated consequences that define the complex cultural and social field within which such disputes occur and take on meaning.

VISIBILITY AND RECOGNITION IN THE POST–CIVIL RIGHTS
AND POSTNETWORK ERA

The second section of *Cultural Moves* considers problems of visibility
and recognition, especially the role of commercial network television in
the production of black subjects after the civil rights movement and in
the context of major transformations in the structure of the global media,
information, and entertainment. I interrogate the assumption of a cultural politics still committed to recognition, representativeness, and
inclusion in a (changing) media-scape and public sphere that no longer
organizes national identity. More specifically, I inquire into the changing
industrial structure and semiotic operation of American network television, most notably our cultural understanding of the "network" as a ritual space for the production of the nation, particularly black inclusion
and visibility through televisual representation.[6] These queries, in turn,
lead me to quarrel with the persistent (cultural) desire for black cultural
inclusion and representativeness in commercial network television, the
(social) nature of black social subjects constructed by industrial, journalistic, academic, and activist discourses, and the presumed (political)
efficacy of network television as the central object of media activism on
issues of cultural difference. Using the example of the "media brownout"
in the summer of 1999, I try to show how the persistent focus of black
cultural and media activism on commercial network television's representation (or lack of representation) of blacks, though still crucial, is
somewhat myopic, and why a cultural politics that neglects profound
transformations in the structure of global media and information technologies will at best produce limited political results. Any cultural politics of blackness concerned with media and representation will notice the
incorporation and aggressive global marketing of cultural difference by
media conglomerates. Some have noted that this strategy is but the latest stage in the cultural logic of capitalism, while others see it as an
expression of ongoing changes in the conception and operation of the
nation, and, perhaps just as importantly, in the role of culture and representation in the production of the nation.[7] My chief assertion is that
American commercial television networks are no longer the primary sites
of mass-mediated theater and performance of the nation, where national
identity—the sense of belonging to and connecting with the nation—is
produced, secured, and maintained through crafting homogeneity from
difference. While the networks certainly remain vitally important, I
nonetheless argue against their continued primacy as a site of cultural
struggle for representation and inclusion. These conditions, I suggest,

also strike at the very core of contemporary debates about black representation and black images: who speaks, who represents, and so on.

Black cultural politics in the United States must reckon, too, with changes in the structure of the media, issues of local politics, global movements of representation, the internationalization (Americanization) of media, and the recognition of difference globally. This is a delicate balancing act, and one, I contend, that offers as many possibilities as it does pitfalls. As with myopic constructs of the nation and the network as the site of cultural contestation, a cultural politics that assumed a central, stable, even national public sphere or coherent blackness is, I believe, no longer tenable. In the post–civil rights and postnetwork era, black cultural politics must reckon with the shifting means of representation, the changing meanings of black representation, and how signs, history, and political economy structure and mediate these meanings. In the context of globalization and the new cultural logic of difference, media and television provide the examples with which I critically engage long-standing assumptions about media politics, surely one of the most hallowed and enduring sites of cultural maneuver in black cultural politics.

This quarrel in turn leads me to questions of aesthetics and visibility, which I take up through the art of Kara Walker, whose works and the cultural moves they enact disturb conventional thinking about black visibility in late-twentieth-century America. My interests in Walker and other artist of her generation are not just with questions of aesthetic judgments and their relationship to cultural politics. As with the case of Marsalis and the Lincoln Center, my interest in the debates and reactions to Kara Walker has to do with questions of visibility, credibility, and legitimacy that are crystallized by disputes over blackness in dominant institutions of representation (e.g., critical scholarly debates, mass media, museums). "The politics of outrage" stages these concerns by detailing and conceptually framing the strong reaction to Walker's work by members of the black art world, as well as the celebrations of her from the "white" arts establishment. Chapter 7 details the contemporary social and cultural contexts of reactions to Walker and contemplates the system (and assignment) of value that designates some work as meaningful and worth celebrating while marking others as unsettling or dangerous. By placing Walker's work in the context of early-twenty-first-century mass-mediated representations in cinema, television, music, and parody, I aim, at the very least, for an understanding of the deep stakes, generational divides, and strategic moves signaled by this controversy. Considering the depth of passion evoked by the polemic, the debates about

Walker's complex and wide-ranging—parodic, playful, even prurient—treatment of slavery, I propose that the response might be understood culturally and politically as a *move* by those offended to otherwise contest, excise, and even repress the historical legacy of black debasement. Ironically, as Walker's work (and her performative staging of it) shows, images of black debasement and abjection were made widely visible and accessible to audiences through forms of mass-mediated representations and popular culture.[8] Because popular representation and memory constitute the highly charged and unstable terrain on which Walker and members of her generation have elected to disarticulate and rearticulate claims for black expressive culture, they expose the complicity and possibly even a libratory role for popular culture and representation in black cultural politics.[9]

## CULTURAL MOVES: BLACK CULTURAL POLITICS

The relationship (or lack of one) between new technologies and the cultural politics of identity animates the final section of *Cultural Moves*. Because of the pervasiveness and prominence of this relationship in the media, there is increasing cultural and social traffic across the discursive borders of race and technology, identity, and information. Despite the quickening pace of this traffic between technology and cultural identity, many of the exchanges still center on questions of privacy and access, and on the growing inequalities for the socially disenfranchised and economically marginalized.

In academic and social policy discourse, for example, the issues of subjectivity, identity, space, and mobility have exploded in recent years, but this discourse, as many critics note, assumes a white male subject. By the same token, in identity discourse that has to do with blackness and representations of black Atlantic diasporic communities, serious discussion about new information and communication technology, and its implications for issues of identity, is often secondary to preoccupations with visibility in Hollywood cinema and commercial network television. In conventional news media coverage of new information and communications technologies, where the issue of race is concerned, industry leaders (and, in some cases, scholars) stress the need for computer literacy, access, and the integrative functions of these technologies for more efficient administrative and consumer needs.[10] One narrative in this coverage depicts politicians and activists, like Jesse Jackson of the Rainbow Coalition, pressuring technology business and industry leaders for assurance that appropriate hardware, infrastructure, and resources for connecting to the information superhighway are available to the poor.[11] What social interest these issues do generate comes from the emerging market potential for the business community, political expedience, and utopian dreams of endless communication and consumer sovereignty, and from the prospect of moving beyond identity, of transcending local and embodied concerns with race and gender difference. These utopian possibilities (and the desires on which they are based) raise a crucial question about inequality, privilege, power, and difference: for whom would such changes take place and at what social cost? Regardless, a good deal of the new technology and information discourse is framed by corporate interests and is therefore concerned with extending market control, consolidating economic expansion, and exercising global domination in the name of better consumer services and endless choice.[12] Although this corporate discourse of control is not always explicit, it is narrated and thus accessible via consumer-friendly representations of the new technologies (and the implicit conception of its ideal subjects). Where there is talk about culture, tradition, and identity (in the press and in technology industry discourse), it is framed largely in terms of managing and controlling any social and political impediments to growth that may come with it.[13] Much of the utopian celebration of new technologies is pitched in the name of better and more efficient consumption and business services, even while it is aimed at gaining control of global infrastructure, hardware, and finance.[14]

By considering the relationship between identity (in this case blackness) and new technology, I aim to place these two discourses in closer critical dialogue, emphasizing, most of all, the implication of the new information technology for the cultural politics of blackness. In "Is (Cyber) Space the Place?" (chapter 8), I question the implicit ideal that the default position of the new technology discourse (with its primary emphasis on business infrastructure) is automatically (and permanently) set to celebrate difference as nothing more than a consumer market niche. That new information technology, like the Internet, will ensure color blindness, or that it will accelerate multiple and shifting identities, making them (in the world of cyberspace) more pervasive (as the basis of consumer choice) and less significant (as the basis for social equality), is what I find intriguing. Ferreting out the terms and logic of this increasingly conventional understanding is my aim in this section of the book.

Since this book examines different kinds of moves or encounters between the technology and identity, it gives culture a more primary role (at least in relation to political economy and technology). Thus, I venture deeper into the world of cultural practices and moves by looking to African American music for productive engagements, historical examples, and imaginative possibilities for thinking critically about the relationship between cultural identity and technology.

In "Music, Identity, and New Technology" (chapter 9), for example, I examine black musical practice for some of the innovative ways in which black performance artists, musicians, and composers productively negotiate the technological possibilities of representation and the modes of information transfer, storage, and retrieval, while locating their work within an explicitly African American cultural framework. I focus specifically on the creative work of composers and performers George Lewis, Pamela Z, and Steve Coleman, because these musicians, among others, effectively use the new technologies to innovate and extend ways of imagining black cultural traditions. Rather than evading the questions of identity, culture, and race, composers and performers as wide-ranging as Sun Ra, Herbie Hancock, George Russell, and Muhal Richard Abrams use technologies of sound, notation, storage, and retrieval to explore the soundings of African American culture and identity. Along with these seminal figures, I also consider the critical commentary and work of Afro-futurists, the vibrant and influential culture of djs, turntable artists, novelists, and cultural critics who work intimately with new technologies and are committed to expanding and extending cultural notions of blackness. These artists enthusiastically insist on the possibilities of the new technologies for imagining their black selves and their worlds differently.

As I set forth in the concluding chapter, "Cultural Moves," I see this work as an argument for the centrality of culture as a political terrain that matters. The chapters in this book consider practices and enactments of cultural politics that sacrifice neither culture nor politics but appreciate the necessity and the imperative of maneuver and tactic in black cultural politics. If it is to continue to *move* effectively and productively, contemporary black cultural politics must get beyond the nostalgic paradigms and moral panics about representation, inclusion, and the threats of technology (and their impact on issues of cultural authenticity and identity). Indeed, rather than moral panics and entrenched cultural fundamentalism, the chapters in *Cultural Moves* encourage vibrant black cultural maneuvers and practices that see, imagine, and engage the world differently, in all of its complexity and myriad possibilities.

PART I

# Strategies

# CHAPTER 1

# The New Conditions of Black Cultural Production

At the start of the twenty-first century, it is clear that black intellectuals, filmmakers, musicians, choreographers, playwrights, and novelists are profoundly shaping the imagination of American culture. What may distinguish this moment is the recognition by the cultural dominant of the sheer influence and pervasiveness of black presence in mainstream American culture. In the language of Raymond Williams, this recognition and influence approach the rudiments of an institutional formation.[1] The institutionalization of black cultural production, especially the reach of its cultural influence, is taking place in a post–civil rights period of global corporate consolidation. Even as American culture travels widely, and corporate ownership and administrative control over the making of culture becomes more concentrated, a new generation of artists, filmmakers, scholars, cultural critics, and novelists are now members, even leaders, of America's major cultural and social institutions. For perhaps the first time, a small but highly visible cohort of black cultural workers enjoys access to institutional resources, especially the forms of legitimization, prestige, and recognition that such institutions bestow.

A complex and often contested terrain of discourse, representation, and politics typifies these conditions of black cultural production. These cultural struggles bear directly on questions of power; in particular, the relationship of dominant national institutions to forms of black culture that remain outside of mainstream institutions. For example, locally and regionally based organizations and communities of musicians, painters, dancers, and writers in Los Angeles, Detroit, Brooklyn, Kansas City, Chicago, and the San Francisco Bay Area nurture and develop artists, some of whom also enjoy national prominence. No less significant are those artists and cultural workers who form local and regionally based operations that produce, train, and reproduce black expressive forms and practices in local lodges, high schools, community theaters, and churches. With very few exceptions, these organizations, networks, and institutions seldom, if ever, appear on the radar screen of national cultural media. It is as if these levels of cultural production and practice exert little if any direct influence on the national cultural and intellectual imagination. Against the enormous public profile and cultural influence of a cultural capital like New York City and the organizational resources of a major institution like the Lincoln Center, for example, local and regional activities can go almost completely unrecognized.

Bringing these smaller-scale and often more marginal organizations and activities into sharper focus complicates institutional conditions and relations of a black cultural formation. The controversy surrounding the 1995 Whitney Museum exhibition on black masculinity illustrates, for example, the depth of cultural debates surrounding the production and exhibition of artistic representation of black expressive culture within mainstream arts institutions, as well as the tension between local and national, marginal and dominant cultural institutions. As the polemic surrounding the Whitney exhibition showed, the political differences and multiple claims on blackness trouble the ease with which such cultural performances can be viewed as expressions of an already finished *oppositional* black cultural politics.

By the same token, such a performance does provide the occasion for a critical interrogation of what the exhibition means, the mainstream institutional spaces in which it was staged, the circumstances through which it derived its legitimacy, and how it came to be constituted as a discursive intervention in black image making. These issues were made all the more vexing and complex by the racial, sexual, generational, and gender-based disputes surrounding the exhibition.[2]

My point is simply this: the successful "occupation" and use of institutional cultural spaces and the political claims that emanate from them complicate rather than simplify the very notion of black cultural politics. As examples like the Whitney Museum exhibition on black masculinity demonstrate, to present black cultural expressions within dominant mainstream cultural spaces like the Whitney Museum is to generate highly contentious political disputes about black cultural practices and images.

Against this backdrop, I view the institutional recognition and legitimation of black cultural production (and the media celebrations which have accompanied it) in political terms. That is, I see this recognition and legitimation as an instance in which black cultural production functions as a site of political disputes over representation, meaning, and the valuation of blackness as a cultural expression.[3] The recognition and incorporation of black cultural production by dominant cultural institutions, in other words, might be taken as a strategic *move* by these institutions. Such a move, nonetheless, does represent a shift in the historic pattern of exclusion and deformation of black images. Moreover, since black artists, intellectuals, and critics have helped to transform these sites of cultural production, I also see this development as *one* tactic by which black cultural producers negotiate and navigate the uneven terrain of an American national imaginary that still remains deeply ambivalent about black cultural presence.

It can be productive to discuss dominant institutions while retaining the focus on the political idea of a black cultural formation. Such an emphasis moves us beyond binary conceptions of cultural politics that rely on locating cultural opposition as either inside or outside of mainstream social institutions and the legitimacy that they confer. By centering black cultural production and the contemporary strategies through which black cultural producers negotiate the contemporary cultural and institutional landscape, I aim to map the discursive, political, and social conditions that structure the cultural and social spaces of black cultural production.

## BLACK CULTURAL FORMATION

Regarding representation of blackness (in the United States), the question of who has a rightful claim on a particular version of blackness as representative, or indeed the need to delimit what constitutes blackness, no longer defines the terms of black cultural production. Most immediately, this means that the still entrenched language of positive or negative images, polemics about the commodification of blackness, and the endless search for authenticating narratives have come under critical scrutiny and finally been put to rest.[4] Black representation produced in the United States has also come in for some rather sustained critical interrogations from black cultural critics, especially critics in England, for its purported hegemonic tendencies.[5] Despite the historical circumstances and the specific social relations in which they are generated, U.S. black cultural productions are nonetheless globally pervasive.[6] That black American cultural representations sustain their global appeal—circulating, borrowing, aligning, and appropriating a wide array of traditions, formations, memories, and desires—is deeply disturbing and problematic for some members of the black Atlantic diaspora. Black American cultural representations involve complex texts, discourses, and narratives that are typically expressed in multiple and overlapping sites and media. Black cultural producers in the United States deliberately mix and match, spillover and cross aesthetic, geographical, technological, and social borders, exemplifying what Dick Hebdige calls a "cut 'n' mix" aesthetic.[7]

Since the mid-1980s black Americans working in film, television, and music video have sustained a sometimes precarious involvement in image making in documentary and narrative film, and to a much less extent in television.[8] These forms of cultural production and the representations they generate are heavily influenced by developments in black popular culture, notably music, fashion, vernacular language, and sport.

Of course, black popular music remains one of the richest and most controversial sources of black self-representation and expression. Black American musicians continue to invent and stretch the complex terrain on which to articulate black imagination and creative possibility. In particular, black composers and performers in jazz, rock, pop, and rap continue to generate musical styles which unsettle and destabilize, if only momentarily, the music industry's racialized approach to musical production, marketing, and classification.

Black critical and intellectual discourse in cultural studies, literary criticism, feminist theory, film studies, critical race studies, and African American studies have opened and in some cases *consolidated* institutional spaces and discursive communities from which to identify, evaluate, and legitimate black cultural production and self-representation. Inside and outside of dominant institutions and organizations, black scholars and critics remain engaged in the necessary discursive work of generating and sustaining cultural communities. Indeed, this critical work has been enabled by the commercial success and critical recognition of black writers, especially in the areas of black women's fiction, biography, and memoir. These genres have themselves become forms in which black writers have made crucial interventions in the area of black self-fashioning and representation.[9]

In some cases, black cultural achievements are enabled by the significant (and often very public) leadership by blacks of prestigious and high-profile cultural organizations and institutions. At its most effective, this leadership has been central to the visibility, circulation, and legitimization of black cultural production in the national life and public culture of the United States.[10]

I am especially interested, then, in the insights these complex conditions of production and representation offer for understanding the contemporary politics of black cultural production, the shifts in cultural imagination and desire, as well as strategies deployed to achieve cultural legitimacy and visibility. In broad terms, these developments, the social condition of their appearance, and their attendant institutional sites, may actually prefigure what I want to call a *cultural formation*. I use this idea of cultural formation as a theater and staging arena from which to explore the institutional character, features, and political implications of these recent cultural developments.

By the concept of cultural formation, I intend something similar to the sociological and cultural characteristics identified by labor historian Michael Denning to describe the significance of radical popular-front cultural expressions in America in the 1930s, 1940s, and 1950s. In *The Cultural Front,* Denning suggests that in literature, photography, theater, intellectual production, and cinema, a radical and progressive sensibility—a structure of feeling—defined the cultural and artistic products of the period.[11] The pervasiveness and impact of this influence amounted to what Denning terms the "laboring" of American culture. Anchored by a progressive labor movement and rooted in local as well as national institutions like art houses, coffee shops, academic departments, books stores, and union locals, the cultural formation to which he refers expressed a distinctive cultural sensibility. It helped give a distinctive acumen to the organizing and political work of the popular front. In addition to Denning's suggestive example, my conception of culture is indebted to the work of Raymond Williams and Antonio Gramsci. Both recognized the centrality and relationship of culture to the consolidation and institutionalization of a progressive historical bloc.[12] It rejects the reductionist and mechanical conceptions of art and culture that characterizes some approaches to the analysis of ideology and culture, particularly in relationship to material life and progressive movements for social change.[13]

Are we perhaps at the threshold of what we might call, following Denning and, in a different context, Cornel West, a *racing* (that is, an explicit darkening, blackening, and coloring) of American culture, at least in terms of the operation of its dominant institutions of cultural production and legitimation? Using his concept of black cultural projection, Merlman seems to think that African Americans have been able to effectively project, as it were, black cultural achievements and a worldview into the mainstream of American society.[14] Cornel West, Eric Michael Dyson, and others also suggest as much in the realm of popular culture. I am interested in black cultural production in itself, not as evidence that definitively confirms (or disproves) the presence of a new black cultural formation. Rather, my aim is to map the social, economic, and technological features of such formation and to assess its political and cultural effects.

## THE SOCIOLOGICAL PRODUCTION OF CONTEMPORARY BLACK EXPRESSIVE CULTURE

Black cultural expression is shaped by flexible conditions of production, new technologies of communication and circulation, regulatory state policies, expanding means and sites of representation, competing claims of ownership and authenticity, and contested discourses of judgment and evaluation. By now, it is rather axiomatic that regardless of genre, venue, or medium, contemporary black cultural production in the United States is, for the most part, produced, mediated, and circulated through commercially mediated sites such as television, video, music, film, publishing, and theater. Black cultural productions (popular and artistic) cross the boundaries of high/low, popular/elite, commercial/noncommercial, and they operate in dialogue with each other as well as those social and cultural circumstances in which black people live.

Thus, social conditions, political struggles, and cultural discourses directly and indirectly structure black expressive culture. A partial list of these relevant structuring conditions include: the racialization of U.S. society; continuing political debates about race, identity, multiculturalism, immigration, citizenship, and nation; shifts in the structure of the economy; transformations in the geographical distribution, circuits, and flows of racialized populations; the social transformation and cultural redefinition of public space. Disputes among blacks about difference, class, community, mass collective action, authenticity, and, of course, representation constitute the discursive field within which black expressive culture and representation is constituted, negotiated, and enacted.[15]

I use blackness here to indicate the shifting cultural fields and social relations and the material circumstances in which black people operate. With my use of the term *blackness,* I am also referring to the discursive work—cultural practices, social meanings, and cultural identifications—that black people use to negotiate and construct meaningful lives. While I am specifically concerned with understanding how blackness operates in the United States, I do not confine this particular formulation of blackness to the United States. The particular articulations of social, cultural, and material relations are critical for the specific ways in which blackness may come to signify. In discursive terms, I use *blackness* as a cultural trope and social category over which competing claims are made and registered.[16] The material and discursive come together when blackness appears as the object of cultural disputes, when conflicting claims are waged, registered, and used in the service of different interests. In this conception, the empirical, political, and moral veracity on which such claims rest are shifting and unstable, depending on the historical and structural conditions within which they circulate and are registered. The deployment of various moral, rhetorical, and political strategies in the name of blackness (or against it) is designed to construct social identifications in order to win the political allegiance and popular sentiments of social subjects on whose behalf such claims are made. Thus, for instance, black cultural critics sometimes use scholarly and professional legitimacy to contest damaging claims of white racists or the exaggerated claims of unrelenting black isolationists, both of which may be couched in the rhetoric of science. On the other hand, black neonationalists and Afrocentricists might just as easily use rhetorical and moral appeals to a noble and glorious past as a corrective to claims that insist on the absence of black contributions to world history and civilization. Liberal policy makers sometimes use the trope of blackness in political appeals directed at the state to call attention to the excessive and punitive sanctions aimed at specific populations (e.g., Latino, Asian, and Caribbean immigrants, Latino and black males, black teenage mothers, and single parents). Finally, (black) neoconservative scholars and liberal individualists mobilize specific conceptions of blackness to attack the political rhetoric of black solidarity rooted in racial kinship as the basis to enlist political support and to advocate social policies against the distribution of social resources based on race.[17] These kinds of public narrative make some implicit claim to black representation; as such, the manner in which blackness is constituted in cultural representation is crucial to the formation of common sense about the meaning of blackness and the identification and organization of interests that such representations and narratives structure. Commercial mediums like network television, cinema, popular music, music video, information technologies, and the Internet, as well as venues of artistic production such as theater, art galleries, and the concert hall are all necessary sites for the organization, presentation, and circulation of these competing claims on blackness.

This is precisely why such structuring conditions are so important. For there is much at stake in how representations are produced, framed, and potentially deployed to construct political projects.[18] Whether publishing, television, cinema, the university, law schools, or the courtroom, black cultural production and representation are variously shaped by industrial shifts, organizational restructuring, state regulation, and economic imperatives which continue to transform the social conditions of production, circulation, and reception. In the case of commercial network television in the United States, to take an obvious example, governmental deregulation and industrial reorganization contribute to the enabling conditions (and constraints) within which the black television market/audience is constructed as a profitable (or ignored as unprofitable) commodity by the television industry. As old industrial circumstances give way to new ones—including new ownership structures, new markets, different pricing structures, and different delivery systems—the visibility, position, and meaning of the black television audience to networks also change.

These shifting institutional conditions are only the most visible signs of the significant transformations in the communications industry. Different sectors of the communication industry (e.g., music, television, and cinema) are constantly packaging, arranging, and vying to extend and exert control over the terms and circumstances in which their products circulate and take on value. This process involves the industry identification of distinctive segments or niches and the assignment of differential market value to distinctive kinds of audiences. This process, in turn, produces various audiences as markets that are easily combined, segmented, aggregated, and dis-aggregated.[19] But as S. Craig Watkins demonstrates in his careful analysis of black film cycles of the 1980s, these processes are mutually constitutive rather than predetermined.[20] Social and political interests both outside of and within black communities also make and register equally significant and meaningful claims on blackness, many of which operate squarely within the logic expressed by the media. Specifying blackness as the subject of different social positions, competing cultural claims, conflicting political interests, and shifting market imperatives highlights the strategic necessity (in matters of cultural politics anyway) of thinking about the processes and relations of black cultural production in institutional, structural, and cultural terms.

Materially and institutionally, the organizational and economic relationships that characterize culture-media-entertainment-information–based global corporations parallel the cultural and political relations of representation. Black cultural expression is increasingly caught in and thus mediated by (and mediates) new so-called media synergy—multiple levels of intertextual and organizational complementarity and exchange. As with workers, commodities, and information, black cultural images circulate across different mediums, national and geographical boundaries, markets, and genres. As central as they are to the operations of various political, legal, organizational, discursive, and technological structures, the movement of black images and representation is never free of cultural and social traces of the condition of their production, circulation, and use. As Stuart Hall notes, blackness is never innocent or pure.[21]

In this circulation, representation of the black social body, like that of the black physical body, is the object of administrative management, legal regulation, social control, and even cultural fascination by the state, the news media, and the entertainment industry. One need only look at network and cable television programming in the United States (and in much of the Western industrialized world) to get a sense of the extent of this cultural fascination and legal regulation. Network television news, talk and "reality" shows, and sports are often the primary (some would argue preferred) genres through which the disciplining effects of racial discourse and fascination with black representation are expressed. Dick Hebdige, John Caldwell, and John Fiske, for example identify the pervasiveness of technologies of image surveillance mobilized around the black body.[22] Examples abound: the low-tech home-video cameras used to record the Rodney King beating in Los Angeles; courtroom cameras; hidden security cameras in department stores; car-mounted camcorders used by the police; and news cameras used by local news units which literally cover the social body in search of the big story. Of course, we should not forget the large-scale technologies of observation and regulation, such as the domestic use of high-powered aerial searchlights, that were perfected by the Los Angeles Police Department's gang division in black and Latino communities like Compton, Watts, and South Central Los Angeles.[23] The U.S. Immigration Service also relies on high-tech surveillance hardware like infrared cameras, night-vision lenses, and heat-seeking radar to police the U.S. border with Mexico.

Discourses about race in the United States are not just the products of structuring influences and regulatory technologies. They are produced in the representations and logic of commonsense racial knowledge constituted in media such as television news and entertainment. Law and legal discourse is crucial as a subject of media representation. The dramatic investment in law enforcement and a fascination with legal discourse are timeless staples of American television. With this investment, television programs about crime and the criminal justice system function as a means of establishing the normative legitimacy and moral propriety of the present legal system no matter how corrupt and abusive. So, for example, story lines about the lives and antics of the rich, famous, and corrupt are commonplace, as are narratives about the arrest and incarceration of black males. Stories about the unbridled growth of global corporate capital, the increasing concentration of the ownership structure of the telecommunications industry for example, are rare. In matters of race and representation, law and legal discourse are especially crucial because they are the structuring scenes or sites in which organizing narratives about fairness, civility, propriety, transgression, and responsibility are framed. Transgressions and conflicts that are seen as racial encourage viewers to ask: Is it fair? Is it right? Is it legal? Is it good? These are all judgments that are inscribed in the discursive logic through which public narratives and representations about racial conflict are presented. Scholars in critical race theory and legal studies have worked to make visible the complex role of race, gender, and class in legal discourse, knowledge production, and legal practices. But in televisual representations of the law, television struggles to render invisible the systemic way in which processes of racialization, gender subordination, and class inequalities are central to the structure of legal practice and the law. Instead the narrative focus in television is on the occupational hazards (or glories) of the legal profession, the character defects of individual criminals, or the fetishization of the technical machinations of the criminal justice (and legal) system. Black musicians (especially in the genre of hip-hop) and image makers (especially music videographers) have commented on the centrality of race to the operation of the criminal justice system and the law. Through vernacular practices of the street, these culture workers seek to articulate their experience of themselves as racial(ized) subjects of the state. In the representation of crime the discursive alliance between the criminal justice system, the legal profession, and commercial television produces stories that naturalize the relationship between race, crime, criminals, and the legal system.

When linked to a technology of representation like television, the discourse of regulation that fixes this understanding of crime and the legal system operates through the production of the black body as spectacle. Discursively, this operation depends on the production of the black body as the site of pleasure and adoration, fear, and menace. In crime discourse in the 1980s, the black male (youthful) body signified menace and the loss of civility in the public sphere. This narrative of loss was expressed most explicitly by media and politicians, through the steady expansion of the coercive arm of the state (e.g., prison and police) and the privatization of key functions of regulation (private police), incarceration, and surveillance (private security forces). Television represented and thereby constructed the public sphere as the site of an increasing but necessary regulation and surveillance that depended on race, even though it was overtly expressed as moral panic and political disputes over immigration, gangs, welfare, and crime. Culturally, the multiply inflected meaning of black (self-)representation in this discourse of regulation can be seen in the various media constructions of black male criminality, gangsta rappers, and male youths.[24] The electronic mass media (especially news, sport, and music video) are *the* preeminent site where competing claims about black masculinity are waged. Black youth, the sectors of the black middle class, preachers, moral entrepreneurs, police, politicians, black feminists, queer activists, and even scholars all wage claims on behalf of "the" commonsense definition of black masculinity (as, among other things, dangerous and menacing).

Cultural constructions of menace are not limited to black heterosexual men, youth, or gangsta rappers. In a discourse of regulation that uses the rhetoric of traditional values, black gay men threaten the social body in another way, generating a masculine anxiety that cuts across race.[25] This traversal of blackness by an anxious heterosexual black masculinity produces a conception of hyperheterosexual manliness that appears in popular and political discourse and cultural representation as a renewed claim by heterosexual men (of all races) on women, children, family, community, and nation.[26] Hence, in the media discourse of regulation (where fear and menace are the key touchstones of a society seen as out of control), the black male gay body operates symbolically to signify the erosion of morality and threats to manhood and what Roderick Ferguson calls the dominance of heteronormativity.[27] Examples are not difficult to come by: most notably North Carolina senator Jessie Helms's use of the documentary film *Tongues Untied*, by the late Marlon Riggs, as the basis of a nasty frontal assault in the culture wars on gays and lesbians, involving the National Endowment for the Arts and Humanities and public broadcasting. This anxious masculinity also finds expression by protonationalists, religious leaders, and popular musicians within the black social body. Black British filmmaker Isaac Julian's documentary film exploration of diaspora music in the United States, England, and the Caribbean, entitled *The Darker Side of Black,* and Marlon Riggs's *Black Is, Black Ain't,* made explicit the terms of black Atlantic assaults on black homosexual masculinity within black popular culture.

In network television news, national political ad campaigns, and Hollywood cinema, while the physical body of black women has often been present, her subjectivity has not (especially as the primary subject of narrative cinema). In the discourse of regulation, the black body has more often than not functioned symbolically to signal the erosion of family, the deleterious consequence of single-parent households, and the purported threat to a patriarchal moral order. In this discursive universe, women's sexuality and sexual behavior should be strictly confined to the nuclear family and used only in the service of motherhood and (for some cultural nationalists) reproduction. (Here, the black welfare queen/client of the Reagan/Bush presidencies is the most obvious example.) In the production of female heterosexuality (anchored by European myths of beauty and sexuality), black women's experiences have been rendered almost uniformly invisible. Indeed, through their very absence, black women function discursively to consolidate and condense representations that equate beauty and desire with a persistent and pronounced semiotic slide toward whiteness, or of late, an exotic and often indeterminate racial hybridity. In the moral economy of contemporary American discourses of gender, sexuality, and race, black women's bodies operate culturally to mark the boundaries of female (hetero)sexuality, motherhood, family, desire, and beauty.

These discourses of regulation and the moral panics that they helped to mobilize worked for a time in the 1980s to consolidate a neoconservative hegemonic bloc. This bloc routinely used media images of black men and women, the poor, and immigrants to represent social crisis. Gendered and racialized images of poverty and disenfranchisement became the basis for a barrage of public policies and legislation intended to shore up this hegemonic position and to calm and manage the moral panics constructed around race in general and blackness in particular. Typical examples are the erosion of moral standards; the loss of the work ethic (e.g., the 1996 Welfare Bill); law and order (e.g., the 1995 Crime Bill); the decay of Western civilization (the culture wars of the 1980s); and the assaults on whiteness and masculinity (California propositions on immigration and affirmative action). In short, politically and culturally, the image of blacks, the poor, and immigrants anchored a moral panic about the decline and erosion of American civic and public life and fueled conservative and neoliberal public-policy positions on (the sanctity of) citizenship, nation, community, and family. So often media narratives presume and then fix in representation the purported natural affinity between black criminality and threats to the nation. By fixing the blame, legitimating the propriety of related moral panics, these representations (and the assumptions on which they are based) help form the discursive logic through which policy proscriptions for restoring order—more jails—are fashioned.

The production of media representations of blackness (along with those of sexuality and immigration) as threatening the natural fabric and policy proscriptions for reimagining and consolidating a traditional vision of the American nation is challenged with alternative representations. Generated from within black artistic, intellectual, and popular spheres, these black counternarratives and representations might be seen as a rejoinder to the various conservative attempts to demonize, regulate, define, and contain blackness within a right-wing (and increasingly neoliberal) discourse. In some cases, these black representations share much with discourses of regulation, especially on matters of culture, crime, sex, and family. But black claims and counterclaims provide the basis for a cultural assertion of black self-representation that is also deeply engaged with the cultural politics of difference within black cultural discourse, as well as broader American debates about national identity, citizenship, and the public sphere.

## PUBLIC (RELATIONS) INTELLECTUALS AND PUBLIC CULTURE

In the early 1990s Harvard University moved to resurrect its African American studies program by hiring Henry Louis Gates, Jr., as its director. (Similar moves to strengthen African American studies also occurred at Columbia University, New York University, and University of California, Berkeley). At the same time this period saw an upswing in the media fascination with black public intellectuals, a steady barrage of media appearances, talk show experts, and books by black intellectuals and writers. In terms of the conditions of possibility for the emergence of black cultural formation, these developments can be understood not as accidental, but as a moment of historical conjuncture, even articulation, in which all of these events can be seen in relationship to each other. Indeed, one (but by no means determinate) element that links them and suggests that they are more than coincidental is the fact that these moves are occurred at prestigious cultural institutions like the Lincoln Center, Harvard University, Columbia University, Princeton University, the *New Yorker,* the *New York Times,* the Whitney Museum, and the Public Theater.[28]

In a two-year period in the mid-1990s, the *New Yorker* profiled a number of black cultural producers and intellectuals. In a January 1995 article, Michael Berube considered the emergence of a "new generation" of public intellectuals, whose impact on American public life and culture was, to say the least, significant.[29] Among those included in the profile were Cornel West, Eric Michael Dyson, bell hooks, Derick Bell, Manning Marable, and Patricia Williams.[30] A similar profile of black intellectual and cultural producers was featured around the same time in *Time* magazine.[31]

While admittedly a limited case example, when seen together these developments are at the very least suggestive of the point that I have been making with respect to the increasing presence of black artists, intellectuals, and entertainers in U.S. public culture. (This point is even clearer in popular culture, where black entertainers, athletes, and spokespersons are more visible and whose impact on the American popular imagination is registered more immediately.) None of these instances is very significant when taken by itself. Discursively and in terms of a network of social relations, however, the institutional sites in which they took place demand more than cursory consideration. I point to these intellectual interventions as a discursive accomplishment or cultural move, if you will (including the institutional networks and their public recognition), as evidence that black intellectual, artistic, and popular self-representations are increasingly central to the discursive reconstitution or rewriting of American public culture.

Given my emphasis on the discursive and institutional conditions of possibility of this emergent cultural formation, I want to dwell for a moment on the structural features that lead me to such claims.[32] First, there appears to be a very strong relationship between key black cultural producers and the media. Many of the most influential and visible of an emerging group of black intellectuals regularly appear on, write for, and are featured in national news venues. Television talk shows, magazine programs, and feature news segments, along with documentary films, seem especially keen on having at least one articulate and professionally accomplished black intellectual or culture worker serve as commentator and/or talking head. After all, these intellectuals, critics, and artists are extraordinarily accomplished and professionally successful—and, most importantly, many of them make good copy. Second, most are products of a post-1960s civil rights and black power generation that gained access to and excelled in America's elite colleges and universities. They are now well into the prime of their careers—most have tenured academic positions and many hold directorships at prestigious universities, colleges, and foundations. By any measure, all are at the top of their game and thus in the position to watch over important "cultural gates," making decisions that shape the lives and careers of young faculty, emerging writers, and funding organizations.[33] I regard it as more than symbolic that in the late 1990s three of the most prestigious professional academic associations—the American Studies Association, the American Sociological Association, and the Modern Language Association— had black presidents: Mary Helen Washington, William Julius Wilson, and Houston A. Baker, respectively. Like Marsalis at the Lincoln Center, as advisers, foundation board members, and editorial board members of book publishers and professional journals, members of this generation of visible black intellectuals occupy institutional positions in which, at the very least, they helped to establish the possibility that new and different knowledges and forms of representation about black life and culture might be developed. In other words, while there was little guarantee that their outcomes were certain, nevertheless, here were a set of organizational and discursive possibilities where the shape, direction, and definition of black representation at the level of national culture could be influenced by a black cultural formation.

## CULTURAL POLITICS AND GLOBAL RESTRUCTURING

So something interesting, exciting, and consequential was happening through the 1990s at various sites and levels of black representation and American national culture. But do these developments and the possibilities they present add up to anything remotely approaching a cultural formation, even an emergent one? If so, does it exert influence in the realm of American arts and letters? In other words, what difference do these developments make for the remaking of American national identity and cultural imagination? Will the presence of visible and influential black scholars, artists, curators, and filmmakers in dominant and prestigious cultural institutions such as Lincoln Center and the Public Theater, or professional organizations like the MLA or the ASA, matter?

Despite notable institutional incursions and the important contributions of critical black cultural studies of black representation, critics, academics, culture makers, and black audiences continue to express a good deal of worry about the images and representations that circulate in our name. In popular music, for example, Paul Gilroy has expressed concerns about the ethical cultural and political future of black self-representation on two counts: first, he is worried about the chauvinistic implications of a black ethnic absolutism that remains embedded in the concept of race as an analytic and prescriptive political category; and second, he is weary of black popular culture and popular expression that have replaced ethical and political concerns about freedom with bodily and hedonistic preoccupations of sex, drugs, and material acquisition.[34] Ironically, black image makers create many (if not the majority) of the most commercially successful and popular of these representations (and I suppose this is one of the sources of Gilroy's lament). These preoccupations involve a switch from what Gilroy terms ethically based visions of black freedom, guided by (and grounded in) collective struggle, to popular cultural expressions that glibly equate (political) freedom with individual (market) choice, beautiful bodies, a nostalgic glorious past, romanticized racial unity, and immediate sexual pleasure. For Gilroy, the possibility of these values forming the basis of a sublime black sensibility is as scary as it is dangerous. In his view, no matter how pervasive, these representations and popular sensibilities lack political vision and are underwritten by cultural (and market) values steeped in individualism, hedonism, fleeting pleasure, social irresponsibility, isolation, and withdrawal from collective black struggle.[35]

These images are made under very specific discursive conditions and social relations, and such circumstances set the limits of possibility for imagining, producing, and circulating different kinds of representations. This may be the real political challenge of thinking through and evaluating the effects of an emergent black cultural formation and the cultural moves required for its realization and reproduction. For what may be a cause for worry is not so much the images alone, but the frameworks and social conditions out of which they are generated and the desires to which they respond. Together, these conditions structure the assumptions through which such desires are made legible and culturally meaningful. If this is so, then I want to go further than simply to inventory the conditions of possibility for an emergent black cultural formation. In my estimation, what is required is to sustain the challenging (and often vexing) work of critically interrogating the conditions of its production and evaluating the politics that it proposes and enacts. For instance, as I argue in the next chapter, while there is a multiplicity of cultural practices and products circulating in the name of blackness that establish key ground, we must also grapple with the fact that some of these projects are traditional, conservative, exclusionary, and limiting.

One intellectual strategy for thinking through these challenges has been the transdisciplinary practice of cultural studies. Intellectual practices such as critical black cultural studies play an important role in the kinds of cultural moves that I have been describing. It is the primary intellectual and academic practice that maps, evaluates, and legitimates the self-representation of the black cultural production (especially among and within various formations of the black diaspora). Very much like the critical practices it maps, critical black cultural studies challenges and in some cases unsettles various territorial boundaries (disciplines, geographies, ideologies, and genres) that maintain deep and enduring investments in political and analytic stories of the purity, separation, and authenticity of cultural forms and practices. Similarly, as an intellectual practice, it aims for identifying a range of knowledge capable of operating both inside and outside official institutions and formations. That is to say, in addition to interrogating official sites of power, forms of legitimation, and cultural practice, critical cultural studies encourages an interrogation of the spaces and places where the vernacular, the popular, and (sometimes as an expression of both) the commercial often resides. It encourages an interrogation of what sociologist Avery Gordon calls the haunting traces that, while seemingly absent, are socially and culturally very much present.[36] Thus, critical black cultural studies and the forms and practices it analyzes is constitutive and therefore central to the narration, evaluation, and representation of different cultural and political possibilities. As such, it is very much a part of the politics of cultural formation and representation I am concerned with.

In addition to cultural meanings and political effects, black cultural representations are also profitable economic commodities that circulate within global capitalist economies. In the midst of discursive skirmishes within blackness about racial kinship, identity politics, and institutional legitimacy, the commodification of blackness and its global circulation via commercial mass media continues to pose especially vexing questions. For those liberal left critics who are most skeptical of the purportedly negative influence of the market on moral values, market commodification is the obstacle that prevents black collective mobilization. For others, cultural traditionalists, who are most invested in nationalist discourses of authenticity and the central role of culture in the discursive constitution of the black nation, the rapid global circulation and commodification of blackness weakens traditions, historical forms of association and community, identity, and nation. This latter position is doubly ironic, since in an earlier period it was the economic, technological, and global circulation of people and materials that accounted for black presence in the New World in the first place. These factors helped to structure the very conception of nation, identity, and self that black cultural representations aim to express.[37]

Indeed, the wave of black popular culture which exploded in the American (and British) cultural imaginations beginning in the late 1970s was, in part, enabled by a global culture industry. Film, television, and the recording industry were each profoundly impacted by developments in technology, alternative delivery systems, changing formats, and mergers, buy outs, new markets, and deregulation. For black popular culture circulating in this shifting commercial environment, this structural uncertainty and rapid transformation was especially significant. As the global reach of media conglomerates became greater and more precise and as the markets on which they depended became more differentiated, black cultural productions gained a measure of access to global circulation. In the context of structural changes in the global entertainment industry, and driven by the preeminent search for something new and different, black cultural expression came to occupy some of the nooks and crannies of the global and domestic cultural marketplace.

The new global structure that now defines the modern culture and entertainment industry is not merely the only game in town, but the only game on the planet. This new global structure still does not so much dictate the content of black cultural production but rather it establishes the very terms within which such products (including those that are counterhegemonic) are produced, financed, and exhibited globally. One would want to ask, then, how are counterhegemonic and alternative expressions and representations in black culture imagined, produced, and sustained? Any response to such a query must of necessity make visible or at the very least develop a cartography of institutional and social spaces necessary to produce and sustain black self-representation under conditions of global transnational media conglomerates.

George Lipsitz suggests that, in matters of culture, it is important to recognize, account for, and challenge the cultural appropriation and economic exploitation of people around the globe directly at the points of production. He also encourages cultural analysts and critics to explore just how exploited and dominated communities negotiate, make do with, and, where possible, oppose these processes, structures, and social relations at the point of commercial consumption. Like Stuart Hall, Lipsitz recognizes that commercial culture is an important site of cultural politics because it is where popular meanings are made, loyalties enlisted, and identifications articulated. These processes are important, moreover, because these are the social points of articulation required for the political work of constructing new formations, alliances, and identifications globally. In other words, by focusing on consumption and the commercial routes through which cultural products circulate, Lipsitz imagines the possibility of a counterhegemonic cultural politics that operates on the ground of global capitalism without conceding that such terrain is always on the side of capital.[38] This is an important insight for understanding these powerful new organizing structures, the social logic on which they are based, and the conditions of possibility for different forms of counterhegemonic practice. This is the critical challenge we face.

# CHAPTER 2

# Jazz Tradition, Institutional Formation, and Cultural Practice

In 1991, Lincoln Center for the Performing Arts in New York City inaugurated its jazz program and installed its first artistic director, trumpet virtuoso Wynton Marsalis. This historic move, carried out by a major American cultural institution, signaled the emergence of a new period of visibility and legitimacy for jazz in the national culture. Lincoln Center's decision provides a reference point for exploring the operation of cultural politics—issues of aesthetics, race, and institutional formation—within a dominant cultural organization.[1] Moreover, it is an opportunity for reflecting on the sometimes tenuous and misunderstood relationship between the sociology of culture and cultural studies as analytic strategies for making sense of contemporary culture.

Marsalis's centrality here is by no means coincidental. Indeed, given his leadership of the generation of jazz musicians often referred to in the jazz press as "the young lions," his musical formation in New Orleans, his formal training at Tanglewood and the Juilliard School of Music, and his unparalleled recognition and achievements (e.g., Grammy Awards in both jazz music and classical music), Marsalis's role is perhaps singular. I mean, then, to highlight the media's representation of Marsalis, as well as his own use of media and Lincoln Center as platforms, in order to make sense of his impact as a musician and cultural advocate. In other words, I examine the tactical moves, social conditions, and cultural politics of the renewed attention to jazz as a cultural practice in the context of the media representations, debates, and polemics surrounding Marsalis and the legitimation and recognition of jazz by major cultural institutions like Lincoln Center.

While I develop the cultural politics of Marsalis and his work at Lincoln Center more thoroughly, I also gesture toward an alternative cultural approach to the practice of jazz. The set of productive practices and aesthetic approaches associated with Marsalis and Lincoln Center I shall refer to as a *canonical project*. The alternative, a view of aesthetics and productive practices that I locate in the metaphor of *the road and the street*, approaches the jazz tradition as a site for expansion and reinvention. I explicitly mark the social, cultural, and political boundaries of these practices, since they draw on distinct (though sometimes shared) technical vocabularies, cultural assumptions, aesthetic conceptions, and social investments in African American music traditions.

At the level of cultural and aesthetic politics, these distinctive approaches and practices enact different, but important, oppositional possibilities. Thus, while I place these practices in dialogue with each other, I also want to suggest that in the end they involve different ways of seeing the music in particular and (African American) cultural politics in general. I deliberately set into analytic (and political) tension, then, these cultural projects and the cultural politics—aesthetic and institutional—that they enact.

The growing media attention and public interest in jazz—the critical debate over its direction; the installation of Lincoln Center jazz program; the proliferation of philanthropic, public, and corporate financial support; and the growth of research and training opportunities in conservatories, institutes, and universities—signal a significant advance in the institutional recognition and legitimation of jazz.[2] This recognition and legitimation are especially striking when seen from the perspective of the sociology of culture that foregrounds the organizational, structural, and social relationships within and through which such recognition is achieved. In short, I view the activities and debates surrounding Marsalis and his canonical project at Lincoln Center as an effective (and largely successful) struggle for institutional space and recognition within contemporary culture. This effective struggle for institutional recognition and legitimacy is all the more significant when considered from the long view of the historic relationship between jazz and a dominant cultural institution like Lincoln Center, which, as the *Los Angeles Times* described it, is an "institution that has looked down its nose at jazz for decades."[3] Similarly, cultural studies help to clarify the cultural politics involved by alerting us to the racial, aesthetic, and discursive constructions and struggles that also lie at the center of this process.

Wynton Marsalis and his supporters are absolutely central to understanding this move toward institutional recognition and legitimation. In his varied roles as media personality, recording artist, cultural advocate, arts administrator, composer, and performer, one can tease out elements of his aesthetic and cultural project, as well as the institutional strategies for realizing them. Marsalis's vision and the cultural politics that underwrite it are pivotal for grasping the significance of the cultural struggles surrounding jazz since 1990. His effective, though no doubt polemical, directorship of the Lincoln Center program is a useful entree to this instance of contemporary cultural struggle.

### INSTALLING THE CANON

Wynton Marsalis is one of the most accomplished, celebrated, and rewarded musicians of his generation.[4] Indeed, so prolific and celebrated is Marsalis that there have even been the inevitable comparisons in the press to Leonard Bernstein.[5] Marsalis works in a variety of venues (jazz clubs, concerts, and festivals), media and educational settings (workshops, universities, radio, and television), and performance contexts (modern dance, ballet, opera, quintet, big band, and orchestra). His collaborations in related art fields include work with cellist Yo-Yo Ma, choreographers Garth Fegan, Peter Martins, and Twyla Tharp, as well as opera diva Kathleen Battle. His Grammy Awards, lucrative recording contracts, television and radio series, and directorship at Lincoln Center ensure a busy and demanding schedule.[6]

It is not just Marsalis's public visibility, commercial success, and professional achievements that I want to highlight here, but rather how the *figure* of Marsalis, in critical and popular discourse, may be read as an example of an oppositional cultural strategy by African Americans engaged in struggles for institutional legitimacy and recognition.[7] Marsalis himself, in fact, has used the social space of cultural performance and the institutional space of Lincoln Center as platforms from which to issue certain pronouncements about his vision of the music, culture, and tradition. Anchored by a modernist vision of aesthetics, a purist suspicion of the dangers of commercialism, and a deep commitment to racial pride, his is a cultural project—a canonical project, to be precise—which aims for institutional recognition, codification, and legitimation.

From his highly visible and influential public platform, Marsalis articulates a cultural, social, and aesthetic vision which aims to canonize jazz and to ensure it a significant place of cultural recognition and legitimacy for his and future generations.[8]

## Aesthetic Modernism and Anticommercialism

One of Marsalis's most impressive qualities is his ability to forcefully articulate his aesthetic approach to jazz. Tony Scherman observes that "many disagree with him but few musicians or critics have what Marsalis can claim: a thought-out unified view, a cosmology, and aesthetic."[9] Marsalis's aesthetic approach to jazz involves a complex understanding of the music's contemporary cultural context, its historical formation and tradition, its technical elements, and the significance of its key innovators. Socially, Marsalis's aesthetic is founded on what he calls jazz's essence,

> Some of the essential traits of jazz are things that have nothing to do with music. . . . First comes the concept of playing. You take a theme, an idea, and you play with it. Just like you play with a ball . . . so you have the spirit of playing. Next is the desire to play with other people. That means learning to respect individuality . . . playing jazz means learning how to reconcile differences, even when they're opposites. . . . Jazz teaches you how to have a dialogue with integrity. . . . Good manners are important and spirituality . . . the soul of the music comes out of that. You have to want to make somebody feel good with what you play. Many so-called cutting edge forms assault the listener. But that's not the identity of jazz. The identity of jazz is to present itself with some soul to people.[10]

These characteristics form one part of Marsalis's view of jazz as a modern form. This social understanding is very much organized around his conception of the American character and his belief in the possibilities of American democracy. For Marsalis, jazz expresses a modern impulse. It "means a group of people coming together and playing without prepared music. It means negotiating your personality against the personality or with the personality of another musician with no controls over what the other musician is going to play. That's modern to me. That never existed until the twentieth century."[11]

Musically, Marsalis stresses conventional musical elements that characterize and hence distinguish jazz. These include blues, swing, collective improvisation, syncopation, call and response, vocal effects, and worldliness. So central are these constitutive elements to Marsalis's par-

ticular musical approach to jazz that it is worth quoting him directly
and at length on each element:

> *Blues.* Blues gives the jazz musician an unsentimental view of the world.
> Blues is adult secular music, the first adult secular music America pro-
> duced. It has optimism that's not naive. You accept tragedy and move
> forward. . . . Blues is down home sophistication. . . . Blues is such a
> fundamental form that it's loaded with complex information. It has a
> sexual meaning, the ebb and flow of sexual passion; disappointment,
> happiness, joy, and sorrow. It has a whole religious connotation too,
> that joy and lift. . . . And blues gives you a way to combine dissonance
> and consonance.
>
> *Swing.* Swing means constant coordination, but in an environment that's
> difficult enough to challenge your equilibrium. In jazz somebody's play-
> ing on every beat. . . . That's what makes swinging in jazz a challenge.
> On every beat there's the possibility of the rhythm falling apart. You
> have the constant danger of not swinging. Swing isn't rigid. Somebody
> might take the swing in a new direction, and you have to be ready to go
> that way. You're constantly trying to coordinate with something that's
> shifting and changing. . . . A lot of what Afro-Americans did in music
> was refine things that already existed. Afro-Americans didn't invent it,
> but they refined it to another level and put another type of American
> twist to it.
>
> *Collective improvisation.* People getting together and making up music as a
> group.
>
> *Syncopation.* A syncopated approach to rhythm means you're always pre-
> pared to do the unexpected, always ready to find your
> equilibrium. . . . In jazz you're improvising within a form. You chal-
> lenge that form with rhythms and harmonies. . . . It's all connected to
> the notion of playing. You set parameters and then you mess with them.
>
> *Call and Response.* Statement, then counter-statement and
> confirmation. . . . In jazz, the call and response is spontaneous. You
> invent it. Players call and respond freely, all the time. You have two
> types of call and response in jazz. The first is concurrent. . . . That's
> the most fascinating call and response, the simultaneous type. That's
> true collective improvisation. . . . The big bands made call and
> response sequential—that's the second type—and orchestrated it. In big
> band music, the soloist played and then the ensemble responded with an
> arranged phrase.
>
> *Vocal Effects.* There's achieving vocal effects on instruments, vocal effects
> that come, for the most part, from the Negro tradition, down home tra-
> dition. Southern shouts and moans, those slides and growls and crises
> and screams.
>
> *Worldliness.* There is a spirit of worldliness in jazz. You can hear how jazz
> is connected to other musics from around the world. Folk musics specifi-

cally, but also classical tradition. . . . Ellington is the prime example.
. . . He was trying to apply the sound of jazz, not by imitating other
people's music but by understanding how its elements fit jazz; jazz music
is not provincial.[12]

For Marsalis, then, jazz is the expression of the highest ideals of the
black cultural (as opposed to racial) imagination. Jazz emerged out of a
traceable past, structured by a formal set of elements, and practiced by
a recognizable group of composers and performers. In other words, jazz
is characterized by a complex set of social values, a sophisticated tradition of recognizable texts and practitioners, and a systematic means of
reproduction. Recognizing these qualities, jazz, according to Marsalis,
must be formally studied, systematically codified, and practiced through
performance, education, and institutional recognition. It must be supported as well through an informed and critical public discourse.

Marsalis's aesthetic approach to jazz forms the basis upon which he
identifies a particular corpus of styles, players, compositions, and standards by which the music is measured and judged. Within the jazz formation, he draws a rather sharp distinction between what he calls jazz
and the avant-garde, particularly with respect to the seminal contributions of artists like Cecil Taylor and Ornette Coleman. Marsalis is especially forceful about this distinction: "I've talked to Ornette about his
notion of free jazz. I think it's chaos. Maybe it's not, but that's what I
think it is. Chaos is always out there; it's something you can get from
any fifty kids in a band room".[13] While he is quick to note that the family of players loosely known as the avant-garde do not call their music
jazz, his view applies particularly to post-Coltrane stylistic developments in jazz; for example, the work of the World Saxophone Quartet
and the Art Ensemble of Chicago.

> I've listened to it (the avant-garde), I've played with the musicians, I was at
> the first concert the World Saxophone Quartet gave. I played on bills with
> the Art Ensemble of Chicago. It's not interesting to me to play like that. If
> I've rejected it, it's not out of ignorance of it. I don't know any people who
> like it. It doesn't resonate with anything I've experienced in the world. No
> food I've eaten, no sports I've played, no women I've known. I don't even
> like Coltrane's later stuff, to be honest. I don't listen to it like I do "A Love
> Supreme." It was with the type of things that that late period Coltrane did
> that jazz *destroyed its relationship to the public. That avant-garde concep-
> tion of music, that's loud and self-absorbed—nobody's interested in hearing
> that on a regular basis.* I don't care how much publicity it gets. The public
> is not going to want to hear people play like that.[14]

Since, for Marsalis, jazz must be supported by a critical and informed discourse, in addition to avant-garde musicians and composers, he directs some of his most unforgiving criticism towards critics, journalists, and music industry personnel who in his estimation profoundly misunderstand and misrepresent the music. "Jazz commentary," he observes,

> is too often shaped by a rebellion against what is considered the limitations of the middle-class. The commentators mistakenly believe that by willfully sliding down the intellectual, spiritual, economic, or social ladder, they will find freedom down where the jazz musicians (i.e., "real" people) lie. Jazz musicians, however, are searching for freedom of ascendance. This is why they practice. Musicians . . . are rebelling against the idea that they should be excluded from choosing what they want to do or think, against being forced into someone else's mold, whether it be the social agendas of the conservative establishment or the new fake liberal-establishment of which many well-meaning jazz observers are part.[15]

Along these same lines, Marsalis has more recently observed that "in jazz it is always necessary to be able to swing consistently and at different tempos. You cannot develop jazz by not playing it, not swinging or playing the blues. Today's jazz criticism celebrates as innovation forms of music that don't address the fundamentals of the music. But no one will create a new style of jazz by evading its inherent difficulties."[16]

It is in the deployment of his aesthetic vision against critical excesses and misrepresentations that one begins to get a glimmer of Marsalis's cultural politics; as early as 1988, in the editorial pages of the *New York Times,* and in his own volume, *Sweet Swing Blues on the Road,* Marsalis intervened directly in the public discourse about jazz.[17] These interventions are key, for in them Marsalis offers a corrective to what he sees as misrepresentations of jazz; the objective for Marsalis is, of course, to restore to musicians the authority of judgments and representation of the music and thus reestablish levels of competence, musicianship, and artistic integrity. This is how Marsalis put the matter: "Right now we're trying to get back to people playing at a competent level of musicianship. Another battle is for musicians to be recognized as authorities on music. That's never happened in jazz. And we're battling for the recognition of the ritual aspects of jazz, of the fact that jazz music is not like European classical music."[18] Marsalis's attempt to distinguish jazz from what he regards as excessive (and damaging) confusion between European classical music and the jazz avant-garde is perhaps matched only by his contempt—aesthetic and technical—for the corrosive effects of commercialism on jazz. As such, he has consistently distanced and distinguished jazz from commercial forms like pop, rock, and hip-hop. His aesthetic modernism is complemented, then, by contempt for commercial contamination that threatens the purity, nobility, and integrity of jazz through confusion and mimicry. "Jazz is not entertainment," Marsalis once quipped early in his career.[19] This sentiment captures Marsalis's contempt for the corrupting influences of commercialism on jazz. And he does not mince words to express his feelings about contemporary popular music: *popular tunes are sad pieces of one-chord shit. Today's pop tunes are sad.* Turn on the radio and try to find a pop tune to play with your band. You can't do it. The melodies are static, the chord changes are just the same senseless stuff repeated over and over again."[20]

Jazz needs to be "protected," as it were, from these leveling influences, because in a culture driven by profit and record sales, confusion, misrepresentation, and, worse for Marsalis, a misuse of the term *jazz* can easily result. Again, Marsalis puts the matter forcefully and directly: "Anything is jazz; everything is jazz. Quincy Jones' shit is jazz, David Sanborn . . . that's not to cut down Quincy or David. I love funk, it's hip. No problem to it. *The thing is, if it'll sell records to call that stuff jazz, they'll call it jazz.* They call Miles' stuff jazz. That stuff is not jazz, man. Just because someone played jazz at one time, that doesn't mean they're still playing it."[21]

In a rather ironic twist, Marsalis suggests that while commercialism contributes to the social diminution and loss of cultural respect and legitimacy for the music (in the eyes of some), popular music benefits, aesthetically and culturally, from its association with jazz. This is how Marsalis explains it in his 1988 *New York Times* editorial: "I recently completed a tour of jazz festivals in Europe in which only two out of ten bands were jazz bands. The promoters of these festivals readily admit most of the music isn't jazz, but refuse to rename these events . . . seeking the aesthetic elevation that jazz offers."[22] In the same editorial he observed, "to many people, any kind of popular music can now be lumped with jazz. As a result audiences too often come to jazz with generalized misconceptions about what it is and what it is supposed to be. *Too often, what is represented as jazz isn't jazz at all. Despite attempts by writers and record companies and promoters and educators and even musicians to blur the lines for commercial purposes, rock isn't jazz and new age isn't jazz and neither are pop or third stream.* There may be much that is good in all of them, but they ain't jazz."[23] Such confusion and mis-

representation, when combined with the relentless commercial imperatives to sell records and at all costs to turn out hits, is, for Marsalis, at the
heart of the matter. This situation, which generates misconceptions, mis-
understandings, and appropriations of jazz, is what seems to trouble
Marsalis most.

### Racial Nationalism and American Democracy

A similar kind of protectionist stance defines Marsalis's conception of
the role of African Americans in relationship to jazz. While certainly not
limited to it, this conception begins with and is perhaps most evident in
his defense of both jazz and African Americans against the persistent
and destructive racial myths that still permeate many of the critical and
popular conceptions about jazz and its practitioners. Marsalis confronted this myth directly in the editorial pages of the *New York Times.*
"The myth of the noble savage in jazz," he asserts, "which was born
early and stubbornly refuses to die, despite all the evidence to the contrary, regards jazz as merely as a product of noble savages—*music produced by untutored, unbuttoned semiliterates—for whom history does
not exist.*"[24] For Marsalis, jazz critics and the misinformed commentary
they produce are partly responsible for the perpetuation of this myth:
"This myth was invented by early jazz writers who, in attempting to
escape their American prejudice, turned out a whole world of new
clichés based on the myth of the innate ability of early jazz musicians.
Because of these writers' lack of understanding of the mechanics of
music, they thought there weren't any mechanics. It is the 'they all can
sing, they all have rhythm' syndrome."[25]

In contrast to the "semiliterate unbuttoned" image of the music that
the myth of the noble savage presents, Linda Williams, writing in the
*Wall Street Journal,* describes Marsalis as "a show business rarity: a
black performer who has built up a big mass-market audience while taking a black nationalist approach to his art."[26] Williams suggests that,
for Marsalis, "jazz is much more than entertainment: *It is an important
expression of the 20th century Black experience in America. 'Jazz is,' he
recently wrote, 'the nobility of the race put into sound; the sensuousness
of romance in our dialect; it is the picture of the people in all their
glory.'*"[27]

Given the history, social climate, and deep cultural roots of the myths
that Marsalis has taken on, one can begin to see the crucial role of racial
(and, for some, black nationalist) politics within his larger cultural and

aesthetic project. Indeed, as counterdiscourse, Marsalis attacks this poisonous cultural assault on black people and jazz from a position carefully crafted from his own cultural formation in the black South, his intellectual mentoring by Stanley Crouch and Albert Murray, and his considerable command of musical history, aesthetics, and mechanics:

> My generation finds itself wedged between two opposing traditions. One is the tradition we know in such wonderful detail from the enormous recorded legacy that tells anyone who will listen that jazz broke the rules of European conventions and created rules of its own that were so specific, so thorough, and so demanding that a great art resulted. This art has had such universal appeal and application that it has changed the conventions of American music as well as those of the world at large.[28]

As with his conception of aesthetics and his position on the commercial corruption threatening jazz, Marsalis's racial politics are the source of considerable controversy. He has publicly debated jazz critic James Lincoln Collier on jazz criticism (especially Collier's writing about Duke Ellington). He has attracted bitter and often heated criticism from neoconservative, liberal, even progressive cultural critics like Terry Treachout, Peter Watrous, and Gene Santoro. Neoconservative Treachout has even charged Marsalis with reverse racism, owing to Marsalis's hiring practices, booking policies, and his choices of repertory and commissions in the jazz program at Lincoln Center. While Treachout uses Marsalis's directorship of the program at Lincoln Center to attack Marsalis's intellectual mentors—Stanley Crouch and Albert Murray—his most vehement criticisms are directed toward Marsalis.[29] And while criticisms of Marsalis's choices in programming, orchestra personnel, and musical styles have come from musicians and critics alike, Treachout's is by far the most venomous in its disdain for the way that race in his view underwrites Marsalis's tenure as director. This criticism of Marsalis stems from Treachout's view of jazz as politically neutral, color-blind space of cultural and social practice, a space where, in his estimation, race should not, indeed cannot matter. Treachout suggests, for example, that "so far as can be determined, jazz was 'invented' around the turn of the 20th century by New Orleans blacks of widely varying musical education and ethnic background. . . . *But whites were playing jazz within a decade of its initial appearance, and began making important contributions to its stylistic development shortly thereafter. Until fairly recently, most musicians and scholars agreed that jazz long ago ceased to be a uniquely black idiom and became multicultural in the truest, least politicized sense of the word.*"[30]

Having established his view of jazz's historic multiculturalism, Treachout singles out Marsalis's Lincoln Center program for its race-based hiring policies and commissions. "Under Marsalis and Crouch," Treachout writes, "Jazz at Lincoln Center presents only programs about black musicians; whites are allowed to play with the Lincoln Center Jazz Orchestra, but the historic contributions of earlier white players, composers, and arrangers are systematically ignored, and contemporary white composers are not commissioned to write original pieces for the full orchestra. This policy is so egregiously race-conscious that it has even been attacked by admirers of Wynton Marsalis."[31] Treachout's essay is peppered throughout with direct attacks not just on Marsalis's guidance of the Lincoln Center jazz program, but Marsalis's character, politics, and musicianship. For instance,

> Marsalis is unapologetic about such matters [his controversial leadership at Lincoln Center] and apparently he can afford to be. At thirty-three, in addition to having performed and recorded much of the classical trumpet literature, he is the most famous jazz musician in America. . . . Interestingly, not all of these achievements hold equally well under scrutiny. Technically speaking, Marsalis is a virtuoso by any conceivable standard . . . but his jazz playing is felt by many to be cold and ironically enough derivative.

And,

> Marsalis takes seriously, his job as an unappointed spokesman for Albert Murray's and Stanley Crouch's version of the jazz tradition. . . . He has been quick to criticize other musicians, notably, Miles Davis and Sonny Rollins, for "selling out" to commercial music. And he is adamant in defending his conduct as artistic director of Jazz at Lincoln Center.

And finally,

> Although he uses white players both in the Lincoln Center Jazz Orchestra and in his own group, *it is widely believed that he harbors a general disdain for white musicians,* and the belief seems to be borne out by the facts.[32]

With passing digs at the generation of so-called "young lions" spawned by the success of Marsalis, Treachout details how racial politics in jazz operates: how privileging blackness in jazz works to the advantage of black players, in recording contracts, bookings, and appearances; how it contributes to the misrepresentation of social relations in the music (color-blind multiculturalism); and, perhaps most importantly, how it disadvantages white players. In the end, for Treachout, Marsalis is the most visible, successful, and hence egregious demonstration of the presence of reverse racism in jazz. He notes, bitterly, that one can easily multiply such examples to show how reverse racism has become, if not universal, then potentially legitimate in jazz and indeed, how it has insinuated itself throughout the jazz community. . . . The new reverse racism in jazz is not, of course, an isolated phenomena. It has arisen at a time when such government policies as quota-based affirmative action have made race-consciousness a pervasive feature of American society. In the absence of these policies . . . it is unlikely that public institutions like Lincoln Center and the Smithsonian Institution would lend the prestige of their names to artistic enterprises run on racialist lines, or submit meekly to cynical politicians playing the race card. . . . But that is just what makes the current epidemic in the jazz world so disturbing, and its implication so far-reaching.[33] Marsalis's aesthetic and racial politics make for some strange bedfellows, indeed. White neoconservative idealists who celebrate the color-blind, multicultural aspects of jazz, mainstream critics, and in some cases black radical avant-garde players have for different reasons challenged Marsalis's heady pronouncements and his leadership of the Lincoln Center program. On the other hand, Marsalis has also brought together neoconservative African American cultural critics and intellectuals, young black performers and largely liberal middle-class (white) audiences under a banner of a challenging but accessible middle-brow music, racial pride, and affirmation of American democracy and culture.

Marsalis's racial politics aim to establish the centrality of black presence and contributions to the American experience. Where Treachout sees (and aspires to) color blindness, Marsalis sees (and rejects) racial and cultural invisibility that is sustained by the continuing salience of racism in all aspects of American life and culture. Check out this 1994 exchange between Marsalis and an interviewer:

> Q: How closely is jazz bound up with the experience of African
>    Americans?
>
> Marsalis: It is inseparable—in its inception. They created it. But why has
>    who created it become more important than what was created? It
>    has transcended its inception . . .
>
> Q: One wonders if there will ever be a jazz innovator, someone on
>    the level of Ellington who is white?
>
> Marsalis: There might not, but it's not important. It doesn't make a difference. It is of no significance . . . why is it even an issue? That's
>    the thing you have to examine.
>
> Q: OK, why is it?

    *Marsalis:* Because in our time racism still carries more weight than musical
           fact. Duke Ellington didn't have enough white in him? He's an
           American. He's from Washington, DC.
        *Q:* People probably assume that it's important to you to say that all
           great innovators in jazz have been black.
    *Marsalis:* I don't have to say it. I just say Louis Armstrong. I don't say
           black Louis Armstrong. I mean "what about pride in humanity?"
           Ellington's achievement is his achievement. It's a human achieve-
           ment. Because, remember, the Afro-American experience is
           American experience. *Whenever the Negro is successful at some-
           thing, there has to be an excuse made up for the why. The best
           way to do this is to make his achievement seem like something
           only he can do, for some racially derived reason*—which removes
           the direct competition and exchange that actually exists.[34]

And in the more controlled context of his own book, *Sweet Swing
Blues on the Road*, Marsalis put the matter (the relationship between
jazz and black folk) this way:

> As Crouch says, "They invented it." People who invent something are
> always best at doing it, at least until other folk figure out what it is. If you
> celebrate less accomplished musicians because you share a superficial bond,
> you cheat yourself. Anyway if you ask most black Americans today who is
> their favorite jazz musician, they will name some instrumental pop musi-
> cian. So much for race. The younger musicians of any racial group today
> swing in spite of their race, not because of it.[35]

Regardless of the venue or the occasion, in the final analysis Marsalis's
view of the relationship between race and jazz is a complex amalgama-
tion of deep belief in the possibility of American democracy, a celebration of African American contributions to American culture, and a critique of racism. An individualist ethic drives both his creative spirit and
his sense of possibility for realizing his project in the institutional space
of Lincoln Center.

## INSTITUTIONAL REVOLUTION

If nothing else, Marsalis has certainly used his position as artistic director of the Lincoln Center jazz program as a platform to bring together
and realize a broader cultural project: to establish a jazz canon and create a space for its institutional legitimacy within a premier cultural institution. The conflicts over the realization of that project are as much generational as aesthetic and political. Peter Watrous, jazz critic for the
*New York Times,* characterizes the conflicts this way:

> In many ways the fight is over not only the direction of jazz at Lincoln Cen-
> ter, which has been an exceptional advocate of younger musicians, but also

the direction of jazz: Who has the right to represent it? What will its future be? How will its history be written? And despite the critics' prescriptive sound and fury, it's a fight that is over. The musicians, who commanded the bandstand, have won.[36]

If one accepts Watrous's critical appraisal, and I am strongly inclined to do so on the broader issue of cultural politics, then it is necessary to turn once again to Marsalis. For most critical observers agree he is *the* pivotal figure around which important institutional spaces have been opened and significant legitimation of and interest in the music realized. How Marsalis initially sought to realize this vision was set out in his 1988 *New York Times* editorial (well before his directorship of the Lincoln Center program was announced), where he wrote,

> We designed a Classical Jazz Series this year that deals with the music of Duke Ellington, Tadd Dameron, and Max Roach, as well as evenings given over to singers and instrumentalists interpreting standard songs. This series focuses on two things: the *compositions of major writers and the quality of improvisation.* . . . While enjoyment and entertainment are paramount matters in the Classical Jazz Series, it should be clear that we also see a need to *help promote understandings of what happens in jazz.* An important part of the series, therefore, are program notes by Stanley Crouch, which seek *to explain the intent of the musicians as well as the meaning of the art.* . . . We feel that the proper presentation of notes, song titles and even small discographies will help audiences better understand the essential elements of the music and thereby enjoy the music even more. . . . Classical Jazz at Lincoln Center—whether celebrating the work of individual artists or using improvisational talents of masters . . . is intent on helping to give jazz, its artists and its products their deserved place in American culture. I also feel that the Classical Jazz Series gives Lincoln Center additional reason to regard itself as a center of world culture.[37]

Since 1988, through the Classical Series, commissioned works, collaborations, media and education, performance, and critical engagement with the discourse on jazz, Marsalis has used the institutional space and international reputation of Lincoln Center quite effectively— namely to increase the visibility and legitimacy of jazz.[38] For Marsalis, the recognition of a jazz canon by cultural institutions like Lincoln Center not only ensures the music's survival and legitimation in the society's dominant cultural institutions, but provides him with a prominent public forum from which to engage in political struggles over culture.

The effectiveness of Marsalis's cultural project cannot be ascribed solely to him, in isolation from the social, economic, and cultural transformations that have occurred in jazz since about 1990. Despite his effective intervention into the discursive debates on jazz, there have been notable developments in the political economy of the recording industry, corporate sponsorship of jazz festivals and performance venues, media coverage, education and training, and research on jazz. Many of the performance venues—notably small independent jazz clubs—have been replaced by corporate sponsorship, national franchises, megafestivals, and multicity tours.[39] Remaining local independent venues have to regularly book "name" talent to attract large and affluent-enough audiences in order to make their operations profitable. Although clubs and local performance venues long associated with jazz continue to turn over at a rapid pace, new forms of public cultural and financial support for the music have appeared in the form of foundation support, juried competitions, degree programs, research programs, and repertory programs at colleges and universities. Programs like those at Lincoln Center, the Kennedy Center, and Carnegie Hall are complemented by performance competitions like the Theolonious Monk Institute and research archives like the Institute for Jazz Studies at Rutgers University, the Center for Black Music Research Center in Chicago, the Smithsonian Institution, and the American Research Center.[40]

As for recorded music, the compact disk of course has replaced the vinyl LP as the standard format in which recorded music is presented. Through various distribution arrangements and marketing strategies between record companies and major corporations, jazz is effectively reaching new markets. Notable examples are arrangements between Blue Note Records and Starbucks Coffee, as well as those between cigarette manufacturers, liquor companies, car manufacturers, and jazz festivals.[41] Music videos, television commercials, and special campaigns (e.g., the U.S. Postal Service's commemorative stamp series on jazz legends) also have become an important means through which the music gains exposure. And, of course, public television and cable television (e.g., Bravo, Black Entertainment Television) have become important media outlets for showcasing jazz. For the most part, public and college radio remain the primary radio outlets for jazz, particularly since commercial outlets in major urban areas like New York, Los Angeles, and the San Francisco Bay Area no longer exist.

Audiences for jazz—both those who purchase the music on compact disk and those who attend concerts and clubs—are increasingly educated, affluent, young, and very often white.[42] To be sure Marsalis and his "young lion" associates have also helped stimulate interests in jazz on the part of black middle-class youth, some of whom, ironically, are also drawn to those commercial forms that Marsalis fears most for their insidious effects on the music—rap, acid jazz, house, jungle music, dance hall, and reggae. These styles have brought young people to jazz by way of a search for new stylistic possibilities, as well as a familiarity with earlier players and styles within the jazz tradition.[43]

The popular and critical coverage of jazz, much of which is aimed at young affluent consumers, is limited to a small but energetic jazz press, including publications like *Down Beat, Jazz Times,* and *Jazz Is.* In the press, popular coverage of the music is limited largely to major metropolitan dailies like the *New York Times* and the *Los Angeles Times.* A growing body of independent films (e.g., *A Great Day in Harlem*), biographies, and scholarly monographs have begun to emerge as well.[44]

## THE ROAD AND THE STREET

I want to propose that Marsalis's canonical project at Lincoln Center, while an expression of one form of resistant black culture, is also fundamentally conservative. Musicians and critics alike view this as a project that constructs a classical canon by formalizing it into static texts and confining it to museums, conservatories, and cultural institutions.[45] In fact, drawing on the insights of Amiri Baraka and African American literature, Nathaniel Mackey argues that such projects move jazz from a "verb" to a "noun."[46] In its "high modernist" tone and aesthetic assumptions, Marsalis's pronouncements on the aesthetic dangers and commercial corruption of popular music joins long-standing cultural debates about the relationship of high culture to popular culture and the contaminating effects of the latter on the former.[47] In Marsalis's cultural universe, the move to locate the corrosive effects of the popular arts on the jazz canon is, no doubt, a powerful political move.

In a climate of neoconservative assault on the arts and culture, Marsalis's cultural project is especially appealing precisely because it is built on crucial assumptions about the value of "culture" (and morality) in the still unrealized potential of American democracy. Politically, this scheme accepts a (traditional) view of the erosion of culture and values (which are under assault) and links it to powerful agencies of legitimation and recognition that aim to fix the limits of culture and protect it from the corrupting forces of the market, commerce, and untutored tastes. I find this position and its aesthetics culturally and politically conventional and elitist, the way that traditionalists (both radical and conservative) have always been on the question of popular culture. This vision relies on discourses and institutions of legitimation and power, a discerning and informed public, a critical community of judgment and evaluation, and powerful institutions to value and signal as important the conventions, technical rules, literatures, practitioners, and tradition on which a canon is constructed.[48]

Conservative or not, I do recognize, and even applaud, the strategic and effective interventions of Marsalis. Not so much as a capitulation to Marsalis's aesthetic and cultural politics, but to acknowledge the sheer complexity of the position and the effective results that Marsalis has staked out and enacted at Lincoln Center.

Where Marsalis mobilizes his rhetorical positions and institutional tactics around the need to canonize jazz, to ensure it institutional legitimacy in the broader American cultural landscape, when examined from within the politics of African American music a different set of cultural practices and political possibilities emerge. There *is* another approach to the jazz tradition. Indeed, when one considers the tradition itself and the productive practices and social conditions that shaped it, one finds many of the corruptive influences that Marsalis and his intellectual mentors fear most for their baneful effects on the music—popularity, dance, mass marketing, and the influence of popular styles.

While I can only gesture toward this other approach to the tradition—an approach which I characterize as the sensibility of the road and the street—I do so in order to make a point about the study of cultural practices and to foreground the politics at work in a different approach to jazz as a site of cultural struggle. By indicating an alternative to what I have called a "canonization project," I do not mean to suggest that the sensibilities and practices of a road-and-street aesthetic do not exist in Marsalis's own project. In fact, in *Sweet Swing Blues on the Road,* Marsalis writes quite robustly about the centrality of the road to his own formation and continuing practice as a jazz musician. I do, however, mean to underscore the fact that the locations and conditions of production where jazz maintains its *motion and movement, innovation and expansion,* continue in those cultural spaces outside canonical discourses and institutional practices of legitimation.

I take the metaphor of the road and the street from the great territory bands of the 1930s and 1940s. The road (as opposed to, for instance, the "tour") was an expression used by musicians to describe life on the road—the experience of traveling from community to community, town to town, city to city to perform. The music, social relations, and cultural styles which defined urban black communities in the 1940s and 1950s were, as cultural historian Robin D. G. Kelley brilliantly details, the basis for the formation among many working-class blacks of political consciousness and cultural understanding of blackness.[49] Kelley argues that it was black popular forms and cultural styles found in the streets and clubs of black urban America that gave shape and expression to the cultural and political consciousness of blacks.

On the road, musicians perfected their skills, discovered new musical influences and players, made friends, and constructed communities that extended beyond the immediate confines of geography. Encounters on the road allowed musicians and bands to sharpen their acts, pick up new talent, modify their books, and gauge the response to their music. The literal road and the street, then, were places where musicians borrowed and mixed styles and experimented with new possibilities. In the process, they created music that was dynamic, dialogic, and fashioned out of the experiences and needs of everyday life. While I have no desire to re-create this literal "road and street," I do want to shift the discussion from this literal and historical road and street to a metaphorical one.

Although very much rooted in a jazz tradition, the metaphorical road and street of jazz as a cultural practice depends on a different conception of and relationship to the tradition. It requires a conception rooted in constant change and transformation, where tradition is not simply abstracted, codified, and preserved in critical judgments, cultural institutions and repertory performance. In this image of jazz as a cultural practice, the music lives and breathes, as it were, in the active creations and experiences of changing performance and encounters with contemporary ideas, styles, influences, and performance possibilities, including those in popular and commercial culture. This difference in conception and approach represents far more than a semantic disagreement or conceptual dispute over how the music is represented. The point of the tradition in this view of jazz practice (including its canonical manifestations) is to change it, to reinvent it, to emphasize its "verbal" character, as Mackey puts it.[50]

In contrast to the aim of building a canonical tradition in order to ensure a place of legitimacy and recognition by dominant cultural institutions, an entire cohort of Marsalis's contemporaries—Don Byron, Gerri Allen, Steve Coleman, Cassandra Wilson, Graham Haynes, Courtney Pine, Kenny Garrett, and Branford Marsalis—continually draw from a range of stylistic influences which challenge and stretch the tradition. These musicians, like many of their predecessors, keep jazz moving through its engagement with popular forms, new technologies, and commercial routes of circulation. Instead of protecting the jazz tradition from the corrupting influences of popular and commercial forms like reggae, rap, rhythm and blues, dance hall (as well as Native American, South Asian, and African forms), this cohort of contemporary musicians expands the jazz tradition by reworking it through metaphorical encounters in the literal street. With an emphatic stress on the verbal rather than nominal dimension of the music, these musicians are engaged in a dynamic reinvention and dialogic rewriting of the tradition.

JAZZ AND CULTURAL POLITICS

I want to conclude, then, by highlighting the analytic and political implications of these two distinct, but related, cultural practices. These two kinds of practice operate simultaneously, very often existing side by side, within the same social, economic, and discursive space. And yet I think it is fair to say that, culturally, the distinct political effects and possibilities of each are quite different. Those practices that gain a measure of institutional recognition and legitimacy are privileged in terms of visibility, funding, and reproduction. I believe that this very move also results in the marginalization and displacement of practices (and musicians) that do not enjoy a similar recognition and legitimacy. They point in different ways to different modalities and registers, different aesthetic possibilities, and cultural strategies that challenge, even rearrange, dominant conceptions and judgments of the music.

Marsalis and his supporters effectively consolidated and institutionalized a specific conception of jazz within a dominant cultural institution like Lincoln Center for the Performing Arts. Moreover, the program at Lincoln Center is emblematic of the legitimation of jazz that rests on powerful social and cultural assumptions about the value of art (in this case, "real jazz") as one important source for the inculcation of core American values—morality, integrity, and responsibility. Like the treatments of baseball and the Civil War, this narrative of jazz as both the expression and realization of what is quintessentially American is at the heart of the Ken Burns's PBS documentary on the history of jazz.[51] With Wynton Marsalis as one of the central consultants and on-camera experts (jazz critic and Marsalis associate Stanley Crouch serves as another, as does the writer Albert Murray) in the documentary, PBS's *Jazz* and the installation of a jazz department at Lincoln Center is, I would argue, *the* final discursive move in the canonization of this specific narrative of jazz in the American cultural imagination. It is also crucial to the representation of late-twentieth-century American society and, in

Burns's view (if the documentary is any indication), the culmination of the long march toward racial equality, a march that celebrates cultural diversity as one of the signal achievements of American democracy.[52]

I highlight the importance of these cultural moves by Marsalis and Ken Burns, not because I agree with their aesthetic position or the cultural politics on which they rest, but because I think they illustrate the complexity and significance of various kinds of black cultural moves, especially their political impact in the wider cultural and social arena of American culture.

Popular and critical discourses as well as significant financial support and interest have congealed around Marsalis's notion of jazz, its key texts, and exemplars. Culturally, this has resulted in the creation of a significant social and cultural space for jazz in popular discourse, the marketplace, and cultural institutions. In the context of ongoing wars about culture, values, and art, this is surely a significant accomplishment. And as the polemic surrounding Marsalis's tenure at Lincoln Center indicates, the continuing political struggles over how jazz is constructed, represented, and positioned does matter.

# CHAPTER 3

# The Jazz Left

At the level of cultural and aesthetic politics, the jazz left offers a distinctly different, but no less legitimate, oppositional critique about the place of jazz and black creative music in the national culture.[1] I deliberately contrast with the canon makers this distinct project and the cultural politics that it enacts.

By arguing for the viability of an alternative (and at times related) set of practices and narrative accounts of the music in the most expansive and dynamic sense, I don't want to suggest that such competing projects can be reduced to simple binary formulations of good and bad practices or progressive and reactionary cultural politics, or that musicians and critics aligned with one might not appreciate, be influenced by, or even advocate for the other.[2]

I do mean, however, to make this project—its cultural logic and *moves* (especially its assumptions and politics)—visible. In other words, I want to consider critically the practices, spaces, networks, assumptions, and social relations of an approach to the music that emphasizes the expansive possibilities in jazz in terms of its *movement, innovation, and openness.* I contend that such projects often go unnoticed and are thus relegated to the margins of cultural discourses about jazz and black creative music, because the terms, spaces, and operations that structure them, define their practices, and position their practitioners very often exist beyond the logic of canonical recognition, institutional legitimacy, and conventional discourse.[3]

## MOTION AND MOVEMENT

By using the metaphor of *motion and movement,* evoked by "the road and the street," I emphasize the *verbal and transgressive aspects* of the discourses and practices of the "jazz left." By emphasizing flow, movement, and dynamism, I want to stress the dynamic of change that is also central to the production and practice of jazz and creative music. As mentioned in the last chapter, I take as one early expression of this formulation the great black territory bands of the 1930s and 1940s, for whom the road was an experience of travel from community to community, town to town, city to city.[4] The music, social relations, and cultural styles that defined urban black communities in the 1940s and 1950s were the basis for the formation of political consciousness, cultural understanding, and social affiliation among blacks of the day, especially the working class.[5]

I also use the metaphor of the road and its imagery of movement, openness, and transgression to emphasize the social (and institutional) conditions of possibility—collective forms of social organization, shared experimentation, and a willingness to take risks—that make such innovation possible in the first place. Musicians from Charles Mingus, Ornette Coleman, Thelonious Monk, John Coltrane, and Sun Ra, to the great collectives in the 1960s, 1970s, and 1980s like the Association for the Advancement of Creative Musicians (AACM) in Chicago, the Black Artist Group (BAG) in St. Louis, Horace Tapscott's Pan African Orchestra in Los Angeles, Ornette Coleman's Artist House, Sam Rivers's RivBea Studio in New York, and M-BASE in Brooklyn, all exemplify the kinds of organizational models, musical practices, and aesthetic approaches that I characterize as the jazz left.[6] The music, social relations, and discourses produced by these communities, the aesthetic assumptions that guided them, and the organizational circumstances through which they developed depended on a dynamic conception of the tradition and a willingness to embrace forms that were formally located (by the reigning jazz discourse anyway) outside of jazz.[7] Seminal figures on the jazz left approach the jazz tradition not just as a set of texts and discursive practices organized by strict rules of interpretation and performance, institutions, and formal systems of evaluation and judgment. To be sure, such rules and procedures do exist, as they must in all forms of art.[8] However, in contrast to the unerring devotion to a set of codified texts that come alive through performance, for practitioners of the jazz left the music lives in the active creations and interactions evolving out of performances and encounters with contemporary ideas, styles, and tastes, including those in popular and commercial culture.[9]

The distinction that I want to foreground here, between the formal stasis of a canonical project and the dynamism, openness, and collective impulse of the jazz left, moves well beyond a mere semantic dispute or conceptual disagreement about how the music is represented or who gets to represent it.[10] I am more concerned with the cultural politics of the matter, that is, how systems of evaluation, assumptions, practices, procedures, and resources authorize and privilege one set of musical practices as against another. Canonical or not, all conceptions of cultural production depend on systematic procedures of selection, production, evaluation, and exhibition.[11] Cultural practices that aim systematically to sustain and reproduce themselves depend on some formulation and codification of a past, a tradition. A central point of dispute in the Lincoln Center controversy (and with respect to black cultural politics more generally) is the role of that tradition, how it is narrated and represented, the uses to which it is put, how it is involved in the formation and extension of cultural visibility and authority. For members of the jazz left, in contrast to the canon makers, the point of the tradition is to change it, reinvent it, emphasize its "verbal" character, as Nathaniel Mackey so elegantly puts it. In the politics of culture, reinvention has a price.

## DISRUPTION AND DISCONTINUITY: PRECURSORS

A cohort of Marsalis's contemporaries loosely constitutes what I refer to as the jazz left. Don Byron, Gerri Allen, Steve Coleman, Gene Lake, Cassandra Wilson, Graham Haynes, Greg Osby, Kenny Garrett, James Carter, Terri Lynn Carrington, Vernon Reid, and Branford Marsalis draw liberally from a wide range of musical influences. These players expand and extend the very tradition that Marsalis and the canon makers at Lincoln Center want to formalize and protect from the contaminating influences of commercial culture and untutored tastes.[12] These musicians, like their musical predecessors, keep jazz moving by their active engagement with and incorporation of popular influences, new technologies, and commercial possibilities. Instead of canonizing and protecting the jazz tradition from the corrupting influences of popular and commercial forms like reggae, rap, rhythm and blues, and dance hall (not to mention various experimental, electronic, and world musics), this cohort of the contemporary jazz left expands the tradition by reworking it through their encounters with both the metaphorical and the literal street.[13] As such, these contemporaries of Marsalis challenge and unsettle the jazz status quo, thereby joining a thirty-year "tradition" whose immediate origins go back to the 1950s.

Cecil Taylor, Ornette Coleman, Don Cherry, John Coltrane, Sun Ra, and Albert Ayler represented a generation of avant-gardists who also took an expansive approach to jazz by going outside of the quickly forming stylistic center of be-bop.[14] Taylor and Coleman, in particular, continue to be active and ironically are now viewed in some quarters of the jazz establishment (and the press) as vital parts of the same tradition that they troubled and expanded. At the same time, for canon makers they are occasionally still the objects of lingering and sometimes bitter suspicion. Players like Coleman and Taylor are still accused of not really being jazz players, and derided for having experimented and aggressively pushed the boundaries of the music.

Ornette Coleman is in many ways typical of the earliest generation of experimental players and composers. Still prolific as ever, Coleman has recently enjoyed the kind of modest commercial success and sustained critical support that has ironically led to national prizes (e.g., a 1994 MacArthur Fellowship) and a tribute by none other than Lincoln Center. Today, such accolades may place Coleman closer to the jazz status quo than even he might have imagined. Nonetheless, such longevity and sustained critical acclaim have not dampened Coleman's openness to new ideas or his critical stance on narrow and conventional approaches to the tradition. In 1996 he told *Down Beat* magazine:

> Like everything in Western culture, everything has to have a value more than to yourself, no matter what you do, regardless of how good you are or how bad you are, how beautiful or how ugly. You have to, if you're going to come to the stage of expression, first find the people who will allow you in their territory. To see if the value of what you do fits the image of what they're doing in relationship to wealth. Some people will find that quicker than others. There's nothing wrong with that; it becomes more like a personal privilege than a free opportunity. I think that's the reason why the music in America is so limited as far as concepts of sound. America, it's a young country, and yet the ancestors that ran America came from an old country. I don't think we'll ever catch up.[15]

Ornette Coleman works in a variety of performance settings and venues, with a number of different performance units (including his electric band, Prime Time, that plays creative music ranging from pop and rock to folk and vernacular world musics). He has even included video presentations, poetry readings, and body-piercing demonstrations in his performances. As one writer put it, "Coleman's notions relate to art as a total concept, not something chiseled at and compartmentalized in the ongoing process of creating a global niche culture."[16]

Because Coleman has so consistently worked across many musical boundaries, transforming and extending, merging, and mixing them, to categorize him strictly as a jazz player is to limit and fix him in ways that defy his extraordinary career and influence on music, most especially jazz. Fittingly enough, it is this very broad approach to sound and music that defines Coleman's most significant influence on jazz. In an affectionate letter to Coleman published by *Down Beat* in 1992, music critic John Litweiler wrote,

> You certainly altered the mainstream of jazz. There is a mainline or mainstream of jazz development that stretches from Buddy Bolden and James Reece Europe down to the very latest work by Edward Wilkerson and Dennis Gonsalez. Before you came along, Ornette, a very few individuals . . . and idioms (early jazz, swing, bop and their extensions) dominated jazz. Even though you and some others have exerted a very wide influence indeed, so many separate idioms have appeared . . . that no single individual or idiom dominates; it's as if the mainstream of jazz has become a delta, like the mainstream of other western arts near the end of the 20th century.[17]

Coleman has long insisted on an ecumenical approach to jazz that opened and stretched the music, transgressed boundaries, and reinvented the tradition. Ornette and his contemporaries can be credited with extending its compositional possibilities, taking the music into the concert hall, and opening the way for jazz to engage with sound and personality the way that Armstrong, Ellington, Parker, Davis, and Coltrane did.

Institutionally and organizationally, Coleman codified his Herculean efforts into Harmolodics, Inc. Located in New York and administered by his son and manager, Denardo Coleman, Harmolodics, Inc., is named after the Coleman-invented theoretical system that defines and guides his approach to the music. Part record company, part rehearsal studio and management umbrella for his various performing units and creative projects, Harmolodics, Inc., is the culmination of a life's work and a work in progress.[18]

Coleman's career stresses the gaps and discontinuities of a cultural formation and tradition in contrast to the Lincoln Center construction of the tradition, which emphasizes continuities and inheritances, regularities and signal moments. In the figure of Coleman and others of his generation, one finds the fits and starts, conflicts and tensions of discontinuity and interruption, which result in a very different story of the jazz tradition. As Gene Santoro says about Coleman, "his music, of course, still sets the mainstream on edge, even after his decades on the scene."[19] In his sheer originality and creative imagination, Coleman's music "broke out of what had become jazz's prison house of language: the recurrent cycle of chords, basic to the theory—thirty-two-bar song form—his tunes, which then as now tended to turn on bluesy, boppish figures or near nursery rhymes, were designed to be open, so that musicians could modulate from key to key, chord to chord, rhythm to rhythm when the need struck them."[20]

This approach was the source of freedom that so threatened the conventions of be-bop's stylistic dominance that Coleman and his colleagues were regarded by the members of the jazz establishment as mavericks or impostors or just plain incompetent. As a composer and improviser, this freedom afforded Coleman and his colleagues an incredible range of compositional latitude and improvisational flexibility, since Coleman's music encouraged players to explore and combine different musics, styles, tonal structures, and performance possibilities. The commitment to this freedom accounts for Coleman's still-current forays into funk, pop, and electronic as well as vernacular music. Coleman and his colleagues moved freely through different musics, extending and building on the tradition without being slaves to it.

This freedom, the challenges to convention it produced, and the conflicts that resulted heighten some of the very tensions and discontinuities that narratives of tradition and continuity must, of necessity, make representable by repressing, incorporating, or at least formally confining jazz and its tradition to conventional structures and definitions. In this respect, Ornette Coleman's explorations forced a reckoning with the tension between soloist and the collective, composition and improvisation. According to music critic Gene Santoro, Coleman has an incisive understanding of jazz's peculiarly American dialectic."

> First is the relation between the role of composition and the role of improvisation. . . . Second, like every important figure in the music from Jelly Roll Morton on, Coleman has sought his own way to reconcile the corollary pull between the individual whose need to shape a unique voice out of the past's shards is a jazz axiom, and the group whose ability and need to interact in spontaneity and support the individual are necessary if the music is going to make internal sense.[21]

Santoro argues that such tensions emphasize "improvisation" as the common element in jazz. Rather than pursue a path of music based largely on interpretation and thereby risk sure death, jazz has negotiated these tensions by developing a series of dialects. If one accepts Santoro's proposition, one sees that the contestation over such dialects is probably the greatest source of struggle and disagreement in the controversy about who is in and out, what is jazz and what is not. But I would go further and suggest that at the center of these disputes is a set of discursive operations—*assertions and claims* rooted in appeals to authenticity, a pure history, anointed players, and a *codified set of standards* by which the music's value can be asserted and defended.[22] Where the canon makers look to the past as the basis of cultural authority and social legitimacy, members of the jazz left look to the present and the future without resorting to an implicit hierarchy of claims or styles for what counts and who decides.

Ornette Coleman and his contemporaries introduced new vocabularies, conceptual approaches, and solutions to the tensions between soloist and group, composition and improvisation, voicing and instrumentation. While it may appear that they were not especially effective at consolidating their interventions into formal institutions beyond working bands and recorded collaborations, their lasting contributions were codified into distinctive compositions and performances that have become their own sort of standards. The frontal force of these musical advances has become synonymous with key players, recording dates, and occasionally well-worn compositions like Coleman's "Lonely Woman" or Coltrane's "A Love Supreme." The codification of the challenges of this generation of the jazz left is, I think, the expressive effect of a set of territorial and discursive skirmishes which were played out on the terrain of rather conventional sites and narratives of jazz history. The Burns PBS documentary and the recent Lincoln Center programs are simply the latest expression of such skirmishes.

## COLLECTIVES, CREATIVITY, COMMUNITY

The succeeding generation of avant-gardists on the jazz left learned key lessons from their predecessors. In addition to absorbing the new language, the spirit of experimentation, and collaborative practices of the prior generation, they created or became involved with "community-based" organizations that also served as performance venues, training centers, and organizational sites in which to cultivate new players and audiences. They also articulated complex formulations about their music, practice, and politics. The Association for the Advancement of Creative Musicians (AACM) and its many performance units are emblematic of this organizational involvement and cultural stance.[23] The AACM was the direct beneficiary of the early generation and a formative cultural organization through which many significant members of the contemporary jazz left developed.[24]

The members of the AACM cultivated an expansive approach to the their music. Indeed, among the myriad combinations of performance possibilities and collaborations that sprang from the AACM was the Art Ensemble of Chicago, a group that operated "in the space cleared by the freedom seekers like John Coltrane, Ornette Coleman, Cecil Taylor and Albert Ayler." Accordingly, "the Art Ensemble was busy tinkering with and retooling the tradition, making explicit references to various folkforms, utilizing extended non-energy improvisations, and advancing an expanded notion of multi-instrumentalism with tables of little instruments."[25]

This view of the music and the tradition produced a conceptual approach and practice that considered exploration and experimentation as the rule rather than the exception. The influences of the contemporary music scene (including both experimental music and commercial popular music) provided the musical and social landscape in which musical ideas developed and flourished. The aesthetic gaze was toward the present and the future (with a deep appreciation of the importance of tradition). As such, the tradition was not so much absent or dismissed as it was a building block for new possibilities. Coming as it did at the height of the black power movement and struggles for black political empowerment and cultural autonomy, groups like the AACM and BAG themselves either became central components of community organizations or members joined community-based organizations.[26] BAG and AACM often functioned as the cultural components of community-based movements for cultural awareness and political empowerment that sprang up in local centers. Musicians staged concerts, offered music lessons, ran after-school programs for kids, and participated in local community actions. All of these efforts were locally rooted and guided by a collective sense of cultural tradition and practice.[27] Together with their ecumenical conception of black music and its tradition, these qualities helped to establish and define a model of cultural practice that, while less visible to traditional institutions, is no less effective as a project that seeks recognition, legitimacy, and institutionalization.[28]

For the purpose of establishing the historical and aesthetic genealogy of the contemporary jazz left, following in particular George Lewis, Eric Porter, Ron Radano, and others, I want to emphasize the centrality of the collectivist practice and aesthetic approach of the AACM and one of its most important exemplars, the Art Ensemble of Chicago. This is how jazz writer John Corbett appraises the importance of the.AACM: "The organization is now unquestionably a landmark institution, and recordings like Roscoe Mitchell's *Sound* (Delmark), Richard Muhal Abrams' *Mama and Daddy* (Black Saint), Anthony Braxton's *For Alto* (Delmark), the Art Ensemble of Chicago's *Fanfare for the Warrior* (Atlantic) all bear testament to its overwhelming importance in the lineage of contemporary jazz."[29] Corbett's characterization of the AACM as a "landmark" institution is what interests me most here, for it goes some way toward establishing that the AACM represents a powerful alternative model of institutional formation and cultural practice.

Again according to Corbett, "the AACM is not merely a museumified monument. Rather, it is an ongoing project, a living community of players, teachers, and students who measure their success in terms of commitment to a way of musical life they learned in the Association."[30] Fashioned from the centrality of political commitment and a collectivist community-based organizational structure, the AACM developed, nurtured, and circulated a distinctive aesthetic approach to the tradition. An impressive group of musicians has been trained and supported in this institutional context, absorbing and reproducing its aesthetic approach and cultural practice. Outside of Chicago, the AACM's sphere of influence is perhaps most evident in New York City, where Corbett suggests that "the New York Jazz scene sounds much the way it does today as a result of the work set in motion by this Midwest collective back in May 1965. Even outside the bounds of 'jazz' musicians as far afield as the rock group The dBs and the noise band the Fat have claimed the AACM as direct influence."[31]

Although the AACM claims an impressive list of past and present members, the Art Ensemble of Chicago (composed of the late trumpeter Lester Bowie, saxophonists Joseph Jarman and Rocoe Mitchell, percussionist Don Moye, and the late bassist Malachi Favors Maghostus) is one of the performance units which most typifies its aesthetic approach, collective organizational structure, and political commitments. By the 1990s the AEC was in its third decade as a working unit. Howard Mandel described them as "using African rhythms, modern compositional techniques, be-bop, do-whop, swing, reggae, dixie-land shuffles and struts, subtle atmospheric effects, and raging free improvisation . . . to redefine jazz."[32] Their music has even been described as the "creolization of time and culture."[33] Don Moye, the AEC's percussionist claims that "the term jazz applies to only one of the idioms we deal with. It's all great black and we respect all its forms—they're part of our musical heritage."[34]

The grand sweep of this approach to the music is also expressed in the AEC's stage performance, instrumentation, and process of song selection. Appreciated as much for their inventive costumes and stage craft as for their musical eclecticism, the members regard this as an expression of the group's collective ideals, which they developed as members of the AACM. As Roscoe Mitchell said, "we were musicians in Chicago who had the desire to have more control over our own destinies, that's what the AACM is all about. We were able to sit down together and analyze the past and figure out our plans for the future. The philosophy of the AACM and the AEC . . . has spilled over into other things besides playing."[35] In terms of their expansive view of the music and the aesthetic sources that inform it, member Joseph Jarman describes the band this way:

> The myth and image of the Art Ensemble as a cult group is fading because of the realness of our diverse appeal and the credibility with which we engage in so many different musical forms, and the elements of our performances are not unique to black culture. We face paint, for example, not as war paint but in place of masks, which are used in cultures of every ethnicity to subjugate the personality of the performer so he can more easily become a representative of the community. Masks and costumes make universal statements and are archetypal symbols. We use Afro-American elements because they're closest to our experiences. But it's an American experience too. So even if we don't play rock, rock audiences understand us. So do traditional jazz fans, though we may not play much traditional jazz.[36]

So in musical philosophy, organizational structure, and cultural practice, the AEC's members and their contemporaries push the conceptual boundaries of the tradition, being neither exclusive nor dismissive. Indeed, one writer described the AACM as a "harmony force in free jazz" that "brought back blues, the sound of traditional jazz and swing," along with "long-ignored instruments such as the violin and clarinet, and self-invented and found instruments. They were creating new extended forms and even restructuring the jazz ensemble. Rhythm section–less wind groups and unaccompanied horn solos appeared."[37]

In terms of the rudiments of an institutional structure, a distinctive aesthetic approach, and an enduring cultural practice through which that approach was enacted and reproduced, the second generation of

freedom seekers is important. The AACM and their many contemporaries extended the achievement of Ornette Coleman and his generation,
laying the groundwork for the continuing consolidation and reproduction of the jazz left.


## THE JAZZ LEFT

The cohort of contemporary avant-vangardists and experimenters
expresses what I call road-and-street sensibility because of these musicians' willingness to transgress the boundaries of racial, musical, and
aesthetic categories. Typical of this transgressive approach is clarinetist
Don Byron, who works in a variety of settings and draws from myriad
social, political, and cultural influences, including European classical,
Jewish, folk, vernacular, and Cuban popular and traditional music.
Explaining his use of the term the *jazz left,* which I have borrowed liberally, Byron says, "*I made the case that jazz's left half is being marginalized.* It is being marginalized by people who present jazz in institutions, on the radio, in print and everybody knows that."[38] Going right
to the heart of the cultural politics that concern me here, Byron's elaboration is instructive: "*I thought jazz left of Lincoln Center needed an
institutional home* because it didn't have one. . . . I think Carnegie
Hall and Lincoln Center have really elevated jazz's status and the music
and musicians I know could use that sort of help. The way I see it, jazz
is a two-headed monster, with a Democratic and Republican side, and
without the Democratic side the beast dies."[39]

In their relationship to the music, the quest for institutional stability
and longevity, and the cultural practices and sensibilities that define
their music, players associated with what Byron calls the "Democratic
side" of jazz approach the music like previous generations of experimenters and avant-gardists. In terms of technical competence, imagination, and openness to all kinds of musical influences and sources, Byron
is one of the most gifted and prolific members of his generation. He is
equally at home with the music of Duke Ellington as with klezmer great
Micky Katz, rock, calypso, or classical chamber music.[40] Not surprisingly, Byron's sense of privilege to draw from such a wide range of music
is an expression of his musical formation and commitment to stretching
boundaries, as this *Wall Street Journal* profile explains:

> The upbringing that gave Byron his sense of entitlement combined rigorous
> classical training with the media sensibility of a child of the 60s. "The real
> basis of my aesthetic was the TV show *Shindgig.* I identified with the

backup band. Those cats could play behind anyone—Jackie Wilson, Chuck Berry, the Righteous Brothers, the Lettermen . . . my parents took me to the New York Philharmonic, but I was more interested in Lawrence Welk. His band featured a clarinet and they were on TV."[41]

Byron is passionate about his openness to popular and commercial influences and his refusal of a one-dimensional conception of the tradition. He rejects the press and music industry categories used to define him, his musical approach, and his choice of subjects. Here is Byron on the press's fascination with his interest in (and mastery of) klezmer music: "I'm not doing Jewish music instead of doing classical music instead of doing black music. I play what I like and I don't feel the need to live one genre of music like the young be-bop cats who only listen to be-bop and put down pop music."[42]

Technology has also given Byron access to a kind of global street traffic and musical marketplace, from which he and his contemporaries draw on pop and vernacular resources to extend their rich musical imaginations. Byron's ecumenical approach to the full range of musical options from James Brown to Mickey Katz is what makes Byron and his contemporaries so interesting and compelling musically, perhaps even threatening to the jazz traditionalist and canon defenders.[43] Byron and Marsalis might even be seen by some as working much the same musical and cultural territory (thematically and in terms of their mastery of different musical idioms and styles). But Byron is clearly motivated by a sense of moving the music and the tradition beyond different musical and cultural borders, while Marsalis has devoted much of his public energy and credibility to establishing and then bolstering a narrow view of the jazz tradition. In this rather lengthy response, Byron comments on his conception of the tradition:

> I would say that for me jazz is a new music idiom and so is classical music, even though the majority of what happens in classical music has nothing to do with new music. I don't even think that preservation is really even relevant . . . in the sense that what the idiom is about isn't reproducing, isn't at least all about reproducing a past sound. Like Beethoven isn't a reproduction of Mozart or Brahms isn't a reproduction of Bach, and they all consider themselves part of the same tradition, there is this sense that things have to move on and I consider both jazz and classical music not folk idioms. I think the jazz idiom has to decide whether it wants to be a folk idiom or whether it wants to treat itself as if it's art music, when what it's really doing is creating a folk music atmosphere. We're turning Oscar Peterson's playing or even Wayne Shorter's playing into some kind of music repetition thing. And you can't really have both. You're either art music

and you're about what's gonna happen next or you're not. People who are the most conservative are dominating the talk, the press, the whole debate—a conservative tone. What little money is being spit out by the NEA, some of these conservative cats are dominating sort of who gets what and what kind of music gets funded.[44]

In taking this critical position Byron is by no means unique. His position is typical of other contemporary players on the jazz left.

Greg Osby, saxophonist and cofounder, with Steve Coleman, of the Brooklyn-based collective M-BASE, is, like Byron, passionate and outspoken, ecumenical, and eclectic in his use of popular and commercial influences in his work. Like Coleman, Osby counts among his cultural influences be-bop, Motown, kung-fu movies, and funk. The M-BASE collective was "a group of black musicians, mostly in their late 20s or 30s (at the time of the collective's formation). All but a few of them migrated to New York City after growing up in other rich cradles of black music—St. Louis, Chicago, Mississippi, Detroit."[45]

In the early days of the collaborations that led to the M-BASE collective, two issues seemed to especially animate Osby and Coleman. One was the search for a distinctive individual voice on their instruments. The other was the need for autonomy and control over the creative process, especially control over the social conditions and cultural meanings of their creative labor. In a 1993 *Down Beat* interview, Osby explains the significance of a distinctive sound and its importance in the jazz vocabulary.

> I got the call to play with Lester Bowie's big band when I first came to town (in 1983). Lester is one of the cats that inspired me to pursue an individual voice in the music. I was playing with Jon Faddis at the time and the whole direction of that was what (Hamiet) Bluiette calls "model T-music." Playing with Lester's group—and close inspection of his history—showed me that his approach was more appealing than continuing to regurgitate everybody else's ideas. . . . People that we hold in so much esteem were inventors in their own time. Charlie Parker didn't make his mark by continuing to sound like Lester Young. Without your own sound you can't even hang out.[46]

In the same interview the late trumpeter Lester Bowie also appreciated the importance of developing a distinctive voice: "you could be good, but even local cats wouldn't regard you as hip unless you had your own personal phrasing and sound. That was a prerequisite. Now they try to turn it inside out, make the least developed the most developed. *You do have to go through the music of the past, to learn how to play; but once you do that, that's it . . . jazz is not some academic exercise.*[47]

Along with the formation of a shared working environment, for Osby the motivation behind the development of the M-BASE collective was also practical.

> When me and Steve Coleman started M-BASE, it was a bunch of people getting together and talking, but we didn't have anything established. Lester (Bowie) would say, "So what is that? Whatchyall gonna do for your-selves?" [Weakly in response] "We'll try . . . we're . . . gonna do . . ." He [Bowie] said, "I got all this stuff set up, I can play with this band, that band." That struck a chord; you could create a work base, diversify your skills, using the same core of people—an umbrella structure, like the AACM combined with George Clinton's Parliament-Funkadelic as opposed to working with the same group all the time, putting out the same kind of records.[48]

In musical range and eclecticism, organizational flexibility and inge-nuity, entrepreneurial imagination and drive, it is little surprise that funk guru George Clinton's performance units, including Parliament-Funkadelic, and the AACM were models for Osby, Coleman, and M-BASE. It is also striking that both Osby and Coleman, like Byron, have strong thoughts and clear ideas about the tradition, its exemplars, and the jazz left's relationship to them.[49]

The following exchange between Osby, Lester Bowie, and *Down Beat* interviewer Kevin Whitehead captures the passion that animates their collective commitment and vision about the tradition. Note too the intergenerational admiration between Osby and Bowie.

> *Bowie:* Playing "Bye Bye Blackbird" or sounding like Duke Ellington, that's got nothing to do with where we're coming from. That's the foundation. We got to do the rest of the house. With jazz, its not so much what you play as how you play. It's not some-thing you put into the repertoire. It's a living breathing young baby, music.
>
> *Whitehead*: [mock exasperation]. Jazz is American's classical music. We have to put it into the concert hall to get respect.
>
> *Bowie:* I agree with you. Love to see jazz at Lincoln Center—it should have been there years ago. Every city should have a jazz orchestra with budgets equal to the Philharmonic's. But *don't negate the other things that are happening*, don't stunt the growth of the music. We're not gonna sacrifice the music to get to the concert hall.
>
> *Osby:* These people [folks associated with Jazz at Lincoln Center]

> have to expand their tolerance of other branches of the tree.
> These are all facets coming from the same root source. I con-
> sider what I'm doing, what Lester's been doing, to be truer to
> jazz's historical motive than playing works reminiscent of other
> times, another climate.
>
> Bowie: It's not a simple music anymore. So it does belong in the *street*,
> on the farm, it needs equal access everywhere, the same as
> country western, rap, anything. Because jazz is all
> these . . . *jazz is hip-hop, dixie-land anything people playing
> it want it to be.* "Man don't listen to that Argentinean shit, it
> might influence you." C'mom baby! Influence me![50]

As this exchange shows, there is remarkable consistency in the jazz
left's discourse about the need to transgress the boundaries of the tradition. From Ornette Coleman to the M-BASE collective, the disposition
of openness toward the music and the tradition is the same. Like the
music collectives that preceded them, the M-BASE collective initially
came together to develop a distinctive aesthetic approach, musical language, and collective organizational structure which would allow them
to transgress the boundaries and conventions of the tradition.

In the late 1980s, M-BASE (which refers to Micro Basic Array of
Structural Extemporations) began as a musical collective of young musi-
cians each of whom eventually established their home base in Brooklyn,
New York. The original members included Greg Osby, Steve Coleman,
Cassandra Wilson, Gerri Allen, Robin Ewbanks, and Graham Haynes.
Although each has gone on to establish successful careers, many mem-
bers of the original collective remain in touch with each other and occa-
sionally perform together professionally.

By way of explanation, some journalists and some of the members
refer to M-BASE as "the interaction that goes on between musical structures and improvisations on them."[51] Comparisons to Ornette Coleman's Harmolodic system or George Russell's Lydian system are
inevitable and, I think, justified.

Along with Osby, much of the heart and soul of M-BASE revolved
around saxophonist Steve Coleman, a Chicago-born musician who came
of age musically under the tutelage of Von Freeman, Muhal Richard
Abrams, George Lewis, and the general influence of the AACM. Coleman's musical and cultural influences include African and Eastern philosophy, kung fu, be-bop, funk, and the Cuban new-song movement.[52]

Along with establishing an organizational structure and formulating
an aesthetic approach to the collective's work, Coleman developed an
ambitious program of outreach and education designed to cultivate new

audiences and spread the word about M-BASE. Coleman and fellow members insist that the collective model on which M-BASE is structured is not simply another stylistic intervention vying for dominance and recognition in the cluttered history of stylistic displacement driven by the quest for the next new thing. Rather, their collective approach (as with similar efforts in the past) represents a fundamental

> way of thinking about creating music. It is not the music itself. The idea is not to develop some musical style and play that forever. . . . The conception of M-BASE is in many ways a non-Western conception of how to use music to express experiences. The concepts of M-BASE are based primarily on Africa and creative music of the African diaspora. The music is unique primarily in the area of spiritual, rhythmic, and melodic development. Finally, the concept of which style is better than another style has no place here. Since the goal is the experience of culture and philosophy, there is no "better."[53]

To implement this conception of the music and ensure the working and creative conditions necessary to perform it, Coleman (echoing Lester Bowie) created a series of distinct performing units: Steve Coleman and Five Elements; Steve Coleman and Metrics; Steve Coleman and the Mystic Rhythm Society; Renegade Way; and Steve Coleman and the Secret Doctrine. Each performance group provides Coleman with the opportunity to develop, integrate, and present different aspects of his musical interests and personality. Coleman's name appears with each unit, he says, as a concession to the vagaries of the market and the requirements of sustaining a collective approach to musical production and collaboration in an environment where egos and fame dominate and pull players in different, often conflicting directions. Coleman has reflected a lot on this point, and his observations are worth quoting at length:

> I started these different groups to provide some way to allow me to work with others in a creative environment. You see, when I was working with Cassandra Wilson, Greg Osby, Gerri Allen, etc., we made it a point to try to have a group that did not have a musical leader (or business leader). I was one of the pushier people in the group in terms of trying to advance our musical way of thinking. When the press began to write about us as a group they decided to make someone in the group the leader. In every interview that I've ever done and when I talked to anyone I made it a point to tell them that I was not the leader of M-BASE and that there was no leader. This made no difference to Western-thinking journalists who insisted that there was a leader, and it was nominally written that I started (or was the leader of M-BASE). This led to problems as others wanted to be looked at by people outside of this process (critics, writers, record company people)

as doing more things of a leadership nature, they wanted to be looked at as leaders. Eventually egos came into play and this is one of the reasons why this particular group of people are not really working that much together today. So I decided to just start the group myself and lead in a more obvious way so there would be no argument and therefore no ego battles.[54]

For Coleman the original idea of forming a collective or set of working associations to make music was natural and rewarding.

My goal was, and is, to express the relationship of mankind, myself in particular, to everything else through music (or some sort of organized sound). Since I do not live in this universe alone I feel that this is best done by more than one person at a time, or group of people. I've always wanted to be around other creative individuals so that is why I took up with others, if it is called a collective or not is not really the point for me, it's the work that gets done and trying to stay on this path of creative expression.[55]

It was but a few short steps from this philosophy to the formation of M-BASE. Again Coleman:

Getting together with the other people who have been considered in the past as being a part of the M-BASE collective just happened as a result of me expressing myself and others doing the same. . . . I will always be working with people and since the frame of mind that I and the people that I work with are generally in M-BASE (and not the music itself), then maybe you could say that M-BASE is a collective. For me, the M-BASE collective is the group of people who have contributed to a way of thinking about creating this music. It is not a group of people who create a certain style of music.[56]

Given his philosophical and aesthetic proclivities, and perhaps because of his experiences in the evolution of the M-BASE experiment, Coleman draws a rather sharp distinction between M-BASE, or what Cassandra Wilson called "a way of life," and the various performance units with whom he tours and records.

This alternative sensibility, this way of life as Coleman calls it, is not just articulated in abstract philosophical and aesthetic terms. It shows up in the music of Coleman and the other former members who actively cultivate experimental approaches to sound while remaining open to a wide array of musical influences.[57] The sensibility is also expressed in a musical and cultural practice that, like Don Byron's, is decidedly political. For instance, on at least two occasions Coleman has taken his band on extended tours (including to Cuba and California) where he has established residencies at universities, community centers, and churches.[58] While in residence, Coleman and his group (which included dancers, per-

cussionists, and rappers) gave workshops, lessons, lectures, and performances (many of which were free) at the community-based venues.[59]

Even in these contexts the notions of collectivity and community were
on Coleman's mind: "It's a community music that we're playing, not just
in the sense that we play for the community, which we do, but that inside
the group the music depends on a team effort."[60] Beyond the internal
dynamics of personalities, business, and the general rigors of running and
maintaining a band, Coleman is also committed to establishing the visibility, legitimacy, and institutional infrastructure necessary to sustain and
nurture the jazz left. According to the *San Francisco Bay Guardian,* Coleman's activities on behalf of education and community are a far cry from
Wynton Marsalis's conducting a lecture-demonstration in an elementary
school or a church basement.[61] Although this is true in the strict sense of
venue and visibility, as a *cultural move* designed to establish and promote
a specific approach and vision the aims are the same. In other words, and
this is the dimension I want to stress, Coleman and his colleagues actively
established networks, cultivated knowledge and information, and developed explicit criteria for judgments and discriminations about the music,
as Marsalis did through concerts, television broadcasts, and educational
outreach through the auspices of Lincoln Center.

For Coleman, this meant trying to "do a lot of community things"
and finding "different ways of getting the music to the people in ways
that are conducive, like having people pay less and having more open
situations which are ideas I got from people like Coltrane and Mingus."[62] In 1996, for instance, Coleman set up shop in Havana, Cuba,
and later in Oakland, for extended periods with his band, the Five Metrics. In California they "rented a large house in Oakland's Fruitvale dis-
trict," where through meeting people and hanging out, Coleman cultivated new audiences and established musical friendships.

So the contemporary ideals, transgressive cultural practices, and cultural politics inherited from an earlier generation of avant-gardists like
Ornette Coleman and the AACM continues with work of Don Byron,
Greg Osby, and Steve Coleman. The aesthetic approach, cultural practices, and organizational strategies of these contemporary members of
the jazz left help complicate and reckon with where and how different
cultural practices operate and are positioned in the shifting politics and
structures of black cultural production. With the canon builders who
occupy the jazz mainstream, the jazz left forms part of a broader and as
I have tried to suggest, contested cultural formation. This contested field
involves significant disputes over the terms and shape of a cultural

vision, a political critique, and aesthetic imagination, all in the name of culture and identity. What is at stake is nothing less than claims to the representation of black cultural tradition and the inscription of that tradition into the organizational, aesthetic, and political landscape of twenty-first-century American culture.

In terms of the contested claims on jazz and black music traditions, what the case of the jazz left shows are the strategies, tactics, network, organizational structures, and performance sites through which a generation of contemporary players (like its counterparts at Lincoln Center) gains (and sustains) a measure of cultural authority and legitimation. Now I want to consider these cultural moves for recognition and legitimacy in terms of what the canon makers and the jazz left share, to see where they diverge, particularly in terms of the vision (and effects) of the cultural politics that underwrite their respective projects.

As I argued in the previous chapter, the most explicit and politically enduring effect of the canon makers is the fortification and consolidation of their relationship to major cultural organizations and institutions like Lincoln Center. As a major institution of cultural authority and legitimation, Lincoln Center provides the platform, resources, status, and visibility that the canon makers draw on to construct and advocate for their particular notion of the jazz tradition.[63] Through their relationship with Lincoln Center, the canon makers are in the position to define, defend, and advance their perspective. The availability of resources with which to stage productions, generate press coverage, commission works, and employ artists provides the financial and organizational basis from which to assert sustained recognition of jazz in the public imagination.

In the hands of the canon makers, the tradition is produced and defended through the identification of key composers and figures (Armstrong, Ellington, Parker), key compositions, recordings, and performances that are codified into a body of work which then becomes part of the canon. A key discursive operation in this process of canonization is identification, collection, codification, and evaluation of texts (e.g., recordings, compositions, and performances). This process allows for the perfection, mastery, and reproduction of an identifiable body of work that can be reproduced by a community of practitioners, evaluators, and consumers. These key figures and texts constitute the contours and boundaries of the tradition and a musician's relationship to it. Popular, vernacular, and commercial influences are screened out and cordoned off, devalued, and marginalized, for their allegedly contaminating and corrupting influence on the anointed work. Sources of replenishment and extension to this canon are to be found in the periodic attempts to update, perfect, and replicate as close as possible the original sound, intent, and performance.

Institutional legitimacy and cultural authority are produced and subsequently reinforced in the press and media. Cultural capital and social status flow in the direction of key players, spokespersons, and works because of their identification and affiliation with each other and powerful institutions.

In a limited but nonetheless important sense, the cultural politics produced in this process might be seen as oppositional, for black cultural politics anyway, to the extent that jazz music and the jazz tradition have heretofore remained outside of, if not beyond, the cultural, financial, and organizational reach and interests of dominant cultural institutions. The *cultural moves* by the canon makers like Marsalis and his colleagues at Lincoln Center can be considered oppositional to the degree that their efforts secure a measure of institutional recognition and support on par with other forms of art and culture. These strategies might also be seen as oppositional to the extent that they articulate a vision of blackness and black experiences in those cultural spaces that have heretofore not recognized such experiences.[64]

Nonetheless, as an oppositional cultural practice, the politics of the canon makers can be muted, moving between social liberalism and aesthetic conservatism. Liberal because the construction and defense of jazz tradition is, in their view, very much part of an African American cultural tradition. In a climate of political conservatism, attacks on affirmative action, and suspicions about multiculturalism, this view defends important cultural terrain. Indeed, conservative scholars and journalists doing battle in the culture wars continue to respond to this position with charges of racism and reverse racism. At the same time, the project of institutionalization—including Lincoln Center and the Ken Burns documentary—is conservative, in my estimation, because of its unyielding commitment to a conventional conception of the jazz tradition, its seminal contributors, and its key texts.

Taking a more transgressive approach to the tradition, the jazz left, by contrast, operates without, and hence beyond, the formal institutional, organizational, and financial infrastructure and resources necessary to get and sustain the recognition and stability enjoyed by the canon makers. I see the jazz left as a more amorphous, loosely structured, but no less important intervention in fashioning a public imagination and, more powerfully, an alternative understanding of jazz and black diasporic cultural formations.

Like the canon makers, the members of the jazz left value the importance of a distinctive and unique voice as the hallmark of jazz expressiv-
ity. Because players and composers are in constant search of new
approaches and grammars, they look to popular, vernacular, commercial, experimental, and global influences as sources of new possibility
rather than of contamination and suspicion. One of the major consequences of these choices, especially the greater range of aesthetic freedom
and cultural autonomy that comes with it, is the absence of visibility and
sustained recognition, regular employment, recording opportunities,
and lucrative salaries.

Members of the jazz left, thus, often remain marginal to dominant
institutions of legitimation and visibility—recording companies, mainstream press, and even cultural institutions like Lincoln Center. Players
rely frequently on alternative institutions or social organizations like
music collectives to develop their work and to cultivate audiences, while
supporters and critics depend on such venues for regular access to the
music. Small museums, galleries and restaurants, music festivals (especially in Europe), arts grants, independent recording companies, community-based social and political organizations, and increasingly the
Internet serve as sponsors and performance venues that provide opportunities for financial and organizational support.

In rare cases, cultural visibility can come from affiliations with prestigious arts organizations and even press coverage. It is more often the case
that professional and social networks, collaborations, and locally based
performance venues serve as the basis for building the social infrastructure necessary for musicians on the jazz left to develop their craft, nurture new audiences, and sustain their practice at a reasonably high level.
In other words, cultural legitimation comes not so much from affiliation
with dominant cultural institutions, but social networks, word of mouth,
and local circuits of information generated through performance,
recordings, and reputation—in a word, the road and the street.[65]

Like the wider context of black expressive culture, the jazz scene is
complex, contested, and vibrant. Despite these cultural tensions and
structural conditions, the presence of jazz in the American national
imagination remains visible. Both the canon builders and the jazz left
are in their own ways constructing and advocating for the music in
social and cultural spaces that have heretofore not recognized and
appreciated the music.

With the kind of resources, recognition, and legitimacy that the
canon makers now enjoy, the institutionalization of jazz in dominant

mainstream institutions will likely find acceptance.[66] That, after all, is one of the intended aims of cultural institutionalization. But, as the Burns documentary shows, this institutional power has also marginalized and isolated the music of the jazz left.

With notable exceptions, the conventional wisdom in the jazz discourse is that the music's history can be understood dialectically (e.g., as a succession of stylistic displacements and successions).[67] In this view, two (or more) competing styles vie for dominance and hence need each other for the continued survival and periodic revitalization of the music. This narrow and conventional understanding of jazz tradition is increasingly dubious.[68] For despite the presence and acceptance of jazz in the mainstream, it has never been so aligned with dominant and legitimating institutions of culture power. The prospects for its continued mainstreaming and acceptance in the wake of the success of the Lincoln Center program seem quite healthy.[69]

The internal dynamics networks and practices operating on the jazz left, while certainly shaped by the circumstances of institutionalization, do not depend on them. Musicians regularly look to new sources for expanding the tradition and the boundaries of their aesthetic conceptions, musical practices, and cultural identities. These musicians continue to be attentive to soundings in other spaces and places throughout the world. A measure of the maturity of black cultural politics illustrated by the debates, practices, and tensions within African American creative musics can be gauged by the fact that the discourse on black cultural production and politics, as the comparison of the canon makers and the jazz left shows, has moved beyond issues of identity and nationalism.[70] The musical sources in the streets, and in other places and regions outside and inside of black communities throughout the world, offer vibrant imaginative possibilities. In the culture wars over the tradition, the jazz left has not so much lost or even conceded to claims of the canon makers as shifted the sites of imagination and the sources of expression.

It has taken over seventy-five years for jazz to finally reach a secure a place at Lincoln Center. That is a major accomplishment, never mind a lot of years for America's so-called classical music to finally get some recognition in the halls of the nation's dominant cultural institutions. Meanwhile, on the margins and at the boundaries of this recognition, the jazz imagination and its practitioners on the left have staked out different objectives and politics.

# PART II

# Tactics

# CHAPTER 4

# Where Have All the Black Shows Gone?

Much about American network television changed between 1992, when I completed *Watching Race*, which ended with the close of the 1992 television season, and 1997, when I looked at the new season for an update on black progress.[1] At the end of the 1992 season I was disappointed with the cancellation of several favorite programs, but I remained hopeful about the prospect of black representations on American network television. In subsequent seasons, black-oriented shows like *The Cosby Show* and *A Different World* moved from premier network schedules to the lucrative orbit of reruns and syndication. Although a shift from a focus on the middle class to urban youth briefly appeared, they were replaced in the network schedule with black shows preoccupied with domestic families, parenting, and social relationships. For a while, Fox Television continued its quest for legitimacy and financial profitability with black shows like *New York under Cover* and a staple of hip-hop youth and urban-oriented comedies. Inevitably, even these offerings gave way to the cash cow of reality programming, old staples like feel-good comedies (aimed at white youth), and sports.

Two mini-networks—Warner Brothers (WB) and Paramount (UPN)—joined Fox in challenging the dominance of the three major networks.[2] To wage this challenge the new networks used black-oriented programming to anchor their fledgling evening schedule. This business of using black-oriented programming (especially situation comedies) to get a scheduling toehold continued the programming strategy that the Fox

News Corporation used in its nascent years.[3] With a calculated financial risk and little to lose in terms of reputation as a network, Fox Television pursued urban and youth audiences interested in this sort of programming.[4]

By 1997, black cast and black theme-oriented shows were still confined largely to the genre of situation comedy and entertainment variety. That year the major networks scheduled a thin slate of nighttime dramas featuring black lead characters: *NYPD Blue, ER, Law and Order, Chicago Hope, Homicide: Life on the Street, Touched by an Angel, 413 Hope Street,* and *Players.* The network also scheduled the usual fare of black-oriented situation comedies with identifiable black actors like Bill Cosby, the late Gregory Hines, LL Cool J, and Jaleel White.

There was little new here. The network strategy of offering programs featuring all-black casts and themes, accompanied by a smaller number of short-lived shows with a sprinkling of black-cast members, continued a pattern of black visibility and invisibility on television that began the early 1970s, following the urban rebellions of the 1960s. I am intrigued with this ebb and flow of black television representations from season to season, and so I explore in detail, in the next chapter, the context, history, and cultural implications of this pattern. For now, I want to analyze the 1998 television season as a basis for considering some of the more general questions raised by the episodic nature of this institutional production of visibility and invisibility.

According to a 1998 *New York Times* piece, the prospect for black television representations in the 1998 season seemed considerably more dismal than prior seasons.[5] Ironically, it seemed that the hour-long drama was finally about to deliver the goods, presenting programs with multiracial casts, devoting story lines to complex depictions of black life, and locating such programs in integrated workplace settings. It was no surprise that television did not show multiracial representations of the intimate spaces of home and family. Not only did the representation of blacks remain largely confined to situation comedies, but it seems that there was some general apprehension (if not outright fear) on the business side about the financial risks involved in pursuing racial crossover dreams.

Just as interesting is the discursive frame through which journalists, critics, industry observers, network executives, and studio heads talked about television representations and race. According to conventional wisdom, black, brown, Asian, and white television viewers watch different programs. But since they remain the idealized subjects of television advertisers, studios, and networks, the culturally pressing question is still whether white viewers will watch shows about the lives of people different from them, and whether networks and studios will take the financial risk of programming these shows.

In the late 1990s American television audiences were migrating in record numbers to other forms and sites of service delivery.[6] In this context, the racial politics of audience composition, viewing preferences, and financial risks indicated by the consistency of data on the racial character of audience preferences could be read as a cultural crisis. That is, the structural transformations in the global media and information industries were articulated culturally, and so too was the racial logic that structures audience choices and preferences. Television, especially television news, is a particular and important kind of public sphere, hence the problem of diversity in television representation was both cultural and structural.

Black television representations are shaped by shifting conditions of possibility that include new global markets, larger and more powerful interlocking structures of ownership, newer and more complex relations between products and means of distribution and circulation, and even less regulation by local, national, and international governments. Among the most far-reaching and consequential transformations affecting American television was passage of the 1996 Telecommunications Act, the changes in corporate ownership of media conglomerates, the emerging structure and global reach of entertainment/media/information companies, and rapid advances in new technologies and program delivery.[7]

In the years since the close of the 1992 network television season (where the concluding episode of the season's most popular program, *The Cosby Show,* was broadcast opposite news coverage of the flames of the L.A. rebellion), a new industrial logic took shape. Within this logic, larger but often more nimble corporate entities emerged, with the hope of ensuring access to more profitable shares of the global entertainment/information/communications market. Through joint ventures, buyouts, mergers, and new investments, by the late 1990s global companies like Fox News Corporation, Warner, Time, TCI, and Microsoft solidified their positions as global players. These companies acquired television stations, movie studios, cable operations, satellites, publishing houses, record companies, theme parks, film libraries, communications infrastructure, and movie studios. While maintaining large complex bureaucratic organizations, they were organized into smaller administrative (and creative) units designed to strategically and efficiently identify markets, generate products, control distribution, and move those products anywhere on the globe at any time. In other words, larger and larger, yet more nimble and flexible, administrative and financial units were intended to generate and distribute a diverse range of entertainment and information products. The goal was to establish greater access to and control of global markets.

In this new media-scape, distinctive creative, technological, and financial entities and activities—computers and related information technologies, cinema, telephony, broadcasting, publishing, satellite, theme parks, cable, music, and electronics—were combined to form giant global media firms like TCI, Time-Warner, Fox News Corporation, Disney, Bertelsmann, and Seagram. While this kind of reconfiguration was anticipated in the late 1970s and early 1980s, one of the immediate political and legal factors that ensured its realization was the passage of the 1996 Telecommunications Act.[8] This act restructured major aspects of the telecommunications industry. These included the scope of federal regulation and oversight; the size and composition of firms; the assignment of broadcast frequencies for television, radio, and cellular telephones; the upper limit on the operation and ownership of broadcast stations; the control of delivery systems; and the complementarity between various media technologies.

The 1996 Telecommunications Act dramatically deregulated the telecommunications industry which essentially gave major American corporations like Time-Warner, General Electric, Fox News Corporation, Disney, TCI, Microsoft, Seagram, and Disney the green light to pursue mergers, joint ventures, new research and development, and world-wide expansion with the blessings (and supposed oversight) of the U.S. Congress. So profound and far-reaching was the act that no aspect of American telecommunications was left unaffected.[9]

As the major corporate players acquired new properties, entered joint ventures, and otherwise pursued the globe as one giant market for media, information, and entertainment, newer, more powerful, and diverse corporate entities appeared. Microsoft, the computer software giant, was suddenly in the television business; Fox News Corporation was in the sports and satellite business; General Electric was in the sports arena business; and Time-Warner and its competitors either own or were busy pursuing deals for news, cable, movie, publishing, and music entities.[10] Television production companies, television stations and networks, and cable operations are all components of these global media giants.

In this global environment, media companies must maintain consistent sources of content or software that can be moved efficiently through multiple delivery systems (e.g., cable, wireless, terrestrial, satellite) to destinations (computers, television sets, CD players, movie screens) across the globe. The technological distinctions, organizational partitions, and cultural meanings that once defined technologies, delivery systems, or media are no longer meaningful in any productive sense. Media content moves just as easily from novel to cinema screen to television to video to theme park and programming.[11] With such a voracious demand for content and information, telecommunications companies needed to contend with increasing production costs, greater consumer choices, and different systems, all the while trying to exert greater control over production, distribution, and markets.

Through joint ventures, multiple ownership (TCI, for instance, owned controlling interests in the black cable network operation, Black Entertainment Television, which was purchased in 2000 by Viacom), and cooperative development agreements covering hardware and software, the major corporations extended their control.[12] As consumers, we experience these forms of control at the point of our most familiar, mundane, and ritualized encounters with the telephone receiver, the cable box, the computer screen, and the television set.

## WHERE HAVE ALL THE BLACK SHOWS GONE?

The summer of 1999 saw the decade's final installment of the serial television game of "now you see us on TV, now you don't." In the two years prior to the NAACP's call for a boycott of the television networks by black and Latino media activists and political organizations, the contours of the impending confrontation were already visible.[13]

The 1997 fall season of American network television was revealing with regard to black television representation, so it is worth recalling the networks' programming choices. In that television season, black television shows were still rather plentiful in the schedule; however, they were concentrated largely among the program offerings of the newest television networks. Programs slated to air were also mainly situation comedies. Of the six commercial television networks, WB, UPN, and Fox had a combined total of *sixteen shows* that could be identified as black or black-oriented prime-time programs. Of the traditional majors, CBS scheduled three and NBC one. ABC did not schedule a single black show that season.[14] Fox scheduled three shows (including the only nighttime drama), WB scheduled four, and UPN placed a total of five shows on its fall schedule. Most of the scheduled programs were returning from the previous several seasons; of these, the most popular and well-known black show on Fox was *Living Single*, starring Queen Latifah. *Living Single* was initially canceled, but was quickly revived by Fox after a successful letter-writing campaign by the show's fans. The often controversial *Martin* and the popular *New York Undercover* were not renewed for the 1997 Fox season.

In addition to Queen Latifah, familiar stars like Bill Cosby, the members of the Wayans family, Jamie Foxx, Brandy (Moesha), Steve Harvey with the addition of Cedric the Entertainer, Jaleel White, and Malcolm Jamaal Warner all returned to the prime-time television schedule that year. It should come as no surprise that situation comedy was still the dominant genre, and households and workplaces the preferred settings, for shows that season. Stories about adolescent maturation, relationships, friendships, and roommates provided continuing story lines and narrative action. That season's televisual black Americans were drawn largely from the middle and working class, and included small children, students, and retirees. Characters could be found in various domestic arrangements, including extended families, shared living spaces, marriages, and nuclear families. All of the shows stayed close to the predictable conventions of the genre—medium camera shots, lighthearted narrative dramas, and familiar settings in which everyday difficulties and relationship tensions are the stock in trade. These conventions moved characters through predictable experiences and situations that provided momentary transformation. The action and emotional cues were pumped up and pushed along with laughter provided by enthusiastic studio audiences and laugh tracks. Contemporary music, fashion, language, and information gave the shows the feel of being steeped in contemporary urban black popular culture, whose currency was enhanced and style made more explicit with regular guest appearances by entertainers and athletes. Recognizable figures—mostly athletes and musicians—found their way to the small screen. At the same time, former television personalities like Will Smith (star of *Fresh Prince of Bel Air)* and Martin Lawrence (from *Martin)* moved from the grind of sustaining a weekly series to the more lucrative world of film. But, for black viewers, this mattered less since in a visual economy of scarcity the traffic between the small screen and cinema was not all that important. Being visible was.

While not particularly remarkable aesthetically, the fact is that these shows helped to sustain a black presence, albeit separate, in the media-scape of American network television. This stubborn separate (and not always equal) racial representation on American commercial network television was the source of continuing frustration and concern, especially on the part of media activists, journalists, and scholars. Upon closer inspection, it is evident that the most integrated casts and story lines in those years took place on hour-long dramatic programs like *ER, Homicide,* and *NYPD Blue.* Like their sitcom counterparts (and contemporary progeny), these shows were most often set in the public spaces of work. On the other hand, the genre of situation comedy—long associated with intimacy, family, romance, and domesticity—is still the site of some of the most benign but persistent segregation in American public culture.

Furthermore, while the television industry continued to maintain a minimal commitment to black presence on commercial network television, the shows that survived were located, structurally at least, in the least risky part of the network schedule (and the low-investment sector of corporation). Following the leads of cable, WB, UPN, and Fox—all among the newest networks—used the principle of narrow-casting and the strategy of niche marketing, with youth as their target audience. Even though ABC, NBC, and CBS enjoyed a considerable share of the commercial television market, when cable and the new networks were factored in, the traditional network share was below 50 percent. Traditional networks like NBC and CBS also adopted niche marketing strategies by positioning their operations as name brands that appealed to white middle-class professionals, with shows like *Friends, Seinfeld, Frasier, Cybil, Suddenly Susan, Third Rock from the Sun, ER,* and *NYPD Blue.*[15] As with cable, the newest networks made the greatest inroads into the traditional network share by targeting youth and urban markets. That is, these new networks pursued such programming strategies until they established a brand identity with advertisers in key sectors of their market.[16]

Considering these two television seasons in terms of business and the financial interests of media corporations, what appears on the social and political radar as segregation, the containment of black shows, and the regulation of black visibility is, I believe, the beginning of the new industry logic. By the appearance of these two seasons the television environment was no longer dominated by three major networks—hence the force of various new delivery systems, global media operations, and marketing clutter was felt more immediately and directly. This means that in order to remain competitive, television programmers had to be clear about their audiences or market niches, efficient in the production and scheduling of their programs, and strategic about cultivating their brand identities. Despite their claims to the contrary, to remain competitive networks long ago abandoned the strategy of aiming the least objectionable programs at the widest possible audiences. Cable operators, new networks, and old-line majors made explicit marketing decisions to use their programming to reach distinct demographics, including black urban markets.[17] Black shows, where they are developed at all, were and are selectively developed and deployed by major commercial networks as part of their overall marketing and branding strategy, a strategy and ideal demographic that in all likelihood does not include black people as a prime market.

These operations are in pursuit of smaller, more sharply defined demographics, lifestyles, and disposable incomes. They schedule relatively inexpensive shows (including reruns, movies, game shows, and, most recently, reality programs) with identifiable stars and personalities.[18] They combine various forms of programming and service delivery, including cable wire, the traditional broadcast signal, and satellite service. Accordingly, Fox, UPN, and WB have modeled their approach explicitly after cable.[19] The more nimble approach to marketing, scheduling, and program development on the part of cable television helped to reshape American network television.

## THE CULTURAL POLITICS OF BLACK REPRESENTATION

In light of the new technologies, sophisticated means of circulation, and reconfigured systems of production, I want to think about black visibility and recognition, especially what they mean and the role of television in the production of that meaning.

Just what exactly *is* a black program and what does it signify? I still want to insist on the cultural significance and historical specificity of black television programming that emanates from the United States. This significance still rests with the fact that such images function as cultural sites for the articulation of specific desires, meanings, relations, local histories, and struggles of black life in the United States. At the same time, the significance of black television programming can no longer just be limited to local and specific meanings and politics in the United States, since cultural encounters are not specific to this country. American network executives' actions since the advent of television suggest that for the most part they remain deeply skeptical that black television programming can do any more than generate short-term profits in American television markets.[20] But can the new technologies of exhibition, circulation, and delivery broaden the field of play and, for black cultural producers, change the terms of the game?

It seems to me that black program makers and buyers can seriously consider how black television programming will play in the distant reaches of the markets made more accessible by satellite, cable, the Internet, and other forms of service delivery, information circulation, and cultural travel. Given this circumstance, is a prerequisite for black television shows (and films) simply that they travel well? That they speak in a universal language? And if so, what is that language(s) and what is the embodied representation(s) through which it is expressed? Is it the naturalized (racialized) athletic and dancing black body? Perhaps it is the body endowed with musical prowess? Is it the black corporal body of the liberal civil rights subject? Perhaps it is the neonationalist subject of hip-hop discourse?

Shows that finally do make it to a network or cable schedule (or a Cineplex screen) now more than ever are required by the global structure of ownership, delivery, and markets to speak in a universal language. All of this means that black shows now signify in relation to a rapidly changing political and cultural field of finance, production, exhibition, and circulation of media content, including sports, film, information, music, games, fashion, and style. The meanings, pleasures, and identifications generated from black television representations, no matter where and how they travel, still bear the perceptible traces of the specifically American circumstance in which African American blackness is constructed and operates. This means that the global journey of media images of blackness is also an occasion to consider the role of media and television in the cultural production of the United States as a structured racial and national formation.

## BLACK REPRESENTATION AND THE POST–CIVIL RIGHTS PUBLIC SPHERE

While liberal journalistic discourses about segregation and integration, crossover and separation persist in the United States, the shifting global media environment raises a different kind of question about the racial politics of American network television and its programming practices. In particular, one wonders about the continuing relevance of a public sphere organized by the media and defined (on questions of race) by the discourse of civil rights. The persistence of racialized programming patterns and viewing preference among racial and ethnic groups may well suggest the presence of a post–civil rights public sphere.[21]

The new logic of television broadcasting—the logic of the neo-network—in the United States may have two seemingly contradictory social implications for television representations of blackness. In purely economic and marketing terms, television shows about blacks continue to appeal to networks to the extent that they add value to the brand identity of their networks. As traditional network identities—expressed through their logos and stable of programs on a given evening, across the schedule, and throughout the season—become more focused and explicit, the defining market characteristics (regardless of regional or national location) and aesthetic parameters of a network drive the demand for programs. The genre, star power, program conventions, and scheduling strategies constrain studios and networks, even as they guide their decisions. While it may fulfill demand within identifiable genres designed to attract a particular market niche, this conventional strategy, which was developed to reduce market uncertainty, means that the program offerings that manage to find their way to a network's program schedule will remain safe and conventional. As buyers and schedulers of programs, network executives continue, indirectly at least, to shape the range, look, content, and style of a show that it seeks to program.

At the same time, despite their domination by Western corporations, a broader range of service delivery options and the rising importance of television programs as sources of product identity for global media companies promise greater possibilities for black and minority representations to circulate more in market niches. Take, for example, the persistent finding that in the United States blacks and whites view different programs; black-oriented programming widely viewed in black households seldom if ever registers with white viewers.[22] As I explore more fully in the next chapter, rather than interpret this finding as a failure of the integrationist ideal of the post–civil rights public sphere, one can see it as a statement about black tastes, interests, and pleasures. For me, the real question is whether or not program makers and buyers will respond to these expressions of tastes and preferences or continue to see them as a minor market and hence of little financial consequence because they have no crossover appeal. In terms of cultural politics I think that this expression of black interests begs for a different reading of the post–civil rights public sphere and the role of television in the production and organization of that public.

This expression of black cultural tastes, and the post–civil rights public, together with the logic of the neo-network focus on niche markets and flexible production, suggests the possibility of producing programming driven more by the demand to reach such publics and less by the demand for intelligibility and relevance by broad audiences who may speak a given language or know the intimacies of a particular cultural experience.[23] Though small and marginal (albeit with increasing implication for global companies), the success of ethnic programming on cable stations, Internet developments with file sharing, downloads, radio, music production and circulation, and the production of film for the Internet are all examples of potential possibilities. Politically, these possibilities make for some interesting opportunities for new cultural articulations, for engaging memories, histories, and stories that are particular and specific at the same time that they require information and understanding rooted in identifications, loyalties, and interests that transcend local concerns.

If this is to occur at the level of global media and not just below their radar, then global corporate entities must remain open to identifying and serving such niches (and they must be profitable). Although they continue to slip in terms of audience share and innovative programming relative to cable, the American television broadcasting remains hegemonic. Giant entertainment/information/media companies continue to control the libraries, film holdings, book lists, and software around the world. With their vast financial resources and through their control of telephone lines, satellites, broadcast stations, publishing houses, and software, they are still the major purchasers and schedulers of programming content around the world.

No matter how hegemonic, the logic that drives this global structure still must respond to and organize the uncertainty that exists at the local level. Even as new forms of corporate power continue to structure identifications and alliances that can be realized through the new technologies of communication, they can never completely discipline or absolutely control such possibilities. Thus, we might ask, where is it possible for blacks, Asians, Latinos, gays, and lesbians to establish representation in an industry whose raison d'etre is to package our desires and identifications? Several models are on offer—the cable route illustrated by Black Entertainment Television (BET) and Univision, the small cable operations of ethnic television, the niche strategy of mini-networks.[24]

The immediate problem for black program makers is not just making black programs—though widely dispersed and wildly erratic, they are available—but how to make a greater variety of programs and how to communicate them to desirable audiences. In addition, negotiating the logic of the market as a terrain on which forms of community, identification, and association is constructed and structured is as tricky as it is potentially productive. Program makers will face the onerous task of generating programs that speak to the specific concerns of particular and local markets. Spike Lee, Walter Mosley, Oprah Winfrey, and other filmmakers, novelists, and entertainment figures have recognized this challenge and tried to respond with television programming aimed at specific segments of blacks. Latinos have also recognized the opportunities presented by the shifting structure of the television industry and have responded with, for example, children's programming aimed at multicultural and bilingual audiences.[25] Some of these efforts involve old traditional networks, while others are aimed at cable channels and networks; among the most responsive and innovative has been Home Box Office (HBO). By the same token, since these programs must travel to distant markets and audiences with different histories, traditions, languages, and experiences, the meanings (and politics) of culture, including blackness, will have to be negotiated within the terms of these competing aesthetic and economic demands.

How does one speak with confidence about what such shows mean, when the audiences and the markets they organize do not always share histories, identifications, and experiences? To be sure, in a global media world, neither immediate experience nor shared identification is required for a given program to produce meaning and pleasure. (Indeed, one might argue that our global media-scape itself—whether the Internet, cinema, music, or the satellite—constructs identifications and shared histories through its very existence.) On the other hand, representations, no matter where they circulate or how they are generated, are more than free-floating signifiers cut loose from the social and historical mooring that makes them intelligible. Though media representations do obviously signify at multiple levels and in different times and places, they continue to bear the traces of their conditions of production and the historicity of their time and place.

# CHAPTER 5

# Television and the Politics of Difference

The debate over diversity in American network television is, I contend, the expression of a much longer struggle over the production of a national imaginary and the role of commercial television in the construction of that imaginary.[1] As it concerns governing and order, the integrative function of television is central to this process, as are underlying assumptions about culture and representation. Thus the periodic crisis in television over racial representation is less about the network's loss of markets and audience shares than about governance and order. The focus of this chapter is the history of this struggle, the cultural logic that structures the debate, and the role of television as a major discursive site for managing difference.

In the 1950s, the problem of difference was largely based on class, ethnicity, and gender. One of television's aims was to offer representations of experience based on a model of integration that transformed persistent ties to place, ethnicity, and class into the basis of a new "national" identity guaranteed through upward social mobility and the middle-class suburban ideals of the nuclear family and consumption.[2] By the 1960s, the challenge of constructing a national imaginary through television confronted a conception of difference expressed almost exclusively in racial, class, and ideological terms. This challenge produced a tension between integrative models of the nation, based on the ideal of assimilation, and the pressure of racial groups whose notions of pluralism appealed to television to represent distinctive cultural identities based not just on a homogenized view of the nation but also on race and culture.

The industrial television system to which contemporary racial groups appeal for diversity is organized on the basis of a few monopolies; the state exercises some control over the size, number, location, and capacity of these monopolies to reach audiences. From the perspective of the contemporary media structure and regulatory environment (in the aftermath of the 1996 Telecommunications Act), this dominant logic has shifted again, in part because of the introduction of new technologies, a new regulatory environment, and transnational corporate media entities.

As we saw in the last chapter, despite this fundamental change in the logic and structure of the global media environment within which American commercial network television operates, communities of color continue to appeal to traditional cultural and political institutions, older forms of media, mainly broadcast television, and the state for legal recognition and cultural representation. These appeals continue to assume that commercial network television remains organized by an integrative ideal of national identity. Moreover, they assume that the state—through its regulatory oversight—remains the key player in realizing this integrative function.

My argument is that the discourses of politics and media activism that periodically appeal to network television for greater visibility and recognition are organized by a view of television as key for fashioning a national imaginary through cultural pluralism. At the level of viewing practices, the structure of the industry and the regulatory role of the state are defined by a different logic. I suggest that the complex and related discourses of liberal pluralism emanating from journalism, politics, and the academy have failed to grasp adequately the gap between their discursive commitment and the contemporary realities of this transformation.

I think Ien Ang is right to see such discourses as modernist mythologies of American national and nationalist identity constructed by and through television.[3] Ang argues that social theory (primarily functionalist sociology), communications theory (transmission models), and, to a lesser extent, semiotic theories that analyze cultural meaning have played significant roles in organizing how we think about the television system (including television audiences) in the production of this national imaginary. By challenging the purported integrative functions implicit in these academic discourses, Ang argues that we have a crisis of modernist myths, a crisis that emerges precisely because of modernism's inability to manage difference. She encourages us to make sense of the play and effects of differences and the disorder they produce (a disorder produced also by television) from the vantage point of active audience studies.

Accordingly, activists, industry insiders, and, in some cases, scholars continue to interpret the viewing habits and preferences of black, Latino, and Asian audiences, compared to whites, as the periodic expression of grievance by disaffected political subjects. This unwillingness, even inability, to see communities of color as more than aggrieved political subjects is evidence of the lingering effects of a post–World War II liberal discourse of national identity.[4] This discourse, and the image of national identity that it sponsors, continues to shape contemporary perceptions of television's moral universe as one where the absence of blacks, Latinos, gays, lesbians, and Asians is understood as a shortcoming of American society and television.

How might this set of circumstances be read differently? What is required is a different way of reading the operation and management of difference for what they say about the present order and about the possibility for imagining a new and different kind of public. This means, most of all, developing an analytical viewpoint that sees the programming preferences and viewing habits of people of color as something other than the failure of a liberal pluralist discourse to produce a coherent national identity. At the end of this chapter, I consider some of the conditions that make possible a reading of the programming choices and viewing habits of blacks from the perspective of what Ien Ang calls "orderly disorder or disorderly order."[5]

ACTIVE AUDIENCES AND DESIRABLE SUBJECTS

The final summer of the twentieth century proved to be busier than usual for American network television. Yet another round of mega–media mergers were announced—between Viacom and CBS—and commercial network television was the object of public criticism (and a threatened boycott) by black and Latino communities fed up with the absence of racial and ethnic representation on the small screen.[6] The summer of 1999 saw a plethora of news articles, television news stories, and talk shows announcing the lack of diversity in the programs scheduled for the fall television season and exploring why. This story was widely covered by the *New York Times*, *Variety*, *San Francisco Chronicle*, and the *Washington Post*. However, I want to single out for particular attention its coverage in the July 20 issue of the *Los Angeles Times*.

Entitled "Networks Decide Diversity Does Not Pay," the *Los Angeles Times* story is emblematic, I think, of some of the complex discursive moves and assumptions which frame how we understand issues of diversity, national identity, and the role of television as a representational system. The controversy itself serves as a vehicle for thinking about the logic of difference and the shifting, yet pivotal, challenge it presents to American society and network television.

The *Los Angeles Times* article is not especially remarkable. It appears under the byline of *Los Angeles Times* staff reporters Brian Lowery, Elizabeth Jensen, and Greg Braxton. It is straightforward reportage that includes statistics on audience shares and viewing habits, as well as quoted commentary about the state of television from political activists, industry observers, network spokespersons, and media scholars. The story ponders why network programming continues as it is, and it does a good job of explaining the relationship between program suppliers, advertisers, and the networks. All of this is ostensibly so readers will get a sense of what members of the industry (and its critics) think about the issue of diversity in network television and the responsibility of television to represent diversity. To get a better sense of the story consider the lead:

> A splashy magazine ad for ABC recently boasted that the network offers the "broadest range of programming" on television. The ad features ten of the network's biggest stars—and not a single black, Latino or Asian face among them.
>
> ABC is not alone. In twenty-six new prime-time shows slated to debut on the four major networks this fall, every lead character and nearly all the cast regulars will be white, even those on shows where the action takes place in urban high schools and New York City night spots.
>
> After years of promises by network executives to make prime-time television look more like America, what's going on?
>
> Industry sources say the answer boils down to a harsh economic equation: there's not enough money in diversity to make it a priority.
>
> As the country turns more diverse, TV viewers are becoming *more racially fragmented*—choosing to watch shows with characters that look like they do. And networks, seeking to preserve a dwindling share of audiences, one that gets siphoned away by cable and the Internet, have chosen to aim squarely at the target they hope will offer the biggest economic return—delivering to advertisers as many young white viewers as they can.[7]

There we have it. The issue of diverse programming based on racial and ethnic differences poses a conflict between the political economic interests and representational responsibility—or, as Ien Ang would have it, the political economic conflicts with the semiotic. In this construction of the desirable audience, the ideal subject of television networks and their advertisers is imagined on the basis of specific qualities—discretionary income, tastes, scarcity, and viewing habits. It is on the basis of such a conception of the desirable subject of network television that the conflict over diversity erupted.

As the article makes clear, subjects are not equal and do not possess in equal measure qualities that advertisers and networks deem desirable. Indeed, by their logic, race and ethnicity operate as indexes by which to determine suitability for programming designed to attract the attention of the network's ideal subject. This slippage of subjectivity and the role of race and ethnicity in that slippage require a distinction between the kinds of subjects that (in an economic sense) matter in television and those that do not.

We might say that in the early twenty-first century, viewers are constituted by network television as cultural subjects, economic subjects, and political subjects. By cultural subjects, I mean to emphasize the traditions, practices, identities, and representations that are generated from and recognized to exist within a specific cultural tradition and social location. With economic subjects, I refer to the constitution of individuals and collectivities as consumers whose desires and preferences are registered in the structure of the marketplace organized by the television industry (flawed though it is), through its advertiser-driven system of funding based on audience measurement and accounting. Political subjects are characterized by the ability of audiences to constitute themselves as political entities or, in this case, interest groups, and to have their interests raised and represented to the industry and the state.

These conceptions may appear to give primacy to an industry conception of individual viewers as voters and consumers free to make choices in the market. This is not my intent. Indeed, I mean to emphasize the different ways of characterizing subjectivities made within the context of the signification and representation of media. In other words, we can also think of audiences in terms that are often antithetical to, outside of, and far more complex than conceptions defined solely in terms of market and institutional conceptions of audiences and their viewing practices.[8]

Journalists, scholars, and media activists often refer to viewers as if these different modalities of subjectivity were perfectly symmetrical and coherent. But a careful look at the *Los Angeles Times* article indicates something else at work. Take the modality of what I call political subjects. Throughout the article, there is explicit attention to black, Latino, and Asians viewers in terms of their political marginalization. These viewers consistently appear as the subject of the article and the object of the public controversy in which the industry finds itself. Nevertheless, complacent white viewers are the *subjects* of a television discourse in need of the agitation of media activists, the expertise of journalist and scholars, and the courage and imagination of network executives and program makers.

Consider, for instance, this passage taken from the article: "some insiders maintain that the *real cause* of minorities being marginalized has simply to do with *audience tastes.* Just a decade ago, industry executives say, *white viewers* were much more willing to watch shows that featured predominately African American casts. . . . Not so today. Don Ohlmeyer has called it the 'Balkanization' of television, with *viewers* gradually dispersing to watch programs *designed for them.*"[9] This claim suggests that blacks, Latinos, and Asians will watch programming featuring whites, and, if given the opportunity, these viewers will disperse in search of programming designed for them. But the passage intimates the viewing habits of whites is the constant object of industry programming decisions. In the end, it is white subjects who must be appeased. It is they who must be satisfied and thus not lost to competition from cable, the Internet, and other forms of service delivery.

But this assumption about the desired subject of commercial network television is not just cultural and social. It is also economic. Race and ethnicity play a pivotal role in the production and organization of this institutional desire. Whites are the ideal subjects of consumerism and representation, while people of color are simply political subjects on whose behalf civil rights advocates must make special appeals for recognition and representation. The cultural traditions and identities of blacks, Latinos, and Asians must be transformed and thus made to appeal to whites, whose economic and cultural capital is assumed to be paramount.

Even on the issue of difference within whiteness, the political and semiotic meet to guarantee whiteness as the ideal subject of network television's cultural and economic desire. This dynamic is most clearly illustrated by the network response to the representation of sexuality and sexual orientation in television. In this passage about gays and lesbians from the *Los Angeles Times* story, we see the merger of cultural, economic, and political subjects around whiteness: "the television industry's profile has allowed at least one minority group, gays and lesbians, to actually flourish. Some say this is because gays are disproportionately represented within the industry, allowing many program creators to feel more comfortable writing gay characters than ethnic minorities."[10] Despite the fact that gays and lesbians have been some of the most vocal political critics of television representations, it is this seamless fusion of the cultural and economic dimensions within whiteness that is especially notable in light of the controversy over diversity. Neither the reporters nor the industry insiders with whom they spoke ever mention the possibility of sexuality serving as a cultural deterrent to the industry's economic commitment to whiteness.[11]

This complicity and confusion of television's desired subject is evident even among African American advocates who speak on behalf of blacks and people of color as political subjects. Here, too, it is striking how the normative value of whiteness is considered to be the subject of network television that must be courted at all costs: "Without any question, *viewers today* have a lower tolerance and are not crossing over as much as before," said one veteran-programming executive. Dr. Alvin F. Poussaint, director of the Judge Baker Children's Center on Boston, suggests another reason: 'Past black oriented sitcoms . . . had a quality of writing and tone that crossed over to a *mass audience*. Current African American sitcoms,' he said, 'have more of a specific tone that targets blacks. *White America* got tired of black sitcoms after *Cosby* and *The Fresh Prince of Bel-Air.*'"[12]

What had been implicit throughout is finally made explicit. Namely, whites are the subjects of commercial network television: "Given this trend [a lack of racial crossover], the lexicon of diversity is changing. *Networks can't afford to alienate whites, who make up the vast majority of potential viewers, and remain the ones advertisers privately concede that they want most.*"[13]

No matter how active they are in registering their tastes, preferences, and identities as cultural and economic subjects, blacks, Latinos, and Asians are required by circumstances to act primarily as political subjects. As such, they are visible to the commercial network television industry (this recognition may even produce momentary changes in the racial representations on the American television). But this semiotic and political (economic) pressure may also come at considerable cost, for it means that audiences from communities of color are seen (and hence responded to) largely as political subjects (rather than as economic and cultural subjects).

In the current climate of network television and changing media, I believe that this controversy indicates a deeper and more profound crisis, one that, like the culture wars, bears on the cultural struggle over the production of American national identity.[14] The persistence of these issues reveals the deep and persistent way that race and ethnicity operate to structure inequalities (not all subjects and subject positions are equal) in the United States. At stake is the national ideal of integration and liberal pluralism, most especially the social and cultural discourses through which such ideals were made representable (including television as a chief means of popular representation and circulation).

This postwar ideal remains a defining assumption of scholarly and journalistic discourse, as well as the basis of political initiatives of civil rights activists and liberal media-industry insiders. This postwar liberal ideal is a defining motif of the *Los Angeles Times* article:

> The lack of integration in this year's new shows—in settings that would *normally be diverse,* such as the west wing of the White House—left even people who work within the industry *grasping for an explanation.* . . . "The entire broadcast industry *has a responsibility* to make sure that there's *diversified programming* on the air, and this year, as a group, *we came up short,*" said Garry Hart, president of Paramount's TV production arm. "We've got to do *better next year,* and *anyone who feels otherwise is wrong.*"[15]

Somewhere between accepting the responsibility for presenting diversified programming and being made to admit that they came up short is the management style of a liberal idealism that has not yet learned to do more than tolerate social and cultural differences.

Despite pronouncements to the contrary, the liberal discourse of diversity and inclusion endlessly desires a subject whose whiteness it believes ensures cultural, political, and, most of all consumer legibility. Crossing the borders of this discursive commitment is risky business, and threatens to produce a costly indecipherability. Hence, the discourse relies on periodic reminders (from colored peoples) of its moral commitment, and after a few minor corrections (like adding minority cast members to prime-time programming) returns to business as usual.[16] But how did things get this way? Why with each periodic correction does the conflict seem to deepen, each time ignoring the principle of national identity forged out of difference and diversity, to which network television seems so committed and yet does little to effect?

## THE PRODUCTION AND MANAGEMENT OF DIFFERENCE

From its inception, coping with difference has been endemic to commercial network television. From the advertiser's need to differentiate products, to attract desired audiences, to the need to form viewers into distinctive markets, television has always produced and managed some form of difference.[17] A series of smaller but related problems stems from the basic contradiction in what Raymond Williams calls television's cultural form.[18] The prospect that audiences would not view, that they would turn away, that they would get it wrong or that the wrong ones might get it, is a consistent concern of network executives and advertisers.[19]

The networks (as well as journalists and, in some cases, scholars) adopted a discourse in which the power of the medium was thought to lie in its potential to plug each of us into the same events and viewing experience. According to the logic of this discourse, at the very least television would form the basis for a feeling and (electronic) experience of national identification and belonging.[20] But this vision of national belonging and identification depended on the exclusion or, at the very least, domestication of the image of Native Americans, Latinos, blacks, Asians, and the transformation of white working-class ethnics into suburban middle-class consumers. For American television, a crucial moment of discursive production of American national identity was the 1950s postwar period of suburbanization and economic expansion.[21]

Television's role in the production of national identity depended on the careful articulation of social, cultural, political, and economic dimensions. It depended on a construction of Americanness targeted domestically at the transformation of ethnic and gender identities and practices from working-class realities into middle-class aspirations and mobility. On the international level, it depended on America's ability (during the Cold War) to contain communism and make the world safe for democracy.[22] The television industry has, of course, always been concerned with managing uncertainty and reducing the economic risks of market instability through the rationalization of production and through extending control over those markets. Economically, the middle-class ideal of American national identity and belonging was articulated in American network television through advertising.[23]

Socially, the middle-class ideal of Americanness was staged in the theater of domesticity, where social ties and identities based on gender, family, and tradition were its primary targets. Labor and time-saving appliances were aimed at white women, whose work and social domains were increasingly defined in terms of the good mother—a nurturing and unselfish figure who remained at home providing for the husband and kids.[24]

Television programming and advertising encouraged working-class white ethnics to abandon the habits, practices, and identifications based on old ties of neighborhood, family, and community in favor of suburban life filled with consumer goods that announced and confirmed achievement of the mythical American dream. The sphere of domesticity, complete with national brands and new forms of association and community, competed with, transformed, and in some cases displaced social relations formerly defined by clubs, bars, and work.[25] Consumption was the hallmark of what it meant to be an American, and as the latest piece of domestic technology the new medium of television, controlled by advertisers, was the emblem of arrival and the primary means of expressing both modernity and Americanness.[26]

At the semiotic level, the dominant genre that came to define (and dominate) American network television, the situation comedy, was a complementary means to ensure identification with home-centered consumption and entertainment. By combining, hence regulating and managing, images and stories designed to ensure familiarity and sameness, predictability, and consistency, television structured the management of certain kinds of difference into its day-to-day operation and strategies of representation. Through the use of genres such as soap operas, situation comedy, and entertainment variety underwritten by sponsored advertising, network television worked hard to articulate its semiotic and economic dimensions to the rhythms of everyday life in the domestic sphere.[27] Implicit in this articulation was the recognition of social differences such as gender, ethnicity, class, public/private, work/leisure, spatial organization, and generations.

In perhaps its most unsettled (and hence most adventurous and innovative) period, the articulation of the social (domestic) and economic (advertising) with the semiotic was applied to disparate sources of the symbolic materials out of which television would fashion a distinctive identity—film, radio, vaudeville, musicals, entertainment variety, and comedy.[28] Combining these disparate sources of programming was a way to symbolically manage differences in location, identity, tradition, and experience of audiences (largely, but not exclusively, within the domestic sphere), in the process forging them into the constitutive elements necessary for the production of a symbolic national identity. Effectively combining the social, cultural, and economic dimensions of the industrial and semiotic system in this way was made possible by a conception of commercial television's political function as integrative.

As both Lynn Spigel and George Lipsitz have shown, these strategies produced mixed results at best, since this symbolic construction of what it meant to be American had to contend with the stubborn countermemories of deeply embedded cultural traditions and social realities of everyday life. In particular, Spigel demonstrates that life in the suburban homes of the newly arrived middle class was anything but ideal.[29] Working-class folks, white ethnics, women, and people of color folded the new media and the consumer dreams they sold into lives lived not just in front of the television screen but also beyond it. Some refused the idealized constructions of and identifications with televisual versions of the dream, others selectively incorporated bits and pieces, while still others harbored suspicions about the world they were being taught to desire.[30]

If this discursive management of difference was to be successful in its use of television, the cultural contradictions of the specifically "American dilemma" could not be kept off television. In the 1950s television's role in the production of the national identity was management through selective incorporation, a kind of incorporation that had to grapple with the root problem of attracting and keeping audiences through differentiation. In order to gain and keep its ideal viewers, consumers, and members of the television nation, the networks had to acknowledge audience differences. From the very beginning, then, television's construction of this idealized America was fraught with contradiction, principally the production and management of a difference that always presented the prospect of rupture and refusal.

Lynn Spigel, for instance, shows the centrality of assumptions about work, gender, and the domestic sphere in the structuring of television programs and advertising aimed at women.[31] Although her discussion on this point is not explicitly about black, Latino, or Asian women, her insights are useful for identifying how the problem of race and its management was considered. According to Spigel, industry executives helped to organize "the experience of watching television." They were guided by assumptions based on notions of sexual difference and what were assumed to be distinctive differences between men's and women's relations to the domestic sphere—domesticity was assumed by program makers and network executives to be the site of men's leisure and women's labor.[32] While Spigel's critique of the view of women's labor as unproductive is significant, its assumptions about the raced and gendered division of labor is suggestive in another way.

The subject of television's 1950s family discourse (and, I would add, the nation's) is white and middle class. This is evident in representations of family situation comedies of the late 1950s and early 1960s. But what about the presence of black people in these domestic spaces—particularly black women—for whom such domestic spaces were not just sites of white male leisure or unrecognized reproductive labor for white women? For black women domestics, suburban households were also the sites of racialized wage labor. For this raced and gendered class of workers, domestic work is best defined in public terms rather than the private spaces of domesticity. Black women domestic workers were subjected to the discourse of television, except that they had specific and particular gender and racial relations to television and domestic labor, a relationship defined in terms of wages and public labor within the private sphere of domesticity. My point is simply that black female workers in television representations and at work were invisible, and necessarily so, because they represented an intractable expression of difference with which television's discourse of integration (from which the emerging national identity was forged) could not cope.

In the formative years of American network television, it seems that race was too unruly a point of difference in the production of the medium's most cherished subjects—consumers, television viewers, and white suburban members of the imagined nation.[33] Nevertheless, as Sasha Torres argues, the encounter with race offered by the civil rights movement provided both television and the emerging genre of television news documentary some of their most dramatic pictures and stories. At the same time, in its encounter with television the civil rights movement found a potent if momentary ally, capable of circulating the movement's powerful moral message and struggle for recognition to the far reaches of the country and the world. In short, television's role in relationship to black participation in the nation coalesced around questions of television's visual style and authority as a news-gathering and reporting institution and the movement's moral claims on nonviolent resistance as the route to legal enfranchisement.[34] On the question of ethnicity, ties of language, religion, and tradition remained the major social obstacles to making the nation out of differences. But the issue of race presented more deeply structural and intractable obstacles, since the American system of racial subordination was still held in place by the residues of scientific racism, Jim Crow practices of racial terror, and the legal enforcement of the doctrine of separate but equal racial segregation. This related set of factors really enabled the production of the white middle-class suburban consumer as the desired subject of the postwar nation of unlimited abundance, infinite possibility, progress, and homogeneity.

## RACE, RUPTURE, AND THE MANAGEMENT OF DIFFERENCE

In the wake of the civil rights movement and the emergence of black power, the late 1960s provided a formidable challenge to this televisual ideal of national identity, and explicitly raised the question of how to manage a dimension of difference that had heretofore remained repressed through exclusion. As with the nation, race remained the touchstone of America's management trouble; it became, and remains, it seems, the explicit difference most in need of management.

The legal end of segregation and the emergence of cultural pride in racial identity (as a result of anticolonial movements in the third world, racial nationalism, ethnic studies in the university, and antiwar movements in the street) made race more, not less, visible in the American national consciousness.[35] Race (and a shared history of oppression and political struggle) as a significant social basis of cultural identities (fueled by social unrest in American cities) complicated and troubled the lessons TV taught about belonging, citizenship, and national identity. Blacks, Latinos, and Asians no longer remained the silent and servile other to the televisual image of a homogeneous America basking in the spoils of postwar suburban expansion. These heretofore invisible members of the nation demanded *recognition, visibility, and inclusion* in the national imagination. Politically, blacks and people of color demanded to be treated as subjects of the nation and not just as consumers whose spending power was harnessed through race-based marketing strategies, while their cultural traditions, experiences, and identities (occasionally and selectively included for a bit of color) remained beyond representation.

Culturally, race was threatening and disruptive. Threatening, that is, to the logic of a universal, normative, and invisible whiteness on which the national imaginary (as recently as the 1950s and 1960s) depended. This threat required management at the level of television's response (both representational and industrial) and at the level of scholarly and journalist discourse that provided the principal account of how to imagine the nation. Integration did this work. The discourse of integration was deeply rooted in the logic of assimilation, which, in the aftermath of the civil rights movement, was codified into a social project of color blindness, a legal project of equal opportunity, and a moral project of individualism and self-responsibility.

The racial politics of the period, however, proved considerably more intractable and complex. Where many working-class white ethnics aspired to middle-class suburban life, as Lipsitz argues, such aspirations were fashioned out of a historically entrenched structure of racialization that facilitated this aspiration for mobility and its realization. This was the active production of the nation in action. Guaranteed low-interest federal housing loans, massive highway construction, college scholarships, and job training were made available to white service members and other white ethnics to ensure their social and physical mobility.[36] Redlining practices in real estate, together with race-based lending policies of banks and other financial institutions, helped to contain blacks and Latinos in segregated inner-city neighborhoods, entry-level jobs, and limited educational opportunities.[37] Materially, then, the construction of the nation out of white cultural aspirations to realize the American dream was fashioned out of specific historical and material conditions of possibility, in which race-based social practices and legal policies were the order of the day. Culturally, these mobility aspirations were shaped from a desire to move away from the population centers where blacks, Latinos, and Asians were the newly recognized citizens and potential neighbors that many "real" Americans wanted most to avoid. Despite the legally and morally charged language of equal opportunity and color blindness, by the middle decades of the 1960s many whites identified with the dream of segregated suburban middle-class worlds promoted by television representations and, more importantly, they equated these lives with what it meant to be American.[38]

The discourse of color blindness (as distinct from equal opportunity) posed problems for communities of color as well. In the wake of the black power movement and the strong thought of racial and ethnic nationalism, some (black) folk simply rejected the principle of invisibility and the slide toward whiteness as the universal subject of television and the imagined American nation. Blacks wanted cultural membership in the imagined nation constructed by television, but on different terms. At the very least, such terms meant acknowledging significant differences in cultural tradition, experience, and history. Indeed, while many blacks did aspire to the suburban middle-class life promised by the American dream and promoted by television, others insisted on black-generated ideas about the (black) nation that could be programmed within the context of the existing network structure.

These discursive, political, and material circumstances placed the problem of the representation and management of racial difference on a semiotic and economic collision course. Where the racial politics of television's golden era provided a model for managing issues of class, ethnicity, and gender, after the civil rights movement and the onset of racial nationalism, there was little assurance that such a strategy of incorporation and containment within the domestic sphere would result in effective semiotic and political economic management of racial difference. By following the integrationist logic, the gamble was that extending television's national imagination to include racial groups in the sphere of domesticity would sufficiently loosen suspicions about racial and cultural difference. Accordingly, whites would eventually come to feel comfortable with people of color as televisual citizens, friends, neighbors, and family members as WASPs had done with working-class European immigrants. But with the new militancy and nationalism there was little guarantee that communities of color, with their different and particular histories, conflicts, and traditions, would aspire to membership on these terms.

The potential (and actual) rupture occasioned by the problem of race opened complicated debates about the national identity, belonging, and citizenship that have continued to define controversies over network television and racial inclusion. Race is the repressed that returned in the 1970s and 1980s, rupturing the integrationist ideal of the homogeneous middle-class America constructed on network television. So dramatic and far-reaching was this return of the racially repressed that along with the need to extend network control over an unruly and chaotic market, the confrontation with race forced a modification in the semiotic and political economic order of American commercial network television. In the industry vernacular of the period, the turn to relevant programming included the representations of racial and ethnic difference. Representations of race opened the way for other points of social difference such as class, region, and generation as the basis for distinctive cultural identities with which television (and the nation) had to contend.[39]

The civil rights movement produced blacks, Latinos, and Asians as full political, legal, cultural subjects that television could no longer ignore, marginalize, or blatantly stereotype. At the same time, commercial network television had to figure out how to economically harness and culturally recognize these new legal subjects of the nation. Networks had to figure out how to incorporate the cultural traditions and identities of the new subjects in such a way as to make them profitable and yet not to scare away whites.[40] African Americans did indeed become visible (if contained and limited) subjects in the semiotic landscape of network television, if only as a result of the moral imperative and political pressure on television to meet its responsibility to offer more inclusive and racially diverse programming. The networks still had to avoid alienating whites, and it fell to the discourse of liberal pluralism as a strategy of management and containment to do both—that is, to make blacks visible and to hold the racial center by not alienating whites.

Instead of homogeneity created out of difference through consumption in the suburban domestic sphere, liberal pluralism constructed parallel universes in which different cultural identities based on race were acknowledged but contained (within genres, programming strips, and networks schedules). Rather than one version of domesticity, now there were several—white, black, working-class, middle-class, and so on. Organized into markets based on class and race, consumption and commodities became the currency that held the imagined American national identity together. While the ideal subject of the nation imagined by television remained white, middle-class, and suburban, the discourse of liberal pluralism ensured that television representations would now include blacks (and, to a far less extent, Latinos and Asians) and women. The ideology of equal opportunity could be represented (through consumption and culture) without threatening the political gains of the civil rights movement or the cultural and political hegemony of whiteness. Most of all, this separate but equal universe solved the problem of alienating white viewers and appeasing blacks ones, all of whom were still connected to the dominant network structure.

This was achieved by the network's organization and structure—its political economy, which was defined by the dominance of the three-network system, and its semiotic economy, which rested on a representational logic that moved between the ideal of racial integration and the reality of a liberal pluralism expressed as racially identifiable programs.[41] Managing black representations through the logic of the three-network structure and explicitly identifiable programming enabled the commercial networks to respond to moral and political pressure (from blacks) and to capitalize on the potentialities of these new audience segments. As the television industry continues to restructure itself, the persistence of this logic produces a periodic crisis around the representation of race. The problem is neither that people of color are absent on television nor that television continues its press toward the representation of the national imaginary as white and homogeneous.[42] Rather, the structural (and representational) logic of difference (e.g., the three network system) around which television structured itself made network television the site least able to construct and hold a coherent view of a national imaginary like the one that network programming presented in its golden age.[43]

Paradoxically, commercial network television continues to hold a powerful political appeal for many activists, journalists, and people of color as the cultural site most desirable for struggles over the representation of difference. This paradox expresses the lingering and powerful discursive, moral, and political effects of these defining cultural discourses, discourses that first clarified and then solidified television's moral and economic investment in symbolically representing the nation through the incorporation and management of racial difference.

## INSTABILITY AND THE NECESSITY OF DIFFERENCE

In the neo-network era, is it possible that we have finally reached the limit of the purported integrative function of commercial network television in the symbolic and imaginary production of the nation?[44] I believe that the answer is yes, owing to structural changes in the organization, production, and circulation of the television industry, to repurposing and recombining of content along a new logic, as well as to conceptions of the nation and struggles over its constitution.[45] In other words, this discursive limit expresses the failure of a liberal pluralist vision of a national imaginary achieved through the management of cultural difference. The three-network structure of commercial television in the United States has proved to be a limited, if not outright ineffective, means of realizing this desire. To the extent that television ever did produce effective national identifications by managing racial difference through exclusion and eventually incorporation, it did so primarily through representation and consumption. In a three-network system built on relative market stability, the search for the certainty that was guaranteed by increased audience share over competitors was achieved through periodic restructuring that simply divided and redivided a finite market among the three major television networks. From the beginning, network television established its defining cultural identity as a medium of communication located primarily in the domestic sphere. Culturally and socially the home-centered experience of network television produced real access to the symbolic televisual representation of the nation and an imaginary sense of belonging that linked subject, consumer, and citizen within the domestic sphere.[46] This home-centered experience is the basis of the link between citizenship, family, nation, mobility, and consumption that Spigel and Lipsitz saw as so important to the production of the nation and the management of difference from the 1950s through the 1970s.

But American network television is no longer organized simply to manage difference and reduce market uncertainties that threaten the dominance of a limited number of players. The logic of difference and the recognition of unlimited possibilities for new markets have been grafted into the very structure and organization of commercial television, but on a global scale.[47] Conceptions of a finite domestic-centered American market have been replaced with the recognition of the global centrality and possibility of difference.[48] Indeed, a host of scholars including John Caldwell and Michael Curtin suggests that it is no longer accurate to describe the American television system in terms of a network structure. These scholars use the terms neo-network and post-network structure to evoke cultural as well as structural dimensions and transformations in American television.[49] Similarly, John Hartley captures the structural and cultural dimensions of changes in television with his characterization of television as "transmodern."[50] With the cultural and structural changes signaled by Caldwell, Curtin, and Hartley, the specific problem of symbolically making the American nation through television's integrative function in the domestic sphere has moved, first, from erasure, repression, and transformation of difference in its early years, through integration and pluralism in its golden age, to explicit recognition of the centrality of difference in the neo-network era. The corporate brand name and network logo have become the means of expressing distinction and thus the recognition of the intractability of difference on a global scale. Problems of race and ethnicity have given way to the question of how to link a brand name to specific kinds of difference—culture, nation-states, gender, sexuality, and tradition—in order to establish distinctive brand identifications and loyalty through consumerism.[51]

At the level of political economy, new global entities have been formed through massive restructuring, the emergence of new sites of production, and the introduction of new technologies. Niche marketing, narrow-casting (marketing to a specific demographic segment), repurposing (combining and recombining programs with the purpose of creating new products and attracting new audiences), technological convergence, and alternative forms of service delivery now define the political economic terrain of television and new media.[52] Difference, diversity, and diversification of all sorts are the hallmarks of the industry's political and symbolic economy. Built on diversification, difference, and commodification, the massive restructuring of the global media industries located chiefly, but by no means primarily, in the West is designed precisely to pick up the smallest changes in the market and to respond to them instantaneously.[53] I do not mean to suggest that the market structure of capitalistic media has solved the problem of difference through a restructuring of the market and the proliferation of commodity choice aimed at specific niches. This strategy of rearticulating social and cultural difference into a matter of consumer choice has been the hallmark of capitalist media in the United States from the very beginning.

American network television's structural response to the increasing centrality of difference for its global project, and its recognition of the necessity for diversification as the basis of technological convergence has its counterpart in cultural representation as well.[54] The proliferation of academic fields devoted to difference and identity, debates over university curricula, and, of course, the culture wars are all indicative of the intense cultural struggles over the national identity, the crisis of national unity, and the subjects of the nation.[55] They are indicative, as well, of the rise of critical approaches to television and cultural studies that posit conceptions of television audiences as active, fragmented, unstable; and conceptions of cultural identities as actively produced in language, discourse, and representation. These new subjects and the identities they craft are the products of active engagement and use of symbolic meanings.[56]

The proliferation of discourses about difference and the representation of difference also found its way, as might be expected, into the television programming schedules. By the middle of the 1990s, American network television schedules were populated with outward signifiers of all sorts of cultural difference—gays and lesbians, blacks, liberal feminist, even extraterrestrial beings.[57] Program makers and advertisers, in particular, promoted a sensibility that quickly recognized and acknowledged differences of all sorts, especially cultural difference.[58] In the 1960s and 1970s, television played a major role in circulating and translating the civil rights discourse of equality to the level of everyday life and common sense. By the 1990s, television played an equally powerful role in deconstructing and rearticulating that political common sense to a neoconservatism that culturally reinscribed and socially reinstalled white males as the universal subjects.[59] It did so by emphasizing the principle of color blindness and the absence of racism.[60]

Against the backdrop of the cultural politics of difference, the correspondence between market segmentation, service delivery, and identity is no longer just aimed at the incorporation of unruly manifestations of difference that threaten the imagined nation or its ideal racialized subjects. This transformation in the recognition and representation of difference has had a profound impact discursively on the role of television in the making of the imagined nation. That is, television networks, program providers, and viewers are all driven by a logic of difference that ends up (re)structuring the national identity through the recognition and embrace of difference rather than through its elimination, repression, or incorporation.

Differently located and socially constituted active audiences of all sorts seek out, migrate to, and ignore programming now available as a result of the very restructuring forces that were initially designed to reduce the uncertainties of difference. Program scheduling options, though still structured by a few large global players, are no longer confined to three commercial networks, whose operations are defined by the classical monopoly logic of "broadcasting" that dominated the golden era. There is a significant distinction between contemporary active audiences—in their refusals and migrations—and the image of the passive viewer from the 1950s who was purportedly all too eager to join the imagined television nation. In the neo-network structure of transmodern television, specialized markets, narrow-casting, dispersed production centers, and differentiated profit centers depend on the simultaneous operation of different logics able to recognize and respond to the proliferation of differences of all sorts.[61] It is the centrality of difference and recognition of its multiple logics that make up the terrain on which notions of a collective national imagination is necessarily constructed and represented.

The tension between television as a transmodern media of representation and the liberal pluralist desire (including its neoconservative and neoliberal forms) for a national identity is the problem that concerns me here. This tension, I believe, still compels media activists and civil rights advocates to focus on the major commercial networks as the objects of political pressure, whereas the evidence on racial differences in viewing practices suggests that audiences (especially those of color that can afford to) regularly migrate to other places. Finally, it is through commitments to the ideal of liberal pluralism as a solution to the problem of national identity that some scholars, media activists, and journalists remain tied to the hope that television will live up to its purported integrative function in the making of the nation.

Tamara Jacoby, for example, argues that the concept of crossover remains an enduring ideal for television representations of race and that it can still provide a hedge against segregated viewing patterns that have emerged in the wake of cable and the recognition of difference as a productive, even realistic expression of the integrated society.[62] Like many journalists, Jacoby seems troubled by the emerging patterns of segregated viewing and reads these as anomalies in need of correction. She contends that the emergent patterns of niche programming and segregated viewing are the products of the loss of market share by major networks, the pursuit by advertisers of new market niches (which, by her lights, still have to include whites), and by the disinterest of blacks (and other people of color) in the programming that depicts integrated settings. This view continues to hold out hope for the integrative function of the network for making the nation. In a rather sophisticated way, Jacoby also wants to split the difference on the more pressing matter of difference and how it functions in the post–civil rights, post-network era. I find it curious, for instance, that she clings to idealizations of the black subject produced by liberal discourses of color blindness, but she does not engage with the kinds of racial identities and subjects produced after the civil rights movement. The unwillingness to consider what these new subjects might mean for the image of the nation and the role of television in producing the nation means, perhaps, that Jacoby is not particularly interested in the kinds of subjects out of which the nation has to be fashioned or in emerging and contested concepts of nation.

The continued focus on major American television networks as objects of political pressure is largely due to cultural concerns. Thus, while the structure of the network system has changed dramatically, for most citizens the major commercial networks continue to hold meaning culturally and symbolically. They continue to be regarded politically and culturally as operating at the center of the national social and political culture, and they remain in the best position to reach the greatest number of people, especially on issues of perceived national importance. As a result, then, the very idea and meaning of the "network" continues to hold value culturally and politically.[63]

## DIFFERENCE, ILLEGIBILITY AND INSTABILITY

I want to conclude this chapter by returning to the problem with which I began: the role of television in fashioning national identity through the management of difference structured by specific conceptions of the nation and networks. As I have explained, these discursive investments result in a cultural politics fashioned out of commitments to a liberal pluralist model of society. To my mind, such politics are at best critically impoverished and at worst ineffective because they fail to expose and exploit the discursive gaps and fissures between lingering modernist conceptions of the nation and the shifting logic of television as a transmodern, post-network media (situated in a global information economy).

The signature assumption of liberal pluralist discourses on which idealized conceptions of the national imaginary rest is a notion of stable,
orderly, and manageable social order that tries to manage (racial difference) through market choices, electoral politics, and the production of a
common cultural identity rooted in consumption. However, following
the example of Ien Ang, I want to begin with a different analytic tactic,
one that does not assume a bounded social order with some prior notions
of national coherence and identity to which we all aspire. I want to begin
with instability rather than order, where "variation does not come about
as a result of the division of a given social entity into a fixed range of
meaningful identities," and where "the infinite play of differences
. . . make all identities and all meanings precarious and unstable."[64]

In its global reach, the contemporary state of American network television is in just such a condition. The central point here is that nations
are limited in their ability to manage and contain difference and to produce homogeneity on the basis of such management. It is the "proliferation of difference that liberal pluralists cannot account for and which
the functionalist technology of audience measurement attempts to
account for, suppress and tame in the form of ratings or statistical measurement."[65]

Beginning with instability as the basis of a productive theorization of
cultural politics suggests, then, that indeterminacy and diversity are the
persistent social and cultural realities that structure and economically
distinguish contemporary global media. No longer is the primary
emphasis just on integrative functions aimed at producing a coherent
one-dimensional narrative of homogeneity—the management of difference through incorporation or even its regulation through recognition.

Instead of seeing the network's unwillingness to show more diverse
cultural representations as a lack of moral courage, a poor business
choice, or a periodic lapse in social judgment, as media activists contend, we can look to the circumstances where such decisions are routine
and culturally acceptable in the first place. Furthermore, rather than see
audience deficiency when we look at data on viewing patterns by race,
what if we reconsider the viewing patterns of (active) audiences of color,
regarding their viewing practices as a refusal, an expression of the bank-
ruptcy of the integrative promise of television in the making of the imagined nation.[66] Global media companies, including network television,
face a new set of symbolic and managerial challenges. The drive is not
just to control the global proliferation of difference, but also to exploit
it. This instability and uncertainty are two elements of the new cultural

logics of post or neo-network American television; it is the orderly disorder or disorderly order to which Ang refers.

From the perspective of the infinite possibility of difference we might
see the active recognition and structuring of difference by commercial
television, where the imagined nation is concerned, as the active production of a kind of illegibility of the nation. As I've said, because "the
networks" play such a pivotal role in the production of national recognition, it is the object of moral and political scrutiny by journalists and
activists, who see illegibility as a state of abnormality, a failure of the
integrative function of television. But from another vantage point, that
of audiences and the global movement of programs and images, it may
be that many television viewers respond to the loss of meaning and legibility of television's imagined nation by negotiating the television system on different terms. That is, national legibility, social integration,
and cultural belonging may no longer be the cultural logic that defines
television's relationship to the American nation-state.

The infinite recognition and representation of difference do imply a
change in how audiences are conceived, and following Raymond
Williams, political and cultural analysis are focused within a specific set
of determinations and limits. Working within the context of a highly
centralized system of program distribution, Ien Ang appreciates the
active and critical dimension of the audience's relationship to television's integrative pull. According to Ang, this active negotiation does
imply the presence of an active audience but it does not necessarily
equate such active negotiation with a resistance that guarantees in
advance a shift in the balance of power. "It would be a mistake," she
cautions, "to see the acting out of difference unambiguously as an act of
resistance; what needs to be emphasized, rather, is that the desire to be
different can be simultaneously complicit with and defiant against the
institutionalization of excess of desire in capitalist postmodernity." Nor
does it ensure that the active audience has moved beyond the industry's
sphere of influence, since "resistance is not built into the system so much
as ambivalence and indeterminacy . . . all of which are created by the
institutionalization of infinite semiosis."[67]

Ang's theoretical and political point is suggestive for posing questions
about television's representation of the nation as legible (and how this
legibility negotiates the issue of racial difference), especially when we
reach the limits of the integrative function of television. I want to claim
for the active audiences of color (within limits, of course) a similar kind
of productive potentiality of retreat, withdrawal, and negotiation with

television, especially its symbolic production of the nation.[68] Active audiences are both the subjects and objects of modern consumer capitalism. In the United States, the ideology of free access and viewer choice is the primary means by which people are drawn into the system of consumption and reproduction. The choice is, of course, made available within determinations that are by no means infinite and open-ended.

This conception of choice by active audiences within a set of structural limits is important for thinking about audiences of color as active—seeking, retreating, rejecting, and pursuing images and representations they "choose" across the televisual landscape. Politically, it is this active component to the expression of desire and difference that is lost in the polemic about network representations of communities of color. That is, within the options available, black audiences, for instance, seek out and follow (black) programming on Fox, Warner Brothers, and United Paramount. This pursuit is also a refusal, the flip side of passively accommodating to programming offerings that they do not find to their liking. Such choosing and refusing follow the systemic logic of the television system, based as it is on measuring audience viewing patterns and deciding from among them which consumers to pursue.

This logic, and the periodic moral panics and the political initiatives they spawn, are rooted in a liberal integrative model of society, governing, nation, and citizenship, one that the current global circumstance renders illegible. It seems to me that political and moral advocates who continue to desire this integrative model of television in the production of the national imaginary implicitly accept a view of the relationship between modernity, broadcasting, and the state born in television golden era. Despite its moral and cultural rhetoric, in the universe of commercial television, not all viewers are equally desired. Nor is it the case that the consumptive powers of all audiences guarantee a measure of visibility and exchange in the marketplace of consumer choice. Advertisers simply prefer some kinds of consumers, tastes, and desires to others. Liberal journalists, television executives, and activists continue to cling to a liberal model of the power of the market and the state to ensure the integrative management of racial and class difference in the face of this evidence. In doing so, these advocates ignore and reject the forms of popular legibility and cultural practice of active audiences of color whose very moves and negotiation of the television system serve, at the very least, to question and critique discursive constructions of nation rooted in the cultural politics of recognition, representativeness, and integration.

Of course, as a political strategy and galvanizing force of media activism, the integrative promise of network television as an expression of the social and cultural national imaginary continues to have appeal. The logic of this discourse produces politics and moral suasion that periodically pressure the commercial networks to schedule and broadcast programming that includes people of color, women, gays, and lesbians (both in front of and behind the camera). At the level of the industrial organization and media industries, these politics square with the market logic of consumption and commodity choice. This cultural logic also leads to periodic restructuring, which is global in reach, differentiated in structure, and designed to make difference and distinction (rather than incorporation and homogeneity) the basis of profitability.

This cultural logic, which of necessity acknowledges and seeks to exploit difference, appears in expressive forms of poplar music, television, cinema, advertising, fashion, and print; it promotes the unstable, fragmentary, and momentary nature of cultural identities made in and through representation.[69] Television makers must increasingly deal with active audiences who register their desire and identities through refusal and retreat, cynicism, inattention, and suspicion. These dispositions now form the basis of critical and active relationships to television representations of the social world and the nation. As such, they can potentially form the critical basis for the realization that nations "are not the natural destiny of pre-given cultures; rather, their existence is based upon the construction of a standardized national culture that is the prerequisite to the functioning of the modern industrial state."[70]

# CHAPTER 6

# Different Dreams, Dreams of Difference

In *The Mask of Art: Breaking the Aesthetic Contract*, film scholar Clyde Taylor examines the multiple positions, strategies, and effects of Western aesthetics on peoples of color throughout the world.[1] Taylor's focus is on "palace discourse," those systems of thought and habit of mind emanating from the crystal palaces of Western power/knowledge (of which aesthetics is merely one).[2] Taylor's immediate aim in this book is both deconstructive and reconstructive. It is a project of cultural criticism and reconstructive possibility. Taylor's critical investigation makes visible different discursive strategies used by "the palace" to construct and sustain advantage. But he also examines the tactical maneuvers of subalterns to subvert and challenge the palace. For Taylor, a critical project of cultural deconstruction and radical reconstruction demands an exacting self-reflexivity that is alert to the ironies of palace discourse.

Angharad Valdivia's concept of discursive diversity and Gregg Barak's of replacement discourse are comparable to Taylor's notion of discursive irony.[3] All appreciate and encourage the perspective of the subalterns. In short, Taylor, Valdivia, and Barak advocate the use of discursive strategies that reveal, critique, and help to establish the conditions of possibility for alternative and emergent imaginations. To be productive, "replacement discourses" must be able to discern and distinguish between cultural strategies of representation that mimic, signify, recode, riff, and otherwise reproduce and reinscribe palace discourse from those that offer critical alternatives.[4]

In the case of cinema, Taylor argues that critically responsive "replacement" discourse generates tactical alternatives that are opposite to the Hollywood discourses that emphasize beauty, symmetry, closure, and heroism. Films from Spike Lee's *Do the Right Thing* to Julie Dash's *Daughters of the Dust* offer visual and discursive strategies which, at the very least, expose the ironies, gaps, and fissures in the dominant regimes of representation.

In the popular language of our time, theoretical categories like difference, multiculturalism, and diversity present active sites of palace cooptation and contestation. The conditions of possibility produced by critical scholarship in fields such as critical race theory, cultural studies, feminist theory, queer studies, and ethnic studies provide a unique opportunity for critical scholars concerned with representation and criticism to move beyond simply reinstalling the virtues of difference. I refer not just to difference based on race, sex, gender, and class, but also to historical and spatial relations, where difference is the critical basis of engagement with palace discourse and the source of an alternative imagination.

This is critical and important work, since palace discourse applies the following strategies to questions of difference: to *ignore and repress* difference; to *conflate* it so that it becomes an expression of indifference; to *hierarchically order* difference where it can serve as the basis of narrow claims for inclusion; to *celebrate* difference as the goal of multicultural identity claims, which elides the history of difference as a basis of oppression and domination; finally, simply to *mark* difference in such a way that it is regarded as an impediment to grander narratives of global twenty-first-century homogeneity. In this way, focusing on the social, cultural, and historical role of difference in the production of palace discourse and the national imagination provides a productive point of entry for critical debate and dialogue that recognizes the productivity of difference as a conceptual and historical matter.

One challenge is to generate critical scholarship, cultural criticism, dialogue, and cultural expressions that identify the procedures by which alternative discourses challenge rather than reproduce palace discourse. But such critical cultural work must also encourage and enable us to imagine the world differently, to think outside of the categories that now dominate palace discourse. At the level of creative expression, such a critical imagination demands the equivalent of a tactical shock effect, something that disturbs and destabilizes the order of things, jarring us to see and imagine differently. At the level of critical scholarship and the professional organization of knowledge production, one tactical shock effect is to transgress actively various genres and disciplinary and conceptual boundaries. With cultural studies, queer theory, and poststructuralism as primary catalysts, the unsettling effects of blurring and crossing of boundaries have already been felt in a number of disciplinary-based academic fields and subfields.

Like some of their more adventurous theoretical counterparts, many cultural producers are aggressively transgressing borders. The work of these cultural border crossings illuminates the way that long-held categories and assumptions that seemed so natural, inevitable, and universal are in fact historically and socially produced in the interest of sustaining the hegemony of palace discourse. Take the field of African American cultural production, for example. The (shock) effect of blurring genres and boundaries has produced the ironic pose of hip-hop (felt especially strongly in cinema, popular music, fashion, and sport). Timeworn distinctions between theory and practice, play and the real, the serious and the frivolous, nostalgia and history, nihilism and morality no longer seem to hold. This slide across borders stimulates vital conversations and confrontation over the question of media influence, control of cultural production, and the role of sexuality, social class, race, and gender in the representation of African American life and culture and the decline of ethnically based political visions.

Independent filmmakers like Lourdes Portillo, Marlon Riggs, Julie Dash, Renee Tajima, Trinh T. Minh Ha, Issac Julian, John Akrumpha, and Thomas Allen Harris, among many others, continue to stretch the boundaries of our cultural imagination on these matters. These filmmakers traverse the world of the academy and the world of filmmaking, theory and the vernacular, the museum and the movie theater. Their works pose vital questions that go to the very core of scholarly and popular issues of difference, identity, and cultural politics. (For the most part, the works of these culture makers explore the subspecialty of identity and difference.)

In many areas of cultural production, both marginal and mainstream, representations and discourses cannot be read clearly and coherently, predictably and correctly in the direction and interest of only one kind of politics or political vision. This refusal and illegibility have generated a good deal of anxiety and rather heated debate about the national future, and whether or not, given so many points of difference, we have a collective set of core experiences that bind us into a nation. The cause for much of our collective anxiety is blamed on the *image* and a sense of the disproportionate influence that the image exercises over us. Implicit in this moral anxiety is some notion of a normative ideal. But normative ideals are made, not given; they are the products of historical struggle and discursive productions.

In its most far-reaching vision, the civil rights movement imagined a post–civil rights nation state in which difference, while recognized, did not matter. Network television was (and remains) central to the depiction, naturalization, and widespread circulation of this desire as a normative feature of the good and just society. But something unexpected (for some, anyway) happened on the way to this national ideal. Difference, particularly race and ethnicity, mattered more, not less, in post–civil rights America. And difference mattered differently on television. As I argued in the previous chapter, the correspondence between the network, as a coherent and stable program and distribution source, and the civil rights discourse of color blindness collapsed under the weight of an increasing emphasis on difference: sexual difference, racial and ethnic difference, gender difference in the case of civil rights discourse and new markets, greater market segmentation, new forms of program delivery, and new technologies in the television system. At the level of cultural representation (especially media studies and media discourses like advertising), a new kind of difference also appeared—parody, irony, indifference, and irreverence are all the hallmarks of a kind of postmodern sensibility that sees the world in terms of the proliferation of difference.

How then to make sense of the persistence of the shifting desire for integration and color blindness as an affirmation of the American ideal in the face of these post–civil rights *(and post-network)* proliferations of difference? I join Gregg Barak in urging a return to the ideal of critical self-reflexivity, by way of a challenge that we critically examine our own investments and relationship to this idealized notion of the American dream.[5] This is the question that filmmaker Marlon Riggs so perceptively interrogates in his film about television, *Color Adjustment*. After each image of desire for African American arrival into the representational body of the nation, Riggs forces his viewer to confront the very foundation of the dream itself, particularly the role of television, in its realization. With televisual images of black arrival represented by (positive) images like Oprah, Cosby, *The Jeffersons,* and *Roots,* Riggs simply asks the viewer to confront the very basis of black inclusion in the American dream, its foundation and contradiction, and the role of television in that construction and representation.

Throughout the 1990s the discourse of color blindness and the civil rights ideal of racial equality were hijacked by an aggressive conservatism that rearticulated claims for racial, sexual, and gender equality into group-based identity politics that purportedly blocked the "true" meaning of the dream. In this conservative discourse, difference is significant only as a matter of individual character and morality. In the face of this rearticulated discourse of civil rights, there is a persistent concern among journalists, scholars, and community activists about identity and difference. On the one hand, there is the constant reminder from cultural conservatives (on both the left and the right) about the exaggerated role of identity politics in the erosion of national unity and national identity. On the other hand, under the banner of unlimited capitalist growth and new technologies, media companies continue to generate new and more precise means of identifying audiences and delivering programming services to them, to the point that we are capable of disaggregating the nation into all sorts of categories.

Critical media scholars and cultural critics continue the work of mapping the steady move toward the global concentration of power in the telecommunications industry, which is, to be sure, an important project. Scholars and activists have also been vigilant about monitoring and registering the shifts, gains, and losses in television and media representations of women, queers, and people of color. Our righteous moral indignation has been duly registered, as it should be, on the question of corporate monopoly, media violence, and the potentially harmful effects of each on our civic culture. We have, no doubt, perfected the fine art of clever and ever more witty readings of media texts.

But these achievements and concerns illustrate and reaffirm theoretical assumptions and moral investments in a very specific social and cultural model of community, nation, public, and civil society. Some scholars, journalists, and activists working in media have been (at best) ambivalent and (at worst) unenthusiastic about embracing insights from the theoretical developments about identity, subjectivity, and the cultural operations though which difference is made to matter socially and culturally. I believe that insights from queer theory, minority discourses, and cultural studies have helped us to see clearly and make good critical sense of media's representation of and engagement with difference. The persistence and precision with which analysts of globalization encourage us to see the virtue and necessity of living in a global world makes good sense. At the same time, we seem unwilling to move away from thinking of difference as persistent sources of division, impediment, and separation to some idealized and imaginary national coherence.

My desire is not so much to fetishize difference or the real historical fact of how difference operates as the basis for cultural and social domination, terror, and repression. By way of thinking through the possibility of replacement discourses that begin from the place of discursive diversity, it seems paramount to begin in earnest by thinking about the play of difference in our national imagination and the role of media in the construction of that imagination.

# CHAPTER 7

# Cultural Politics as Outrage(ous)

In a chapter from *Watching Race* called "Irreverence, Sideshows, and Spectacles," I grappled with the issue of stereotypes, irreverence, spectacle, and parody in network television representations of blacks.[1] I argued that the Fox program *In Living Color* produced mixed results in terms of cultural politics. I took this position in large part because the black poor (particularly women) on the show were almost always the butt of jokes. At the same time, *In Living Color* periodically offered trenchant and unflinching criticism of American racism. Through strategies of engagement that included humor, parody, and a mocking tone, the show served as a touchstone for engagements with racial matters between and within various American racial and ethnic positions.

It is equally provocative and challenging to think about cultural politics in the context of the work of artist Kara Walker. For all of the polemic (and celebration) surrounding it, Kara Walker's body of work seems perfectly to embody and represent our historical time and cultural mood (at least in the United States). Focused as Walker's work is on issues of visibility and recognition, as well as violence, terror, and desire, I want to think about the cultural politics provoked by it, especially the conditions (discursive and historical) of possibility out of which her work (and the polemic surrounding it) emerges. I also want to reflect on the representational and cultural strategies, or moves, operating in Walker's work.

## STAGING THE SCENE

Walker's artwork self-consciously draws on a number of settings, representations, discourses, institutions, scenes, approaches, and traditions. One of the defining qualities of her work is its clever juxtaposition of topics, historical periods, materials and media, and stylistic languages as a means of critically exploring aesthetic and emotional as well as political concerns. Walker's work includes (but is not limited to) sustained meditations on stereotypes, slavery, familiar narratives of American history, romance novels, arts and crafts, museums, mass culture, high culture, kitsch, humor, parody, irony, and the outrageous. Walker's use of these strategies is by no means coincidental; it has been conditioned and enabled by the conjuncture of social developments and cultural tendencies since the dramatic events of the 1960s and the black power period.

Historically black people in the United States have used the expressive arts and popular culture aggressively to imagine and narrate a collective past, the political aim of which was to protect black people. and that (imagined) past from the cultural control of whites. Expressive culture also provided a "scene" or space in which and from which to openly declare black anger and black beauty. Black expressive culture in the 1960s, of course, helped to break the Victorian-like hold that whiteness had on key aspects of our popular imaginations. This break is exemplified by stellar public (and very masculine) displays of blackness at key moments, such as the 1968 Olympics, the visibility and related iconography of the Black Panther Party, and the Memphis garbage strike.

By the mid-1990s, this declaration of black cultural independence turned inward, prompting Ishmael Reed to refer to the ensuing black conflicts and debates over blackness, gender, sexuality, and color-casting as instances of "airing dirty laundry." In the wake of increasingly sophisticated but no less venomous cultural skirmishes between black men and women, queers and straights, light and dark, middle class and poor, the humor—from Spike Lee, to *Def Comedy Jam*, to *In Living Color*—were clearly by us, for us, and on us. But the jokes and the differences within blackness that they often masked circulated unmediated in a public sphere made available by communications technologies like television, film, radio, and recordings.

These tensions, conflicts, and airings of dirty laundry became increasingly more visible and commercially popular in mass culture through forums like popular music, stand-up comedy, television talk shows, and the rituals of public confession, cutting up and putting on in public. American popular media not only enabled this kind of cultural ritual, it aggressively promoted it. For large numbers of black folk, the genie came out of the bottle, right in our living rooms, and there was no getting it back in. By viewing, laughing at, and consuming these images, black folk were directly complicitous in all the stereotypes, ill-considered humor, and worst impulses of our black selves. It was as if we were thrust back to some earlier period of the 1950s, when Amos and Andy (as the NAACP reasoned) were about to blow it for everyone. Then, like now, such violators needed to be called out, stopped for what Tommy Lott has called "racial malpractice." As if this weren't enough, "bitches, niggas, hos, dogs, and mothafuckas" were so common in the music and social language of the black vernacular that it took Professor Henry Louis Gates to mount a cultural defense of black American youth's right to cut-up in the American public sphere.

These cultural developments in and over the popular vernacular of black culture circulated at the same time as feminists, cultural critics, and intellectuals debated the cultural veracity of popular culture, the harmful effects of hate speech, the violence of pornography, and abuses of women and children. And yet it was also popular media like the tabloid press, reality TV, Hollywood movies, soap operas, and novels that staged, displayed, and covered the activities of some of the culture's major marginalized and repressed. Think, for example, of the O. J. Simpson spectacle, including his slow-speed car chase and his subsequent trial; the Clarence Thomas and Anita Hill hearings, with all the lurid details of sexual fantasy, power, intimidation, and terror; or Michael Jackson and his pedophilic troubles externalized as an incessantly repressed and indeterminate gendered, sexed, and raced figment of our collective media imagination. Each of these spectacular media moments spun around the complex relationship between sex, terror, gender, power, and pleasure. Once again, black folk functioned as the cultural and moral image through which white America was reminded of its deeply repressed and vexed relationship to race, sex, and power.

In the midst of this cultural quicksand, some middle-class and professional black folk continued to get ahead socially and economically, while the black poor functioned as their subalterns. In the heady decades of the 1980s and 1990s, the black middle class became the affirmation of American arrival into that civil rights panacea of color blindness, racial equality, and fairness. But what collective and social cost did such an arrival exact from those least able to pay? With the increasing and expanded access to the inner circle of intimacy and recognition came a more strained and tenuous relationship to the stories we told ourselves about ourselves as an imagined collectivity. Perhaps it was time for more cultural regulation. The jokes and stereotypes that used to play to black-only crowds a generation or two ago, when Redd Foxx, Slappy White, Moms Mabley, and Richard Pryor told them, in the hands of the *Def Comedy Jam* generation came dangerously close to violating an unspoken collective code. But with more regulation who was protecting whom? The black middle class, poised to finally get its piece of the American good life? The black poor, poised to be stricken from welfare roles and, in some cases, housed in a prison industrial complex by a moralistic national government that knows best?

In this climate, jokes do not seem funny in quite the same way. Engaging with the black popular vernacular of youth culture seems to be about more than understanding—in the sense of the Rastafarian notion of seen—than grappling with some fundamental cleavage and difference within blackness around issues of gender, class, and sexuality. From *Def Comedy Jam* to *In Living Color,* the jokes were told by a generation of youthful performers who talked almost exclusively about what Bakhtin calls the carnivalesque—sex jokes, food jokes, fag jokes, and bits about getting high, getting laid, and getting over. Some of us excused this turn in the vernacular as mere fun and games; others saw clever oppositional moves of resistance disguised as signifying practices—parody, irony, shock and, most often, in-your-face interpretation—and dead-on critiques of the condition of life in modern America.

But not all were so generous, patient, or tolerant. Some, such as community organizations in Harlem led by Reverend Calvin Butts, sounded the alarm and declared this expression of black youth culture as an assault on blackness and black people. Black politicians joined ranks with some of the most conservative right-wing guardians of the gates, to insist that Congress and the state regulate the "filth" coming from black youth in the name of culture. These cultural moves, and alliances through which they were forged, made for some strange bedfellows; in the end they sharpened the focus on black cultural politics, black cultural production, and the whole question of what James Baldwin called the "burden of representation."

In 1980s and 1990s in the world of the so-called serious arts, let us not forget the outrage, suspicions, and calls for tighter border regulation that accompanied the Black Male show at the Whitney in New York and the Hammer Museum in Los Angeles. Recall also the quite visceral responses that were generated by the Robert Mapplethorpe nudes of black men. And, of course, reverberations were heard all the way to Washington, D.C., and the halls of the U.S. Congress because the late Marlon Riggs dared to depict black men loving black men in his film *Tongues Untied* and PBS dared to fund and broadcast it. Think also of the controversy provoked by filmmaker Issac Julian's engagement with questions of black agency and desire through the figure of Langston Hughes in his masterful *Looking for Langston*. So controversies over black images and black image making, especially as they involve black artists crossing borders and making trouble, is not new.[2]

What is most interesting, even if it is not new, is the sheer volume of black cultural images and representations that draw freely on irony, parody, sacrilege, and irreverence. On a par with the prevalence of these strategies across popular, vernacular, and serious artworks is the range of venues, sites, scenes and media where this work circulates—novels, film, galleries, theater, television, popular music, fashion, and fanzines. Black representations and popular practices move easily and quickly across various borders of aesthetics, politics, genres, and venues, rendering the idea of borders within black popular culture more and more meaningless.

So it is that I come to the work of Kara Walker. Indeed, it seems to me that it is no accident—or at least that is the case I have been trying to make—that Walker's work (and that of many of her generation) draws on and deploys many of the tendencies, strategies, and sensibilities that I have been describing in black cultural production and representation.[3] It is notable that Walker's work has stimulated similar responses (in form if not in context) that engender heightened surveillance, regulation, policing, and pondering about the condition of the black cultural imagination.

I come to a discussion of Walker's work, then, by way of this brief tour through black cultural politics, convinced more than ever that representation still matters for cultural politics, especially for the world out of which Walker's work comes. But I approach her work (and that of her contemporaries), in particular her treatment of the past, for clues for thinking about how historical and contemporary claims on representations of blackness have changed. I want to know more about what this means and how to make sense of this shift and its impact on black representation and cultural politics, especially under the circumstances that, in a bit of a polemic, Thelma Goldman and Glenn Ligon refer to as "postblack."[4] I am interested in Walker's work, then, for what it suggests about a young contemporary black female artist grappling with the past, and for what it offers for making sense of the historical conditions out of which it comes and the cultural mood to which it speaks.

Paul Gilroy, among others, has been concerned with the search for a shared historical condition in which contemporary black artists struggle to find voice. Just what is the problematic and what is its scene? For Walker (and for writers like Shirley Anne Williams, Charles Johnson, and Toni Morrison), this scene is slavery, empire, and race. The problematic: how to reckon with memory, history, terror, and desire, all of which are constituted and produced in that terrible and terrifying moment of chattel slavery. Here is Paul Gilroy on why slavery maintains the cultural and moral force that still requires such reckoning:

> Our imaginations are conditioned by an enduring proximity to racial terror. Whether this is viewed as an effect of oppression or a unique moral burden, it is premised on some sense of Black culture, not simply as a significant repository of anti-capitalist sensibility, but as counter cultures of modernity forged in the quintessentially modern condition of racial slavery.[5]

In an exchange with Gilroy, Kobena Mercer reminds us of the pitfalls of this scene (as the primary source of a black countermodernism). Mercer worries, rightfully I think, that too close a relation to this scene runs the considerable risk of reinscribing both the power of the scene and the cultural politics produced by it. If slavery is the original mise-en-scène of modern black terror (and a black countermodernism), then Mercer is concerned with the conditions of possibility for subsequent stagings and restagings of black cultural imagination. Mercer locates the "burdens" of representation for black artists in the social relations, historical circumstances, and cultural politics structured by these conditions of possibility. For Mercer, conditions of possibility involve both structural and institutional relations to black artistic production and reception. They involve discursive and representational operations and procedures as well.

Concerned with the burdens borne by black artists, as well as the fate of strong criticism and critical discourse, Mercer offers a cautionary tale about the burdens of representation and the enforcement of cultural regulation in the name of a monolithic blackness. Although the specific reference is to England, Mercer's reflections are instructive for the United States.

> Because there has been no continuous context in which to develop mutual criticism, it erupts in emotive and violent outbursts which rarely say anything about specific works of art. But which entail a kind of authoritarian

policing on the part of the black critic, which only inhibits the open expression of differences, perpetuating a state of affairs in which disagreements are silenced and criticism comes to be wielded as a form of punishment.[6]

In this critical state of affairs—whether in the art world or the popular arena—"black art criticism comes to be reduced to a system for making value judgments that are ultimately moral rather than aesthetic in character."[7] What is involved, we might ask, in the social and political move to protect black people and blackness from the "malpractice" of some black cultural workers and artists? And exactly what is involved in constituting such transgressions as violations? The burden of representation, it seems, falls as much on audiences and critics (involved in reception and evaluation) as on the artist and system of artistic production.

SEEN?

To get at the strategies of representation and the cultural politics involved in Walker's work, I want to offer a series of claims that at least try to bring together some of the conditions of possibility and cultural tendencies that I have been describing.

1. Slavery is the site of racial terror out of which black collective memory has tried to forge a countermemory and oppositional culture.[8]

2. Popular culture, expressive forms, and vernacular practices are contemporary sites where black countermemories, desires, fantasies, and representations are produced and circulated. These are major sites for the expression and engagement of the national (in this case American) racial imaginary. This is the organizing theme of Issac Julian's engaging film, *The Darker Side of Black*.

3. The civil rights movement is the contemporary moment when black claims on the civil society were made and asserted in the name of blackness (as an identity and structure of feeling). In the aftermath of the civil rights movement, the black power period is the moment that produced what Greg Tate calls cultural confidence, a confidence that made it possible to explore the ugly side of things. In the wake of this cultural confidence, black difference was forced into the open. Gender, sexuality, and related points of articulation were important points of

challenge to monolithic constructions of blackness (much of which appeared in the guise of an aggressive masculinity and heterosexuality). It is little surprise that these developments generated discourses and practices of regulation and surveillance within blackness as well.

4. Seminal to these historical developments is the role of academic theory in producing specific ways of engaging with the varieties of expressive forms, sites, categories, circuits, and representational strategies for naming, asserting, defending, and critiquing blackness. Such theoretical initiatives have come from black feminist studies, diasporic studies, and cinema studies. In addition to the structural and historical connections to slavery, empire, and nation, blackness is theorized as an unfolding, shifting, multiple, and hybrid set of social relations and discursive positions.

Attention to these theoretical interventions has also brought whiteness, master narratives, and the role of race in the production and maintenance of empire into sharper critical focus.[9] Whiteness and related palace discourses, to borrow a phrase from Clyde Taylor, are the focus of deconstructive projects, and subalterns (including blackness) are subjects from whose vantage points these projects proceed.[10] These deconstructive projects interrogate how the agents of domination (whether of the colonial or national variety) mobilize power and knowledge to "play in the dark," as Toni Morrison put it. Hence it is little surprise that "racial stereotypes" figure so prominently in the work of Kara Walker, where they function as the central tropes of interrogation, shock, play, desire, and pleasure. As Walker notes, "they (silhouette children) took on greater importance when I began thinking about minstrelsy and putting on the other person and interracial desire—when I attempted to see from the other person's point of view, from the point of view of the white male master from American history."[11]

On the terrain of racial stereotypes and palace discourse, black expressive forms use the tactical maneuvers of irreverence and spectacle to inhabit and combine the most shocking, outrageous, and carnivalesque images. These forms and the tactics through which they are deployed produce, for some, dangerous cultural politics that straddle the divide between the pleasures and fun of subversion and the real politics of control, regulation, and reproduction. The political and aesthetic burden of proof faced by black artists and culture workers who use such tactics in the end is decided on the basis of self-reflexivity, location, and level of engagement. The artist is neither neutral nor absent, but always present and engaged. Indeed, for many artists (and the audience) this politics of self-reflection and irony is part of the fun—the point if you will.[12]

This self-reflexivity is, I think, central to the work of Walker, for it serves to place her inside of the cultural operations that the artwork performs. She is in the scene, part of the mise-en-scène, the staging of the scene. This self-reflexivity operates at another level, producing key moments of political articulation and imaginative cultural possibility. Speaking about his own relationship to the Robert Mapplethorpe nudes of black men, Kobena Mercer suggests,

> Without a degree of self-reflexivity black critiques of Mapplethorpe's work that stops simply at the reading of racism and racism alone can quite conceivably be recuperated and assimilated to a conservative cultural politics of homophobic containment. Precisely on account of this ambivalence, Mapplethorpe's photographs are open to a range of contradictory readings whose political character depends on the social identity that different audiences bring to bear on them.
>
> The photographs can confirm a racist reading as easily as they can produce an anti-racist one; they can elicit a homophobic reading as easily as they can confirm a homophobic one. Once ambivalence and undecidability are situated in the contextual relations between author, text, and audience, a cultural struggle ensues in which antagonistic efforts compete to articulate their preferred meanings in the text.[13]

With critical self-reflexivity as part of the modus operandi, and ambivalence as an effect, contemporary black art and cultural practices have generated tactics that liberally use parody, humor, irony, shock, irreverence, transgression, and spectacle. The politics of these tactics of representation depend on or insist on audience and spectator investments. That is, at the very least audiences must do the demanding and often frustrating work of confronting and grappling with the powerful role of race and representation (in Walker's case racial stereotypes) in the national imaginary.

The payoff is worth the investment because, if nothing else, irony and parody help to illuminate the precarious nature of representation (especially racial stereotypes). Politically, the gain is that representations deploying these strategies reveal the degree to which cultural meaning and relations organized through social power are anchored and produced in history (and not in nature). In their appeals to nature, stereotypes and abject representations of blackness repress their roots in history and thereby staunchly resist new and different ways of staging, see-ing, and telling about the complexity of its will to power.

Walker's work, it seems to me, and that of others of her generation, especially in the popular arts, uses these strategies with disturbing suc-cess. For instance, Walker uses silhouettes, together with nineteenth-century melodrama, stereotypes, and romance to explore the intersec-tion of race, sex, and terror through slavery. This work directly engages with slavery, and by doing so compels us to confront slavery as "the" establishing scene of American racial terror. It is this engagement that makes her work so courageous and disturbing.

As an African American artist, Walker's shameless engagement with the shameful and the forbidden dimensions of slavery (as a catalogue essay that accompanies one of her exhibitions suggests) tells us some-thing about why, in matters of American racial slavery, shame and denial are so central to the American national imagination. According to the *Newsletter of the Renaissance Society* at the University of Chicago, Walker's work is unique in its abandonment of historical shame sur-rounding slavery, social shame surrounding stereotypes, and bodily shame regarding sexual and excretory functions. The *Newsletter* notes,

> Walker's work is shameless three times over. In her choice of imagery, she
> has abandoned the historical shame surrounding slavery, the social shame
> surrounding stereotypes, and finally a bodily shame regarding sexual and
> excretory functions. . . . Needless to say, it is the 200-year history of a
> shameful act conducted squarely within our consciousness that makes it
> possible for Walker to not only refuse shame, but to blur the distinction
> between forms of shame.[14]

Walker's work is also doggedly aggressive and assertive in its insistence that slaves and descendants of slaves know a thing or two about white-ness, especially how the fantasy work of whiteness operates, including its production of and dependence on black abjection. The idea of dwelling at the intersections between *desire, race, sex, pornography, gender, and reproduction* is a rough business that always runs the risk of critical paralysis and moral regulation. Dwelling too long and intimately at these intersections is the source of some of the most vexed and persistent responses to Walker's work, especially among African Americans.[15]

But irreverence, parody, and the outrageous are not always effective strategies for engaging cultural politics and struggles over meaning. As the controversy over Walker's work indicates, people are often deeply offended and opt out of investing any time or energy in engaging with the work. As Clyde Taylor shows in *The Mask of Art,* such strategies can and do often miss their intended target of destabilizing dominant discourse. Instead, they help to reinstall and reproduce the very same system of power they intend to expose and disrupt. These polemical works often generate a kind of strong thought aimed at easing the cultural burdens of black folk, but they turn out to exchange cultural and racial protectionism for surveillance, regulation, and censorship. While it may offer protection, such strong thought has its limits. The target of strong criticism herself, Thelma Goldman, curator of the Whitney Museum's Black Male exhibit, argues that "the issue of race and representation is also about transforming the image, creating alternatives, asking ourselves questions about what types of images subvert, pose critical alternatives, and transform our world views and move us away from dualistic thinking about good and bad."[16]

Walker and others of her generation have taken up the challenge of a different kind of reckoning with the issues of memory, shame, terror, and race. This reckoning owes as much to their cultural inheritance as to their personal and collective biography. In this respect, Walker and her colleagues inherited and, in turn, are helping to produce a more complicated way of seeing our collective past and imagining a different kind of future. Like their counterparts in cinema and popular culture, these artists insist on confronting the beauty and ugliness, reality and fantasy, the dangerous, and the repressed in all of us. As Kobena Mercer notes, this complexity must be grasped and appreciated lest these representations are circumscribed, reduced, and made to stand for moral arguments and defenses of a very narrow, nostalgic, and ultimately limiting conception of blackness.

# PART III

# Moves

# CHAPTER 8

# Is (Cyber) Space the Place?

Can black cultural production function as a critical counterknowledge? In the new information order and with the emerging new communications technology, what are the conditions of possibility for the production of such knowledge? In the next chapter, I argue that in the information society, music plays a pivotal role in the production of critical counterknowledge. In this chapter I aim to work through popular conversations and sentiments about the new information technologies as they bear on issues of blackness, difference, and identity. I consider the political salience of identity and representation under conditions that Stuart Hall and Cornel West over a decade ago called the new cultural politics of difference.

## HAPPY PASTORALS OF PROGRESS AND GRIM NARRATIVES OF DOMINATION

Does it make sense, I wonder, to continue to speak about culture and identities as sources of critical counterknowledge, in the context of rapidly shifting global conditions of capitalist production, innovative technologies, new structures of media ownership, and unprecedented transformation of spatial and temporal relations? In the United States and other electronically wired countries around the world, has the digital revolution disrupted something so fundamental as our collective structure of feeling, so that the collective map that gives shape and meaning to our lives and activities is no longer legible? For the most skeptical, the configurations of global economic power enabled by the new communication and information technologies are simply the mature expression of capitalist logic and administrative rationality that Marx and Weber anticipated well over a century ago. The anticipated effect on social relations (exploitation and domination), democratic possibility, and cultural traditions is a very old tale indeed, told by those on the left and the right who are worried about the corrosive effects of a global corporate capitalism on culture, community, and tradition.

An equally familiar tale is the more celebratory and utopian vision of neoliberalism: economic freedom, Western-style political democracy, and cultural openness that is not just enabled by the new media and communication technology but is almost synonymous with it. In this hopeful tale of unlimited economic prosperity, political freedom, and cultural openness, information technology and free markets facilitate the production and circulation of information, and thus are the measure of progress and freedom. Through new communication technologies and the openness of free marketplace culture—including information and entertainment—information is accessible everywhere. Consumer sovereignty, choice, and the availability of commodities—cultural and otherwise—are the economic expression and political realization of this neoliberal vision of democratic possibility and economic freedom. The new town halls and unregulated marketplaces of cyberspace are the sites of participation and choice, all ensured by the efficient operation and coordination of Western market capitalism, neoliberal Western democracy, and new communication technologies. This is the inevitable and celebratory march of progress.[1]

James Carey calls these two sets of tales "happy pastorals of progress or grim narratives of power and domination."[2] My concern is not with rewriting or updating either of these old stories.[3] Instead, I want to try and think through the relationship between operations of knowledge/power around culture and the new technologies of communication and information, particularly for organizing alliances, identifications, and articulations that form the terrain of political struggles for new hegemonies. For starters, consider some of the ways that new communication technologies actually get inscribed and articulated by social relations and logics that produce greater exploitation, domination, and inequality—represented through narratives of freedom, choice, and progress.

In the modern nations of the West, dispersed sites of production, flexible modular production processes, decentralized administrative structures, and the capacity for rapid circulation of information, goods, and people across geographical and spatial boundaries now profoundly organize the flows and encounters with popular commercial media, commercial popular culture, and other forms of information.[4] Of course, these flows and exchanges are variable, elastic, and often uneven, which means (as in the case of cinema or television) that with new and increasingly more sophisticated means of marketing and distribution, both fragmentation and homogenization are the defining logic of global capitalism (and of the production of information and entertainment under conditions of global capitalism).[5] Like the limited conception of "grim tales and happy narratives" of new technology, encrusted binary distinctions between high and low, pure and corrupt no longer make real sense. New production, distribution, and exhibition capabilities are possible, since more dispersed and flexible forms of global production are coordinated and administered through the new technologies.[6]

The historical forms and conditions within which the media/culture complex operates are specific and global as well as abstract and local. Despite their growing technical sophistication, global distribution, and transformation into the digits and bits of the information superhighway, the meanings we make and the uses to which we put them are experienced *socially* and *culturally* in local and specific circumstances. (But, one might be tempted to ask, is this too just another version of a very old story?)

This means, as Allucquere Stone suggests, that technology, no matter how complex, removed, or abstract, must still be understood socially and culturally:

> technologies are visible and frequently material evidence of struggles over meaning. They don't exist outside of complex belief systems in whose social and political frames they are embedded. Their apparent obduracy is an artifact, a technology of its own. A VCR remote control is merely a ritual object in the absence of the dense social networks, capital structures, and manufacturer-driven expectations that manifest as cable and satellite technology, market share, leisure time and entertainment.[7]

By suggesting that media and technology are embedded in social and cultural relations means that their operation and control involve matters of politics and history rather than the mere workings of disinterested technical know-how. John Fiske states the matter directly: "the computer requires categories to link its separate bits of information together and turn them into knowledge. But the categories are *social,* not technological, so *constructing* them is where the power of the computer is politicized."[8]

My own conception of culture, then, emphasizes salience of historical contexts, the centrality of social relations, and the specific conditions of practice and use as the bases for making sense of the social world.[9] I urge a view of culture that stresses the popular and the everyday because I am interested in the practical maneuvers that people use to shape their circumstances and fashion lives out of the cultural and social resources—symbolic and material—at their disposal. Culture (including technologically mediated and commercially produced forms) is particularly important in this regard, for it is also a place for making sense of social life through negotiation, contestation, and struggle.[10]

By focusing on the terrain of the popular (and the specific ways in which popular sentiments and understandings are structured, structure, appropriate, and are appropriated), I want to critically face up to, as George Lipsitz puts it, the contradictory possibilities that the new media and the attendant technologies of information, communication, and commercialization present for thinking about cultural politics in general and black cultural politics in particular. These new technologies—in the form of the Internet, digital storage, retrieval, and network—are now, perhaps more than ever, the predominant places of mediation, transformation, and translation of vernacular and everyday practices into commercial forms. As such, they are easily packaged, taken up, and circulated as popular styles, products, and images where they are registered in the public imagination as the basis of popular understandings. It is where new social relations are forged and where new cultural practices are made from the meeting between the local and the global, the vernacular and the commercial, which to one degree or another are shaped by new technologies that facilitate global flows of people and information. In fact, so profound are these new information and communication technologies as sites of mediation, that Fiske claims that they result in

> images [that are] so promiscuous as to defy any attempt to control and organize them. The mediated world is not only the world that we in the west live in; it is a world that has overtaken one in which an unmediated experience seemed possible. It never was, of course, but the rapid growth of our technological media does make a world of oral language, print, live performances, and nonreproduced (*sic*) visuals appear unmediated by comparison.[11]

Culture, then, is the experiential and representational—in a word the discursive—apparatus through which technologically mediated infor-

mation, experience, and perception circulate, are regulated and contested, and made both knowable and meaningful. Where media institutions and communications technologies are the conduits through which
this information and data circulates, culture refers to the assumptions in
which this information and technology are embedded and the cultural
logic though which and by which this information and experience gain
meaning and coherence. As it concerns communication technologies,
media, information, and knowledge, this approach suggests that culture
is a "conceptual system that creates and defines the world in the act of
discovering it."[12] In the absence of sustained critical interrogation and
political contestation these historically constructed processes and assumptions seem natural and inevitable.[13]

These are crucial matters. In the new global information order,
defined largely by the structuring logic of neoliberalism and free trade,
communications technologies are designed to serve corporate financial
and administrative interests.[14] In the absence of sustained critical sensibilities, forms of social resistance and cultural struggles, forms of
"diversity and difference" which have historically and politically meaningful points of cultural memory, struggle, and aspirations for social justice easily become consumer-focused market indices of consumer
choice—"a multiplicity of commodities, of images, of knowledges and
of information technologies."[15] The distinction here is vital. I agree with
John Fiske and others that there is a significant difference between a
diversity produced by social formations (particularly subordinated
ones) that wish to maintain productive cultural traditions, histories, and
identities relative to other groups and formations (particularly dominant ones), and a so-called diversity that is produced by and for capitalist industries.[16] As we saw in the cases of Kara Walker, Wynton
Marsalis, and the jazz left, culture is a decisive site of struggle over
efforts to make visible and reconfigure the social, political, and epistemological terms of the social terrain. It is to this specific set of issues that
I turn to in order to say something specific and particular about black
cultural politics, cultural struggles, cultural difference, and the new
communication technologies.

## THE CULTURAL POLITICS OF DIFFERENCE AND
## NEW TECHNOLOGIES

In two seminal essays Stuart Hall and Cornel West argue that black cultural politics and, by extension, black subjects have entered a new stage

of history.[17] In his 1990 essay West challenged critical scholars of color, especially black intellectuals, to think about culture, representation, and difference in new ways. In the realm of cultural politics and representation, he called for a project of critical interrogation and cultural production that moved beyond mere contests over positive/negative images or the displacement of stereotyped depiction of African Americans in visual culture. Similarly, in 1992 Stuart Hall challenged critical black diaspora intellectuals to move beyond disputes over *access* to media production and the means of representation, suggesting that a more urgent challenge was to produce work that would show how a politics of culture assumed that difference might serve as a basis for emergent social formations, political articulations, and cultural practices that would change the balance of power.[18]

Both West and Hall recognized that new global processes and capitalist forms of flexible production, coordination, circulation, and accumulation were the structuring conditions of these new critical black cultural politics. Both writers recognized, moreover, that the discursive and aesthetic distinctions between high/low, margin/center, and commercial/pure were no longer salient or especially productive for such a project. The appearance of new technological means and relations of representation, the emergence of new categories of description (postmodernism), and the appearance of theoretical discourses (poststructuralism) are all significant, Hall concedes, because they emphasize the terrain of difference, the salience of identity, and the centrality of the "popular" and the discursive as social and cultural terrain where politics are made.

West and Hall located their analysis of new cultural possibilities in a historic conjuncture where analytic conceptions and cultural representations of "blackness" posit the end of essentialist discourses (social science, cultural, and political) about race. For them, formulations prior to this period were rooted in naive conceptions that took race and identity as natural givens rather than historical and cultural products. Such conceits were not only innocent culturally; they were politically ineffective.

What Hall calls the end of innocence for such naive formulations about race, identity, and cultural politics appeared, more importantly, at the time of erosion of European empire and global hegemony, the subsequent rise of American global hegemony, and the challenge to modernist conceptions of culture. Politically, the social and cultural terrain of the popular and the discursive is necessary for critically interrogating, constructing, and organizing popular understandings. This popular common sense can then be linked to critical enterprises that illuminate and challenge strategies used in projects of conquest, colonization, displacement, exploitation, and domination by the West (often in the name of Western modernism, capitalism, and democracy).

In the decade or so since Hall and West first offered these insights, developments in the structure, organization, and technologies of new communications and information have quickened (as have the scholarly and popular discourses through which these developments are represented and legitimated). The structures of interlocking control and administration of global media and communication technologies are more composite and their reach more expansive. In conjunction with developments in communication and information technologies, the means and relations of representation are being restructured and ordered into new spatial and temporal relations.[19]

Not surprisingly, the direction, control, and benefits of these new structuring relations favor global corporations. For some observers, however, the possibilities for more democratic uses are still an open question, but one that requires a measure of political will and outright struggle. Although he puts the matter in terms that hearken back to "pastoral images" and "grim narratives" of access, MIT's William J. Mitchell, professor of architecture and media arts and sciences, nonetheless seems to appreciate the enormity of the challenge required to change the balance of power:

> By redirecting access to services and opportunities, the growing information infrastructure has the potential to create winners and losers on a vast scale. It is pleasant to imagine a nation of networked Aspens and cyberspaced Santa Monicas peopled by convivial bicycle-riding locals, but the obvious danger is that such restructuring will instead produce electronic Jakartas—well connected, well serviced, fortified enclaves of privilege surrounded by miserable hyperghettos, where investment in information infrastructure and appliances are not made, electronically delivered services do not reach, and few economic opportunities are to be found. The poor could be left with the obsolete and decaying urban remnants and isolated rural settlements that the more privileged no longer need. Surely the most fundamental challenge in building the bitsphere will be to deploy access according to the principles of social equity—not in ways that heighten the privilege of the haves and further marginalize the have-nots.[20]

In places like Japan, Europe, Australia, and the United States, more and more of our daily lives are structured by the capacities made available by the communication revolution. We negotiate even the most rudimentary social activities of school, banking, courtship, travel, entertainment leisure, shopping, and work through some aspect of the new communication media and information technology. For almost all of us, moreover, the cultural terrain of popular entertainment (movies, music, television, electronic games) and information is mediated by the capitalist market economies, administered by global commercial organizations, and structured by the digital grammar of new technologies of communication and information.

With increasing technical capacity and social necessity to manage, coordinate, distribute, and store information also comes the need to make legible and intelligible this information. Where global economic logic, postmodern culture, and new technologies of communication all restructure social relations and produce new spatial territories, can the cultural terrain of the popular ever do more than constitute significant and often intractable difference (for example, tradition, culture, nation, race, gender, ethnicity) as market indicators of "multiplicity and diversity" (age, tastes, preferences, habits, and so on)? Can the cultural politics of difference in the sense that Hall and West suggest ever form the basis of social formations that do more than simply serve as the raw materials for flexible forms of capitalist production or as the basis for systems of subjugation and repression? Exactly what will become of countermemories and alternative traditions of modernism as sources of critique and opposition to such tendencies? Can we produce critical cultural projects that actively contest for popular hegemony when the very representations over which we struggle and the cultural practices in which they are embedded are structured in the logic of global capitalism and grammar of digital bits, cyberspace, and the information superhighway that defines the technological revolution in communications? At stake, then, is not just the "social distribution of economic, technological, and discursive resources" or mere access to those resources, but the very procedures, perceptions, and categories though which we imagine such possibilities.[21]

In some of the scholarly and popular discourse about the new communications and information technologies, there is an explicit and often enthusiastic assurance that with these new capacities come greater possibilities for creating and participating in a truly democratic public sphere.[22] When they are broached at all, questions concerning cultural difference, communities of color, women, and the poor are almost always couched in terms of access or a concern with inequalities of access.[23] In the utopian world of information and connectivity made possible by the new technologies, distinctive histories and traditions are translated, preserved, and accessed through digits, bits, and chips that constitute the defining lingua franca of the information age.

Discussions of black cultural politics like those by Hall and West imagine new hegemonies of subalterns and appreciate the structuring power of new technologies of information and their effect on collection, storage, sharing, and representation. There is a good deal of critical commentary, for instance, on the powerful role of technologies for the production of citizenship, the fortification and control of national boundaries through the surveillance made possible by new technologies.[24] There is also considerable appreciation and hope for the potential use of low-tech forms such as video cameras, low-power radios, copy machines, faxes, and telephones against various forms of high-tech policing and regulation. In the case of new technologies, some see considerable promise for the potential use of the Internet and the personal computer for forging new critical networks of opposition.[25]

For those most hopeful about the capacity of these technologies to help establish a new openness, the specific historical problems of racism, sexism and, to a greater extent, class is still framed largely in terms of the struggle over access. That is to say, from the perspective of those interested in the ascendancy of subordinated and subjugated communities, the issue of cultural politics is largely defined in terms of access; hence there is less sustained critical attention to the historical, epistemological, political, and aesthetic conditions that structure the new technologies, particularly what they mean for questions of cultural politics. The possibilities of the Internet and cyberspace are like a poststructuralist dream (or nightmare) come true: one can be any*body*, disem*bodied*, and re-em*bodied* all at the same time. In cyberspace, subjectivity and identity are indeed severed from the body; gender, race, sex, and age are all potentially severed from their materialist moorings in biological discourse. The raced and gendered bodies that circulate in the material world of history and the cultural discourse through which they are produced and acquire meaning are all potentially interchangeable bits of data that may or may not be revealed in the virtual community of cyberspace.[26] In one sterling exception to the "happy pastorals of progress" that excites many enthusiasts of the new information technologies, Beth Kolko and her colleagues have dealt directly with the issue of race, showing in the process the inscription of racial assumptions and racial thinking in the organization, structure, operation, and experience of various dimensions of these technologies.[27] With subjects ranging from the use of computers in urban schools to the organization of mutual-user domains to the production of art spaces on the Web, the essays in their collection suggest that the new technologies are not and will not serve as the cultural nirvana in which all traces of difference disappear.

In a racial order that depends on specific cultural meanings of race to sustain regimes of domination, we have not yet arrived at the point where the cultural significance of blackness no longer derives from its specific construction and meaning in history. On the other hand, we may be (with the aid of new technologies) at that moment in history when cultural representations of race serve as nothing more than indications of cultural difference which have been emptied out and resignified as cultural commodities indicating mere "lifestyles."

Of course, critics interested in the cultural politics of difference do recognize the necessity to struggle for new alignments, meanings, traditions, and hegemonies on the terrain of commercial popular culture. Some of the most sophisticated and powerful critiques of the logic of globalization and its reliance on the hollowing out and proliferation of differences have come from those who also recognize that counterhegemonic cultural possibilities are articulated, disarticulated, and rearticulated most effectively on the terrain of popular commercial culture.[28] The point of disarticulation and contradiction is in the realm of culture, that intersection of the symbolic economies of culture, the information and coordination systems of global capitalism, and the regulatory and management "acts" of the nation-state.[29]

In instances where such work is most critically and politically far-reaching, the insights have been most relevant to modernist media—the novel, cinema, television, and recorded popular music. But what happens, to return to Hall and West for a moment, to the force of these critical insights and the possibilities they offer when they are applied to the new forms and modes of representation (and communication) offered by the new technologies? Given that forms are already structured by and embedded in social relations and cultural meanings that are historic and specific, can the critiques of modernist cultural operations both expose the cultural logic on which the new technology depends and establish the groundwork on which new possibilities might be imagined?

Perhaps this is too much to expect. I hope not. My query here is really about the project that must, of necessity, inform a critical interrogation of the new technologies, the cultural logic on which they rest, and the operations through which they produce twenty-first-century societies. I

still think it is possible to disarticulate and rearticulate the narrative of
Western progress and democracy in such a way that it does not lead
inevitably to the grim scenarios described by Mitchell in *City of Bits* (or
hearken back to the role of technology in the terror, removal, and subjugation of black people in the new world). Are the critiques and
insights urged by Hall and West (and already enacted by artists and critics like Isaac Julian, Kara Walker, Lorna Simpson, Stan Douglas, Greg
Osby, Pamela Z, Steve Coleman, Anna Everett, Alonga Nelson, Beth
Coleman, Tal Kali, George Lewis, and Paul Miller) simply translatable
into the logic of digital bits, so that even their most progressive possibilities are in the end just so many zeroes and ones in the cyber age?
Under such a logic does the potentiality of "difference," specifically
blackness, as a cultural and political category simply get translated into
one more commercial version of liberal multiculturalism, one more
option in the crowded field of global-style politics?

As with the recognition (perhaps it is capitulation) that the commodity logic that structures the terrain of commercial popular culture is necessarily contradictory, perhaps we must concede a similar point with
respect to the structuring logic of the digital revolution and the new
communications technology. It seems necessary to acknowledge this,
given all that we know about where and how culture is made and its
potential impact at the level of everyday life. Political struggle on the terrain of culture organized by new technologies is altogether more compelling, since we realize equally well that all technologies, regardless of
their historical age or material form, are constituted in and express the
social and cultural relations of their time. This recognition is what
makes so important the linkage between discourses of technology and
discourses on the (black) cultural politics of difference.

Recognizing that the terrain configured by the new technologies is
already structured by dominant political and corporate interests, my
specific concern in the relationship between the debates over the black
cultural politics of difference and the new media technologies is not an
attempt to secure a place for "identity."[30] Neither is it my aim to add to
the debate over the political efficacy or the critical limitations of essentialism. The new communications technologies offer interesting possibilities for reconsidering some of the main positions in this debate, particularly on the issue of subjectivity and its relationship to (em)bodied
experience.

Blackness as a cultural sign still carries significant political and historical meaning—hence the potential for structuring identifications,

affective investments, and understandings at the level of cultural representation. This potentiality is still most obvious in areas of traditional
media representation where race, ethnicity, gender, and tradition still
operate as powerful markers of difference through which to interrupt,
remind, and remember the projects of terror, conquest, and subjugation
that accompanied the formation of the modern West. Cultural politics
mobilized through the sign of raced, gendered, sexed, and former colonial subjects continues to carry specific histories, traditions, and memories of social struggle. In contrast to the political investments in the cultural politics of difference (which critiques difference as the basis for
inequality and nationalism), the discourse of new media technologies
often works to depoliticize difference, making it in effect an inconse-
quential niche market of shared lifestyles and taste. One of the challenges of trying to make sense of the critical affinities and articulations
of practicing cultural politics in the global time of new media is precisely
how to put these discourses in productive conversation so that they
might articulate the terms of a critical cultural analysis of new information technologies, the politics of difference, and cultural politics. To the
extent that the new information order of global media institutions, communication technologies, administrative units, political interests, and
corporate capital makes possible projects of displacement, terror, subjugation, and exploitation, as opposed to projects of justice, equality,
and democracy, then the politics of representation, popular culture, and
difference remains important for the production of counterhegemonies
and new hegemonic possibilities.[31]

In the end, I offer a modest elaboration of the formulation of cultural
politics about difference as it applies to new media and technologies of
communication. The force of both West's and Hall's critical insights
applies most directly to modernist or representational forms of communication media. Their identifications of these modes of representation as
seminal sites for organizing and expressing popular loyalties, sentiments, affective investments, and critical suspicions are signal contributions. Yet, as I argue in the next chapter, the challenge to move beyond
mere questions of access, stereotypes, and idealized representation (i.e.,
homogeneous black subjects) remains as urgent as ever. Engagement
with new communication technologies and the terms they establish for
the practice of identity and the cultural politics of difference is central
to this challenge.

From the perspective of the new information and communications
technologies, as well as global media organizations, the specific concern

with how popular meanings are made and struggled over may pose a very different kind of challenge. Culture and media have always been inextricably entwined, and never more so than at the dawn of the twenty-first century. Commercial culture represents as natural (and inevitable) and preferable neoliberal market logic aimed at control of global consumer markets. By such reckoning, the availability of consumer commodities and consumer choice is equated with consumer sovereignty—progress, choice, and freedom—and thus helps to shore up (and hide) relations of power built on social inequality, labor exploitation, force, and cultural domination. At the same time, popular commercial culture and technologies (e.g., video cameras, cassette tapes, home computers) are still important sites for the circulation (and, in some cases, the production) of local, specific, and alternative cultures and traditions. They are places of potential (and unwieldy) articulations that interrupt, destabilize, and rearticulate (even if only momentarily) the neoliberal logic of global capitalism and narratives of Western progress that equate the free market and consumer sovereignty with democracy and freedom.[32] In either case, the terrain of the commercial and the popular is still potentially vibrant as the political site for exposing and building upon the contradictions of this new global logic.[33]

In a social field organized by a digital revolution that translates signs, commodities, and identities into "bits" of information, yesterday's representation (including the social relations and the politics that structure and produce them) becomes just so much software to fill neoliberal global-market demands for new cultural products that will circulate on the information superhighway.[34] As a matter of cultural politics, then, I want to treat these relations of representation as more than just so much software made available through new forms of communication technology, controlled by and used largely in the interests of global corporations. In the next chapter I look to Afrofuturists, black composers, and performance artists for insights about how music might operate as a productive site of encounter between new technologies and new cultural politics of difference. I explore what the current condition of possibility means for those moving beyond access to critical engagement and production.

Applying the insights of West and Hall about the new cultural politics of difference to the new media might begin by noting the multiple and uneven capacities, means of access, and modes of representation of contemporary media technology. Modern forms of communication media like the press, film, television, recorded music, photography, and radio are significant sites where the politics of representation certainly include, but are no longer just limited to, issues of access. Following Hall, critical understandings of these media emphasize representation as well as the logic, grammar, and history that structure such forms and the representations of difference that they produce. New communications technologies like the Internet, e-mail, Pentium processors, the desktop and laptop computer, and the satellite bear some relation to the social and cultural structure of their predecessors—newspaper, radio, telegraph, telephone, and television.[35] These new forms, moreover, remain linked to the administrative and economic logic of the Western market economies and corporate bureaucracies that generate, finance, and promote them.[36] So long as the content of these new media depends on cultural representations generated in specific historical conditions, a cultural politics interested in production still requires struggles for access and representation.[37] That is, a rearticulation of the possibilities of the new media that struggles to represent the subjects' new cultural politics of difference (as opposed to simply including multicultural representations of subjects as more commodities for the market) requires critical analyses of the logics, structures, signifying systems, and relations of representation not only within the new media, but also between the new and the old medias. In particular, scholars might consider the cultural implications, uses, and possibilities of the new media for how they organize, circulate, represent, exploit, and smooth over differences, including differences of place and class.[38]

What are the specific sites and ways that popular desires and sentiments are organized and made representable under the emergent conditions made possible by the new technologies? In the context of the Internet, for example, can such representations serve as points of identification that might form the bases of cultural and political disruption, transgression, and critical intervention? Or will they simply serve to consolidate and reproduce the existing social relations of exploitation and subordination?[39] In cyberspace and the new communications media and technology that structure it, can difference function as the basis for the production of counterhegemonic cultural representations and formations that link critiques of the existing order with new imaginative possibilities for a very different order. In other words, as Allucquere R. Stone asks, "will virtual systems mean the end of gender binarism? Will virtual systems create a level playing field for everyone regardless of ethnicity, color, gender, age, education, financial status, or the ability to load and fire semi-automatic weapons?"[40] These are, as I see it, some of the twenty-first-century challenges for implementing a critical cultural politics of difference. These challenges are marked by struggles over the meanings of culture and technology that are made in history and not merely given in nature or cyberspace.

# CHAPTER 9

# Music, Identity, and New Technology

Herman "Sonny" Blunt, born in Birmingham, Alabama, adopted the name Sun Ra to signal that he was not of this (earthly) world. For Sun Ra "space was the place" of unlimited human possibility—love, respect, equality, and creativity.[1] The stifling environment of life in the United States, particularly for an African American artist, aroused in Sun Ra the desire to seek a life defined by a different cosmic order, one organized first and foremost in harmony with the grand order of the universe. Sun Ra realized this vision through his compositions (he was a witty and prolific composer), his teachings and lectures, though his organization and support of a musical collective, and though his public performances (which included elaborate costumes, dancers, singers, and his long-time performance organization, the Astral Arkestra). Sun Ra was one of the first composers and performers to explore the potential of electronic instruments and sound. His compositions and performances were distinguished by the futuristic and extraterrestrial sounds of electronic instruments—pianos, synthesizers, harps; but these were also combined with traditional acoustic instruments. Decades before the digital revolution and the information age, Sun Ra looked to space as the place of unlimited possibility.

In the wake of Sun Ra's prescient example, there have been some important moves—critical, scholarly, and performative—in which music served as the productive point of encounter between new technologies and a wide and varied range of black Atlantic, Pacific, Indian, and Caribbean cultural identities and practices. Among the most visible and widely available—at least in popular music—are those musical practices taking place in the dance halls, clubs, concerts, and mediascapes where black soundings (and scenes) go by names like dub, techno, house, jungle, drum and bass, gangsta, illbient, and hip-hop. Scenes in New York, Los Angles, London, Kingston, Berlin, San Francisco, Tokyo, Auckland, Fresno, and Johannesburg bring together imagined communities organized around and through the pleasures of sound and the body. In these and countless other scenes around the world, digitally based phasers, mixers, samplers, drum machines, synthesizers, and computers are combined with older forms like vinyl LPs, two- and four-track tape recorders, magnetic tape, and microphones to loop, sample, cut up, and mix up sounds and movements, memories and experiences. In the long history of black soundings, these sorts of inventions join and extend the practice of using music to make space, craft selves, and perform identities. These most recent popular expressions and performances are stunningly imaginative, however, in their use of vernacular forms and new technologies to reimagine blackness.

In their attention to black popular soundings, writers including Tricia Rose, Greg Tate, Erik Davis, Kodwo Eshun, Paul Gilroy, George Lewis, Beth Coleman, Paul Miller, Anna Everett, and Alonga Nelson, among many others, have been on the case mapping the terms of these encounters. These writers provide useful points of entry for considering some of the ways that encounters between new digitally based information technologies and black vernacular musical practices have changed the terms of hearing and, in the process, imagined different notions of blackness through sound. Afrofuturists in London and New York, dance-hall artists and patrons in Kingston and Toronto, and turntablists in San Francisco, Mexico City, and Tokyo, as well as black avant-garde and experimentalist composers in New York and San Diego, are some of the leading theoreticians and performers of this encounter.

In this chapter, I place the work of these cultural practitioners in dialogue with academic theorists, technology advocates, business entrepreneurs, journalists, and political observers who express differing levels of hope and anxiety about the place of racial identity, especially blackness, in technology and about the impact of technology on black culture. I particularly emphasize blackness, to essay the kinds of moves deployed and positions staked out for what they might tell us about culture and politics, especially the way that music functions as one key area where blackness is being made and remade. In other words, I try to assess the ways that blackness, identity, technology, and cultural politics are being imagined and performed on the ground, so to speak.[2] I do so also in order to show how practices and, most importantly, relations of identity are central, rather than ancillary, to the conception and use of new information technologies. I try to show that black people, in particular musicians, have been at the forefront of using new technologies to extend, reshape, and remix black identities, thereby changing both the cultural terms of the technologies and people's identities.

In *Dangerous Crossroads*, George Lipsitz suggests that popular music often rehearses and dramatizes the conflicts, anxieties, speculations, and even hopes about black presence in the twenty-first century. To Lipsitz's point I would add that this is especially the case in a world organized by information and digital technologies whose potential to render black labor redundant and black culture as nothing more than a commodity is always on the horizon.[3] Anxieties about the loss of subjectivity and community, the transformation of black publics, and the privatization of cultural production are echoed in many a commentary about music's relationship to technology, as are utopian ideas about technology's potential to release social life from the last trappings of modernist encumbrances like race and identity.

To consider some of these moves, I examine the assumptions, claims, strategies, and tropes in debates about the relationship between race and technology. I recognize that notions of belonging and cultural identifications based simply on race or technology are never just about race and technology; nor are they finished and complete projects ready to be placed in the service of political and cultural interests. As an example of a cultural move, questioning the relationship between blackness and technology around music may get us closer to understanding how black soundings operate as a productive way of imagining and enacting blackness in the twenty-first century.[4]

The encounters between black soundings and technologies operate in the context of intellectual, cultural, and political discourses (and desires) that ponder the very meaning of blackness for African Americans in the early twenty-first century. Here I am thinking most notably of debates about memory in the African American art worlds. Examples include the case of Kara Walker; or exhibitions curated by Thelma Goldman at New York City's Studio Museum of Harlem, which she organized around provocative concepts of "postblackness" and "postethnicity."[5] The "techno-soundings" circulating in the black disapora bear directly on discussions of identities, place, space, periodization, geography, and issues of the nation-state that have emerged from scholars working in cultural studies, postcolonial studies, black Atlantic diasporic studies, and African American and popular music studies.[6]

Culturally, the meanings (or at the least contests over the purported meanings) of black identities articulated through music also operate in relationship to cultural formations and intellectual practices like African American studies, black cultural and diasporic studies, Caribbean studies, postcolonial studies, and critical race studies. Scholars and critics working in these intellectual fields (and even in more traditional disciplines like anthropology, ethnomusicology, and sociology) continue to reckon the salience of race and nation as meaningful analytic categories, especially as they bear on diasporic connections and tensions across, throughout, and within black worlds.[7] These moves, as well as the somewhat vacuous notion of politics (cultural and otherwise) and publics that it implies, might be the source of the lament that Paul Gilroy and others have about the loss of ethics, vision, and politics in African American popular culture, most notably black musics.[8]

If we take technology as a point of departure, there is also a complex conceptual map (including political debate and cultural struggle over key figures, origins, and significance of various musics) in place.[9] The apprehensions expressed about technology (of any sort) and its relevance or applicability to black music (and, more generally, black culture) are held largely by purists, traditionalists, and those (politically) invested in very specific cultural ideas about music and identity. Computers, mixers, samplers, phasers, drum machines, and all sorts of software are now available to capture, store, access, mix, and remix sound. These technologies offer musicians, marketers, and consumers new possibilities for making, circulating, and experiencing (existing archives of black sounds), thereby crafting blackness in new ways. Digital technologies make it possible to store, access, and combine infinite permutations of sound, time periods, titles, time, and performers. Chat rooms, virtual listening rooms, and file sharing made possible by digital technologies join radio, bedrooms, home basements and garages, mixing studios, and automobiles, expanding the authenticating tools and spaces, as Gayle Wald puts it, where these musics (and blackness) are produced, travel-transforming time and space, geography, and distance into soundtracks of identification and belonging throughout the world.[10]

One of the significant differences that digital technology has made for recorded sound is to make recordings, collections, genres, found sounds, and bits of sound of all sorts easily stored, catalogued, and accessed.[11]

As such, sound has become not just a recorded collection of tastes and interests accumulated over time, but "archives" that, through digital technology, instantly magnify the possibilities and combinations that can be sampled, mixed, and versioned to make old soundings virtually and perpetually new.[12] As with the infinite possibilities of drafts introduced with the word processor, the language used to describe the music and its significance recognizes this capacity for perpetual drafts or reversioning. In his description of various black diaspora sounds, English critic Kodwo Eshun writes in terms of the *materiality of sound* and its organization and inscription on vinyl, compact disc, or digital files. Rhetorically, Eshun's reviews and commentaries use spatial terms to describe and locate sound culturally in history and materially in the plastic of the compact disc; that is, riffs or takes refer to *tracks, cuts, time, breaks, and sound* in describing the music rather than the more conventional tropes of *titles, bars, measures, arrangements, notes, instruments, chord structures, or solos.*[13] Eshun and Paul Miller (aka DJ Spooky, That Subliminal Kid), among others, deploy their commentary as if they were performing on their turntables and computers in clubs, constantly shifting the language, mood, and modality of their critical engagement as if they were indeed handling so many tracks in a mix.[14] Although they are inheritors and beneficiaries of a generation of cultural studies and poststructuralist theory, those most enthusiastic and versed in making and evaluating black techno-soundings seem skeptical (even dismissive) about the role of critical academic cultural theory for helping make sense of the music and the techno-imaginary that they evoke and celebrate.

Just what do these cultural moves add up to and what does music have to tell us, if anything, about the racing and gendering of digital information technologies? Similarly, what lessons does the encounter between music and digital technology, especially in the context of black musics, offer about notions of blackness, identification, and belonging? In the end, can these black soundings and the practices from which they are they produced point the way to critically different notions of both blackness and the new digital technologies? Does thinking about these issues through music push the boundaries for imagining different kinds of cultural practices and cultural politics with respect to conceptions of black presence and cultural possibilities in the twenty-first century?

While I am primarily interested in music as a point of encounter, I once again want to query the role of identity, the conditions of its production from the angle of new technological capacities, in order to appreciate its role in the creative activity of people who work at the interface between music and technology. Thus, much if not all of what I consider in this discussion is more explicitly about cultural producers and the discourses and conditions of possibility that shape their use of technology in their production of music. While this may seem a bit of a stretch for a book on cultural politics, this focus makes sense for me since, as a cultural matter in which identities are concerned, I think of music as constitutive and not reflective. That is, it constitutes its own subject(ive) experience within its own space and time, and as such is not just ancillary to or simply a product of prior discourses. Music is about making and remaking subjects, and, as such, making and remaking identities.[15]

One of the discursive communities that I find most instructive for thinking about music as the interface between technologies and the production of identity is Afrofuturists, a loose collection of writers, musicians, technologists, critics, and artists. One of my central contentions is this: Afrofuturists use new information and digital technologies to change the terms—expand, really—of imagining and constructing twenty-first-century narratives of black Atlantic identities and representation. They do so by discursively pushing the conceptual boundaries of blackness beyond the historic confinements of place, period, and identity. And they do so by attending, through sound, to the myriad and complex ways that blackness is crafted and travels, pausing, moving, and dwelling in multiple locations, often at the same time and under various signs and in different circumstances. Afrofuturists bring together, discursively anyway, notions of blackness rooted in the connectivity and particularity of black soundings across geographies of time and space. The Afrofuturist encounter with twenty-first-century digital technology, which I detail below, produces different and shifting rhythms of seeing and hearing: thus their musical attempts to imagine blackness in its terrestrial and interstellar travels.

Avant-garde jazz and experimental music composers and performers George Lewis, Steve Coleman, and Pamela Z represent a group of musicians who understand (and show) why music is a critically productive site of encounter between blackness and digital technology. Beginning with clear assumptions about their own relationship to race, gender, and identity, Steve Coleman and George Lewis use those very assumptions to challenge, expose, and unsettle what they regard as the deeply embedded terms in which race, in this case whiteness, organizes new digital information technologies despite their being presented as neutral, unmarked, and beyond cultural politics. In her use of various digital technologies, performance artist and composer Pamela Z confounds conventional notions of identity in general and blackness in particular.

Identity in the hands of these artists forces a reckoning with the imbrications of race, gender, and social interests in digital technologies. These artists exert pressure, not just on the way in which we think about the consequence of technologies on our cultural worlds, but on the way that assumptions about race are stretched and pulled beyond the boundaries of our current conceptions (especially in music). As such, the cultural moves of these composers and performance artists help to open a critique of the raced and gendered logics embedded in new digital technologies that are celebrated, above all, as beyond such matters. Indeed, their work suggests (as have others) that technologies are not neutral, but rather are always raced, gendered, and deeply rooted in particular social conditions, histories, and interests. So I approach this inventory of practices, performers, and cultural politics for clues about the rich possibilities offered by music as a way out of the binary impasse on questions of identities and technologies. As such, black avant-garde and experimental electronic musics and the identities they craft might be seen as guideposts or indicators of how, when illuminated, the cultural logics that structure identity can be used productively in relationship to new technologies to construct different ways of imaging the self and community.[16]

Before taking up the projects of the Afrofuturism and the avant-garde, I first want to review some of the more conventional responses to the relationship between blackness and digital technologies, especially in terms of business narratives and policy discourses about access and competence as solutions to the digital divide. My point is to show that the narrative of the digital divide is underwritten by a market conception of technological utopianism that locates identity primarily in a market model of consumer sovereignty and choice and technology as beyond history, politics, and interests.[17]

## THE INFORMATION SUPERHIGHWAY AND THE RACIAL DIVIDE

Popular discussions of the relationship between black American identities and the new information technologies seem almost always framed in terms of consumer and market access, social-policy options that emphasize the role of the government, business investments, and the moral and political responsibility of corporations, the state, and the black middle class.[18] Accounts about information technology range from critical suspicions at one end to enthusiastic celebrations and utopian scenes of democratic possibility at the other.[19]

Digitally based technologies such as home computers, e-mail, the Internet, microchips and microprocessors, and the software and operating systems that support them, as well as the networking capabilities that link them together, are standard tools of the electronic reality that many inhabit in the routine conduct of daily life in many parts of the world. Whether the popular discourse is about greater access to the information superhighway as the sure route to democratic possibility (especially the elimination of racial inequality), or black suspicion of technologies (owing to a history of terror aimed at blacks and exercised through various technologies of transportation, surveillance, discipline, and punishment), technologies are represented, for the most part, in popular media as largely neutral and beyond politics and identity. Where blacks, Latinos, and people of color are concerned, the new digital technologies are pitched as rich with new (and better) social uses and possibilities. Whether presented as promises to make life better or, for that matter, worse (though this is seldom how new technologies are represented in dominant consumer discourse), the relationship of digital technologies to race and identity is seldom thought of socially, culturally, and politically in terms of their potential uses as instruments of control and regulation.

In the narrative of unlimited possibility for blacks and Latinos, problems appear as issues of limited access. The most salient question is almost always how to increase access of the poor and the disenfranchised to the technologies. The problem of access, then, means bringing blacks and Latinos (and perhaps Native people[s]) along the road of technological (and thereby social and economic) progress by aligning the meaning of information technologies with each group's distinct cultural sensibilities, and in the process reducing the alienation and perceived distance between specific cultural traditions and new technologies.[20] Reducing alienation and making the new technologies more culturally compatible can be achieved, according to this framework, by educating black consumers to make themselves more familiar and thus more comfortable and competent with the technologies. If black people are to thrive in the new century, then the distance between poor and working-class black folk and technology must be reduced, because minimal technological competence is a fundamental requirement for twenty-first-century citizenship in a cosmopolitan world. According to this consumer model of technical competence, moreover, digitally based technologies and the innumerable possibilities they offer are requisite if black people are to continue to progress into the American mainstream.

Although, as some commentators are quick to point out, there are very good historical reasons—ranging from ships and gunpowder to the cotton gin to industrial factories—for black suspicion of technologies, the ideal of creating competent citizens who are able to participate in the mainstream is not incompatible with blackness as a discourse of identity per se.[21] While black suspicion of technology could easily be dismissed as yet another lingering instance of exaggerated identity politics, the historical experience of blacks with technologies of regulation and control remain powerful and the memory of that history still carries moral weight in such formulations. In other words, while there is still work to be done to overcome these lingering suspicions, as black folk we are perhaps entitled to a degree of understanding for continuing to cling to these lingering suspicions. Thus, if we are going to fully realize our potential as modern subjects, so the story goes, blacks clearly need to be more open and receptive to learning about new technologies and must be provided with greater access to them. Such prescriptions mean that considerable work is necessary on the cultural and human side of the equation if capitalism is to turn the large number of poor and disenfranchised blacks into twenty-first-century consumer-citizens.

Where blacks in particular are left out or risk being left behind, the challenge—for civil rights groups, members of the black middle class, new technology entrepreneurs, the corporate information and entertainment industry, and the state—is to develop strategies for achieving a greater measure of black and minority visibility and participation as consumers, members of the new service economies, and citizens. Framed this way, as one commentator suggests, the problem of the relationship of blacks to technological resources and competencies is defined largely in terms of access, competence, and consumption: "What is intriguing, and deeply disturbing," he contends, "is that blacks have participated as equals in the technological world only as consumers, otherwise existing on the margins of the ethos that defines the nation, underrepresented as designers, innovators, and implementers of our systems and machines. As a group they have suffered from something that can loosely be called 'technological illiteracy.'"[22] The hope for greater black participation that underwrites the discourse of access carries political and moral stakes that bear directly on the question of social recognition and

cultural visibility in American society. The new digitally based information and networking technologies provide those concerned with cultural
recognition and social participation an important route into the mainstream of American society. To the extent that blacks, especially the
poor and disenfranchised, remain in a state of technological illiteracy,
we remain outside the national mainstream—at considerable risk to our
own *cultural, economic, and political* future. In the United States, black
citizens (especially the middle and professional classes) enjoy legal
protections and rights guaranteed by the state; in the digitally based
global information economy, these hard-won gains have also resulted in
a measure of social recognition and cultural visibility, but these translate mainly into black consumer visibility and freedom of commodity
choice.[23]

In addition to the waning effects of an aging civil rights agenda, some
observers suggest that blacks are trapped in a condition of technological illiteracy because of culture. That is, black people continue to hold
on to cultural assumptions that privilege knowledge generated through
black vernacular practices and folk wisdom, placing us culturally on a
collision course with knowledge(s) required in the new digital age. For
writer Anthony Walton, who refers to this state of affairs as "technological illiteracy," the problem is straightforward:

> Black folkways in America, those unspoken, largely unconsciousness pat-
> terns of thought and belief about what is possible that guide aspirations
> and behavior, . . . do not encompass physics and calculus. . . . These
> folkways developed in response to very real historical conditions, to the
> limited and at best ambivalent interactions between blacks and technology
> in this country. . . . Not channeled to follow the largely technological
> possibilities for success in this society, black folkways have instead em-
> braced the sort of magical thinking that is encouraged by the media
> and corporations whose sole interest in blacks is as consumers.[24]

As we'll see momentarily, the Afrofuturists invert this logic, looking
instead to Africa, science fiction, and various strands of mysticism as the
epistemological ground for an enabling discourse about new technologies and the centrality in it of black Atlantic consciousness.

In the formulation about access and technological competence, the
challenge for advocates of this position is to move black participation
(and potential participation) from the realm of consumption to production. One popular and well-rehearsed response to this challenge comes
from members of the business and education sectors who espouse the
twin strategies of increasing corporate investments in black training on

the one hand and changing black cultural attitudes about technologies on the other. Calls for a technological and "educational Marshall Plan" are quite common in black, Latino, and white corporations and businesses. In political and business circles, proponents also call for government and the private sector to work together to increase black and Latino access to new information technologies. Concretely this means wiring underserved neighborhoods and communities, making available computers, and teaching competencies in how to use them so as to increase opportunities for black participation in the new information order.[25] Again, Anthony Walton writes, "Why not a technological Marshall Plan for the nation's schools? . . . What if *uber*technocrats . . . used their philanthropic millions to fund basic math and science education in elementary schools, to equip the future, instead of giving away merchandise that essentially serves to expand their customer base?"[26] The leaders of major high-technology corporations like Paul Allen and Bill Gates have actively supported these and related philanthropic projects, including placing basketball courts in inner-city neighborhoods, wiring urban schools and libraries for the information superhighway, and sponsoring CD-ROM projects related to culture and education. In a competitive field where brand names and logo identities are the major means of adding value to cultural products, these responses also have the benefit of enhancing product brand identities like Microsoft in black consumer markets.[27] In other words, the noble aims of good corporate citizenship—which include philanthropy, social responsibility, and public service—and the strategic development of new consumer markets are compatible. Furthermore, while nudging corporations to help create greater opportunities for minority access and participation, Walton, taking aim at culture and identity, also urges blacks to move beyond the limited cultural framework (of identity) which values (almost exclusively) particular forms of knowing and promulgates what he calls a paralyzing suspicion of technology. Accordingly, Walton believes that "blacks must change as well. The ways that served their ancestors through captivity and coming to freedom have begun to lose their utility. . . . Blacks have to imagine ways to encourage young people into the technological mainstream, because that looks like the future . . . and blacks playing catch-up yet again, must reach for it to insure themselves a place at the American table."[28] For Walton and for many others, fuller participation in the information-based economy indicates significant movement into the mainstream, and will in the end represent a measure of real democratic achievement. This formulation and the remedies it proposes are still framed largely as problems of unequal access and consumption; problems, therefore, that can be addressed through training, preparation, and participation on the production side of the production/consumption equation. Blacks must essentially become more modern—in a sense by loosening the grip or fetters of a traditional premodern culture and outlook, including, of course, racial identity. By doing so, blacks enter into full political, economic, and cultural participation in the American dream. In the twenty-first century, such a *cultural move* means embracing digital information technology.

To a large extent, Walton's account of the marginality of black participation in the new technological environment accepts, though not entirely uncritically, the corporate sector's utopian promise of information technology (especially as a consumer-based route to greater participation). He does, nonetheless, recognize the deeply racialized dimension of such technologies, how they operate, their popular perception, and their prospect for productive use and engagement by blacks. While similarly appreciative, Leonce Gaither is less interested in the mainstreaming potentialities of the new technologies than their anarchic possibilities for circulating black cultural productions. He seems to share with Walton the need to reassess the social goals and political assumptions of the civil rights generation. For Gaither, the absence of black participation in the new technologies has less to do with black technological incompetence than the lingering (and now politically realized) ideals of the civil rights objectives—cultural visibility and legal recognition, equal treatment, and access to the mainstream. Gaither observes, "we must acknowledge that the world into which we so desperately sought entrée is dying—and we, like the majority must embrace new and untested worlds if we are to prosper."[29] Training his critical sights on the World Wide Web, Gaither claims that hegemonic cultural, racial, and gender assumptions that structure the Web are still present, especially terms of what he calls the "placeness" of the Web. He acknowledges that the Web has its share of racism, hatred, and predatory behavior, and although he accepts that the Web is culturally raced as white, he seems to think that it still offers opportunities to circulate new politics and new visions: "Rather than avoid the place . . . we should slough off our unconventionalities and hack some new trails through this principally white territory."[30] Less enamored of the corporate (or state) interest in and commitment to moving blacks into the American mainstream, Gaither sees the Web as a place of particular promise, a place where it can be "ours as much as anyone else's." This interest in the Web's possibility for sustaining black identities aims toward very specific and particular objectives. The Web, Gaither contends, "could be an extraordinary disseminator of Afro-American culture . . . an extraordinary political tool and a boon to black business people."[31] While being a slight variation on the theme of access and participation, this formulation expresses what I think of as conventional liberal assumptions about the potentialities of the new information technologies. Both Walton and Gaither clearly recognize the importance of race in the structure and operation of new technologies and both accept the terms of the existing corporate, political, and economic structure. As such, then, the goal of increased participation and access by blacks to the new technology requires at best minimal accommodation by those who control the technology and a somewhat more extensive relaxation of black cultural identifications.

But what if we shifted the angle of inquiry from accepting the existing economic and political terms of new technologies to questioning the cultural logic and social terms that structure and organize new technologies in the first place? This kind of critique has been useful for showing how corporate financial and political interests, as well as business uses of the new information technologies, have come to be represented and naturalized.[32] Similarly, feminists, queer studies, and postcolonial scholars have raised probing questions about the uncritical location of the new technologies on the side of masculinity, the West, and modernization.

Some of the most productive critiques of the presumed neutrality of new information technologies proceed from critical analysis of the spatiality of cyberspace, the semiotic system by which connection and participation are represented, and the use of various texts and language as a means of constructing identity and presence. Beth Kolko identifies several dimensions where the terms of cyberspace are clearly raced and gendered, and so too, she contends, are the terms on which virtual selves and identities are crafted. These dimensions include the actual architecture of virtual worlds, especially the various chat rooms, message boards, and social spaces, as well as the (familiar) objects placed in them; the actual space that is navigated to get from one place to another; the most available and popular identities found in these virtual spaces; and the nature of the interactions that occur among the customized identities that operate there.[33]

In another context, Cameron Bailey also probes for some of the cultural and social assumptions that structure the conception and operation of virtual space. Bailey identifies the cultural sources (which are deeply gendered, classed, and raced), image-scapes, and imagination that form the architecture of cyberspace—from chat rooms and message boards to resources available for constructing avatars and proxies for virtual identities. Bailey suggests that the imaginations that produce these identities, virtual or not, do not exist in a vacuum, but rather that they come from someplace. While the genre of science fiction is among the most widely cited sources fueling the imagination, Bailey believes the American suburbs are also an important source of the order, rules, and etiquette that define cyberspace and the participation that occurs there.[34] Built as they are into the very machinery (both hardware and software) of the new technologies, by the time these forms reach various kinds of users the principal form, logic, and terms of engagement are fully codified. The defining logic and dominant spaces they discursively produce are the terms through which new information technologies produce their subjects. This does not make the inventions and the imaginative use of these technologies by practitioners any less significant culturally. But this circuit does suggest that the terms, limits, and conditions that structure the technologies (and their operations and terms of encounter) are bound up in social, cultural, and political conditions and interests, rather than simply the result of the technology, the circumstance of their operation, or the free market.

OPERATING SYSTEMS AND IDENTITIES

Where politicians, business leaders, and corporate heads might agree that the new information technologies offer the poor and disenfranchised a route to class mobility largely as consumers, some critics reject this discourse (and the assumptions it seems to make about the relationship between new technology, class mobility, and citizenship). Following this critique, our analysis needs to stress the cultural rhetoric, social assumptions, and logical operations and fonts through which technology, identity, and nation are discursively produced. Beth Kolko seems to appreciate exactly the relationships that I am alluding to in her observation that "when you use a word processing program or play solitaire on your computer, you encounter what the *program* produces, not the program itself. The interface . . . is the point at which your experience is grounded . . . interaction with technology is far from apolitical."[35] Kolko's emphasis on the "program" as productive is key. For it is precisely this productive capacity, this generative ability of the program to structure the terms of the relations, that reveals the constructed nature of technologies (as is also true for race or nation.) Therefore, as I look to music for the lessons about the encounter between blackness and new technologies, I want to hold onto this key insight about the constructed nature of technology and race. Again, Kolko states the matter succinctly: "cyberspace and race are both constructed cultural phenomena, not products of nature; they are made up of ongoing processes of definitions, performance, enactment, and identity relations."[36] My holding rather steadfastly to the constructed and productive dimensions of both terms—race and new technologies—is my check against racial essentialism, technological determinism, excessive utopian celebrations, or undue paranoia. In this way I can turn to music for the variety of sites, practices, and rich analytic possibilities it offers for making and remaking both blackness and new technologies.[37]

Indeed, in the critical discourse about race and new technology among various communities collected in anthologies, in popular magazines, and on the Web, there is explicit recognition that race matters—and matters far beyond the question of access. Kolko and her colleagues, for instance, claim that "race matters in cyberspace precisely because all of us who spend time online are already shaped by the way in which race matters off line and we can't help but bring our own knowledge, experiences, and values with us when we log on."[38] They quarrel with the uncritical belief in technology's purported capacity (and desire) to construct virtual identities built on the absence of race, identity, and difference. Cameron Bailey offers a similar critique, especially in terms of the utopian desire for a race-neutral virtual world (or at least one where it does not matter), a desire that is itself raced, gendered, and enmeshed in relations of power.

So perhaps we should abandon utopian claims about the unlimited capacities of new information technologies and consider music more carefully as a potentially productive space of thinking about the relationship between blacks and new technologies. With music as the ground against which to consider this relationship, I think that we might reasonably ask how both new technologies and blackness are transformed in this encounter, and how this creative encounter speaks to the role of cultural politics in the representation and use of new technologies.

So, for instance, are the musics (and by extension identities) crafted in this encounter all that new? Or are they merely old versions made perpetually "new" because of technologies that make it easier to store, access, and narrate them in new ways? Do the new information technologies facilitate the translation and circulation of blackness(es) that reside in coded music and performances, which are, after all, the decoded and recoded imaginings of blackness made audible? If blackness is constantly subject to crafting and recrafting, then what of the impact of black operations and performances—in a word, identities—on technologies? Through critical reimaginings and interventions, can these technologies be made to "speak like a brother," as the composer George Lewis might have it?

Analytically, music offers a productive terrain for exploring the rich and productive encounter between blackness and new information technologies, and it is a significant point of articulation between critical discourse, musical performance and sounding, black techno-culture, and cultural theory. It is in this discursive circuit and exchange, as well as the actual spaces—dance hall, Internet chat room, Web sites, and recording studios—that people come together to imagine, rehearse, and try out new ways of being. In addition, the soundings made and circulated in these black-imagined spaces generate (and manage to sustain) a wide range of provocative critical exchanges, products, and inventions, which expose blackness to constant invention and makeover via sound and representation. Among the most inventive producers of this reimagination of blackness are the Afrofuturists.

## AFROFUTURISM

In the film *The Last Angel of History,* filmmaker John Akrumpha depicts the present as the past from the perspective of the future.[39] Against the barren and evacuated landscape of the late twentieth century, the relics of our present provide clues for tomorrow's data detectives, translators, decoders, and scientists of sound and mysticism.[40] Akrumpha's detectives, decoders, translators, and scientists hunt for traces of a black diasporic past (our present), traces that provide evidence which forms the basis for reversioning the long sojourn of newworld Africans who were forcibly captured and scattered throughout the black Atlantic. In this strong cinematic riff on black science fiction, identity politics, black cultural studies, and black Atlantic soundings, black people are likened to aliens stranded in strange lands. The only hope of metaphorical and discursive escape is to be found in renarrating and reimagining the story of black dispersal and movement. This practice of reversioning these stories and memories can only be fashioned from traces of the creative imagination left behind by the ancestors of those who were forcibly captured and dispersed. In a somewhat conventionally structuralist gesture, these traces appear as popular artifacts that contain clues to black lives whose meanings can only be decoded (and renarrated) by Afrofuturists who traffic in sound, narrative, myth, cultural criticism, and science fiction. Reading the clues to the past is, of course, tricky business, since a "correct" reading is always a double move—a negotiated reading, as it were—that moves both with and against the grain of inherited narratives and dominant but corrupted commonsense understandings about blackness in the late twentieth century. Reading clues are facilitated by digital information technologies that afford access to traces of information (that stretch across physical territories to remap and reimagine blackness as spaceless and timeless), and to the manipulation of that information by constantly subjecting it to new readings and hearings.

A central trope throughout the film—both metaphorical and at the level of evidence—is black sounds contained in artifacts like recordings, musical instruments, written documents, and vernacular practices. Black soundings function for Afrofuturists as perhaps the quintessential body of evidence that can be accessed, read for clues, and re-encoded. Scattered across the vast geographies of the black diaspora, the only way to piece together the puzzle of black life and imagination is by way of the (re)assembly of the cultural equivalent of the Human Genome Project, a sort of *sound archive* in which the traces of a black presence can be recut, remixed, and reassembled not as *the* original but as something new. This is the work of the Afrofuturist. The digital information and communication technologies that make possible the storage, retrieval, production, reproduction, and manipulation of black soundings are their most important tools.

Drawn from equal doses of black science fiction, technology discourse, poststructuralism, funk, blaxploitation, mysticism, black rock, and blues, Afrofuturists are an eclectic mix of erudite, well-trained, and prolific black culture workers, including, cultural critics, videographers, journalists, musicians, turntablists, computer programmers, professors, writers, novelists, poets, and image makers.[41] They constitute themselves as a formation and movement engaging in shared cultural projects that cut across genres, scenes, spaces, and forms. New technologies show up in their discourse as a tool or prosthesis of black subjectivities, a means of extending blackness outward into time, space, and beyond.[42]

Moreover, it seems to me that Afrofuturists offer an explicitly *political and theoretical* reading of blackness in relationship to digital technologies. Drawn from different quarters of black Atlantic musical cultures and cultural discourses, Afrofuturists do not seem particularly preoccupied with African American–inspired civil rights politics of legal recognition, or with market-driven corporate and policy preoccupations with access to the new technologies. Nor are they especially interested in promoting utopian visions of color blindness and using new technologies as a means of achieving such a vision. When they draw on images like alien, data thief, translator, scientist, and mythologizer to craft identities and to perform cultural politics, I think that Afrofuturists are stretching conceptions of blackness.

Afrofuturists use new information and digital technologies to change the terms of a blackness fixed in bodies, place, nation, and even, it sometimes seems, history. They do so by conceptualizing and performing a blackness that exceeds fixed categories like place or genre, and by tracing through sound the myriad and complex ways that blackness travels, dwelling and encountering different notions or versions of itself in different locations and under different circumstances.[43] The Afrofuturists encounter with late-twentieth- and early-twenty-first-century digital technology produces very different soundings and thus ways of crafting identities and performing blackness. The Afrofuturists strike me as already mindful of the fact that technologies are deeply inscribed in racial logics, economic uses, and political interests of the sort suggested by Kolko, Bailey, and others. Recognizing this, Afrofuturists use digital technologies (and conceptions of their possibility) to unsettle, sample, rewrite, and produce new narratives of black presence and participation in the modern world. In other words, their focus is on blackness and identity rather than on the new technologies and their capabilities.

Afrofuturists narrate a black Atlantic tale of origins and (forced) dispersal on planet Earth. Packaged in the imagery of science fiction, poststructuralist instabilities, and computer programming language, these folk look to new technologies to decipher and break the codes to black diasporic survival. In one fashion or another, Afrofuturists are involved in the global project of identifying and breaking codes that hold access to freedom from old narratives and debilitating discourses of black identity. To describe black people and their cultural practices these code breakers use epic tales with tropes of aliens, travelers, and dwellers whose aural soundtracks and imaginative visions are supplied by figures like George Clinton, Sun Ra, Ishmael Reed, Lee Scratch Perry, and Africa Bambatta, among so many others.[44] Using metaphors from the

works of black science-fiction writers like Samuel Delaney, Octavia But-
ler, Nalo Hopkinson, and Greg Tate, Afrofuturists claim that blacks
scattered across the Atlantic world are aliens in an alien land, ever on
the lookout for clues and resources that point the way out of alien
nations and conditions of bondage. Because of the simultaneous and
almost unlimited access to soundings (and the traces of encounter) made
available through the storage and retrieval capacity of digitally based
technologies, black Atlantic soundings hold the master codes to libera-
tion of collective black imaginations around the globe. Access to the
particular and specific soundings of any one group are freed from the
limits of place and linked in new ways to other soundings almost instantaneously. It is possible to rebuild old and make anew different diasporic
connections, as well as to imagine possibilities for inhabiting the spaces
and identities about which Sun Ra wrote. Music functions, then, as an
important vehicle for expressing and performing possibilities for imagining blackness differently. It is the surface on which are performed all
sorts of cultural moves necessary for making and producing blackness.
As such, blackness, like the music through which it is constituted and
expressed, is always changing, always subject to reversioning and
remixing. This tracing and mixing, decoding, and translating constitutes
the foundational work of the Afrofuturists.

If the technologies of the information age provide the Afrofuturists
with the digital tools necessary to decode old codes and imagine blackness differently, then what of the tools themselves, inscribed as they are
with all sorts of commercial interests and racial logics? In the end, are
the uses to which they are put (translation and decoding) and the solutions (new narratives of black identity) they offer any different from the
corporate entrepreneurs or civil rights advocates who promote black
access as the best means for realizing greater black participation, which
they hope will help break the pattern of racial exclusion and invisibility? At their most fundamental levels (the programs and operating systems that produce the fonts and representations with which we interact), aren't these technologies still saturated and structured in and by a
raced and gendered imagination that represents itself as neutral? Are
they not also organized by an economic logic that foregrounds consumer-based conceptions of access and use and a stimulus/response
model of interaction?[45] After all the talk about data, thieves, and aliens,
is it the case that, in the end, Afrofuturists are offering nothing more
than a sophisticated model of consumer sovereignty, clearing the way
for their particular version of software and product content—in this

case cultural identity as opposed to the services and brand identity of some other corporate entity?

Though troubling, this critique does not seem to pose much of a problem for the Afrofuturists, at least according to their various manifestos and pronouncements. The new digitally based technologies, according to saxophonist Steve Coleman and performance artist Pamela Z, function as mere "tools." The encounter between blackness and technology in popular music genres like hip-hop, dance hall, house, drum, and bass, while seminal and inventive, simply accept the cultural terms and social logic embedded in the tools.[46] With the exception of some of the early innovative practitioners, most uses of the technologies are not focused on programming or redesigning the fundamental logic of these tools, except insofar as they can be made to work more efficiently or to deliver "better" results aesthetically and practically. This might mean extending the range of sonic possibilities available, producing new variations in speed, size, and range of access to existing sound sources, increasing the capacity to capture, manipulate, and circulate smaller increments of sound, sustaining looping capacity and the range of tonal responses, and increasing the torque of turntables.[47] For this reason, in the hands of Afrofuturists, the encounter with new technologies (and the discursive accounts through which they are represented) emphasizes the transformative and imaginative work being done on the concept and performance of blackness, rather than on the new digital technologies per se.

Yet these cultural moves are significant. They push farther, harder, and more imaginatively for thinking about the relationship between new information technologies and black cultural practices than corporate marketing strategies that continue to call for greater minority access to the new digital technologies. Although clearly below the radar of policy makers and corporate executives, black diasporic musical communities are already deeply involved with various forms of technological practice—including consumption, networking, and critical cultural exchanges. This involvement suggests that cultural identities and social differences continue to matter as the ground for critical practices and representations. Just as significantly, through their very presence, the discourses, soundings, and representations of Afrofuturists also suggest that proposals that only emphasize technological access, literacy, and participation reproduce and reinscribe the corporate ideal of technology as neutral, moving from the messiness of identity, power, and inequality to the idealized fantasy of consumer sovereignty and individual difference. African American composers and performance artists have taken up some of these questions, and through their example have critiqued the dominant conceptions of new information technologies and suggested how these technologies might be used to rethink African American cultural traditions.

## COMPOSERS AS PROGRAMMERS: HE SPOKE TO IT LIKE A BROTHER

In separate magazine cover stories in spring 2002, the *New York Times Magazine* and *Wired* featured special issues on music, digital technology, and their cultural impact on production, circulation, and experience of music.[48] In articles about developments in new digital technologies and their impact on popular music, there is no mention of race, gender, or identity. Most of the stories seem to assume automatically that their subjects were (to be generous) color-blind or (to be less generous) explicitly white and male. The dance cultures, the gay clubs, and the mixed-race urban scenes around the world where popular electronic music developed and continues to thrive were the focus of an occasional sidebar. But there was little else in either magazine that acknowledged the salience of what one might recognize as cultural identities based on race or gender. In other words, identity (racial or otherwise) was not explicitly present in any of these pieces, and yet was present as their *implicit* subject—in this case masculinity and whiteness. In fact, identity was conspicuous by its very invisibility.

Yet again, technology had been taken to be neutral and subjects assumed to be without meaningful or significant racial and gender identities, traditions and histories. In these idealized representations, technologies are thought to contain unlimited capacities for storage, retrieval, and reversioning, and the particular conditions of production for the music (aside from the lone genius at work in front of the computer, turntables, or mixing console) seem of minor consequence. It is not just music that is being reimagined in these narratives but the very notion of the musician and the conditions of production. Such representations seem to stem at least in part from the utopian fantasy about digital technology that I have been discussing: its neutrality and its unlimited capacity to make such mundane things as identity matter less, if at all.

The one exception to this utopian fantasy was a short (almost throwaway) sidebar about the history and development of the synthesizer in mixing music. In it, Derrick May, pioneering turntablist and mix master in Detroit's techno-scene, offers a cautionary tale about the limits of the powerful program logic that structures and drives much of the new digital technology in music:

> I actually prefer to master all of my music onto a reel-to-reel tape deck . . . with today's technology, everybody's using some form of software to master records, which is limiting them—the program logic says, "these sounds are wrong," that means that no matter how radical you may be, if you don't record within set boundaries, fuck it, you can't do it. So there's this *invisible law in technology that is policing* our music.[49]

Where digital technologies and music are concerned, discipline and regulation appear as discourses and conventions about (aesthetic) value, (technological) neutrality, and the nature of creativity (composition).

Taking these concerns with regulation and policing as a point of departure, I want to pursue the larger point about the relation between digital technologies, identities, and music by showing how (racial) identities are embedded in music. In particular, I want to linger a bit on the idea that soundings enabled by digital technologies are simply neutral and thus beyond mere matters of identity and race.

George Lewis, Steve Coleman, and Pamela Z represent black musicians and composers working at the intersection between identity and technology, who, by their example and work, offer some remarkable insights for thinking about the limits and possibilities of new information technologies. Working in the realm of new music, jazz improvisation, and electronic music, these composers and performance artists are interested in new information technologies and what they mean for the production of black soundings. Therefore, how these artists account for, use, and negotiate their claims on identity (blackness) in the context of the tools and epistemologies that structure the digital revolution provides yet another move through which we can imagine the relationship between identity and technology. Hearing the sounds of these artists, listening to accounts of their own practice, and understanding how they work, it is clear to me that it is not so much that black identities are interrogated in their work (as is the case with the Afrofuturists), but the technological possibilities for producing and reproducing cultural practices and traditions. To understand this relationship, I interviewed, studied the work, listened to performances, and visited the Web sites of Lewis, Coleman, and Pamela Z to understand some of the challenges they faced in using new communications and information technologies.[50]

Positing the relationship between bodies, race, and music is at best a tricky business. With considerable insight scholars like Olly Wilson, Ron Radano, Paul Gilroy, Jocelyne Guilbault, Jon Cruz, and Georgina Born appreciate that while race is a social construction whose meanings and systems of signification are organized culturally and circulate through oral, auditory, visual, and linguistic signs, in the end one can make claims about the existence of something that is agreed upon as black (American) music.[51] Evidence for such claims is taken from scholarly studies of traditions, practices, the organization and structure of music, the social uses and reproduction of the music, and the cultural production of various discourses through which such musics are represented (and reproduced). In other words, the discernible elements of black music are always discursive and therefore cultural and social—and not biological, physical, or auditory alone. The case for understanding the practices, traditions, contexts, and meanings of soundings generated by blacks (in the Atlantic diaspora) as music is possible because of the discursive operations and procedures through which these soundings are transformed into something that we recognize as black music. These practices and operations include specific conditions and techniques of production (and reproduction), traditions, bodies of work, interpretive and critical communities (especially the characteristics, attribution of meaning, pleasure, and value they signal). I locate identity within this corpus of elements and practices and the meanings they come to signify. Black musical soundings are never just about sound, any more than blackness is just about race or black bodies. One cannot be reduced to the other—sound to race or race to sound. If one accepts the proposition that blackness can and does signify cultural meanings whose very viability is connected to its visibility and the constellation of meanings that have congealed around that visibility (including its sonic meanings), then it seems to me that racial invisibility and color-blindness as the realization of an expressly American identity is ridiculous. The cultural meaning of color-blindness, its historic and semiotic alignment with whiteness, and its productive possibility depend on the presence and visibility of blackness, or at the very least some notion of "other" as the site of an absence. Given the history of race and representation in America (and especially the powerful complicity of whiteness in organizing the racial logic) the very aspiration to color-blindness is a fantasy, a condition of impossibility. In other words, the meaning of identity is summoned through the power of a marked other that signifies a lack, in this case blackness. And what about the identity of this claim to invisibility in the context of the new technologies, which, through their social logic, produce the notion of invisibility to escape from identity in the first place?

Cultural sociologist Jon Cruz gives us some insight into the complex relationship between claims to invisibility, the production of whiteness and the disavowal of identity, and the dependence on marked or dark bodies, soundings, and the production of racial subjects.[52] Working in the context of nineteenth-century racial meanings in the United States, Cruz argues that the formation of what we have come to recognize as modern American identities of the (white) self were fashioned out of nineteenth-century crises of the social subject. For Cruz, this condition, which he calls "subject crisis," arose in the nexus between old-world logics and values and the shifting conditions and demands of the new world. Accordingly, this crisis required work on the new-world subject. Ironically this work on the subject (or subject work) focused on African slaves, whose soundings (and, by extension, humanity) were illegible and were heard as noise to white slave owners, intellectuals, abolitionists, and opinion leaders of the period. The slaves thus needed to be *made* human—that is, transformed into subjects of human comprehension and visibility—according to the dominant political, moral, cultural, and racial codes of the period, and in terms of the debates and discourses of humanism, reform, and abolition. This work on the subject, according to Cruz, led to the production and circulation of new discourses and intellectual disciplines like folklore and sociology, and to subfields like race and ethnicity, urban studies, and to concerns with identities, but identities of racial, ethnic, and cultural others. In the process of this social and cultural work on the subject, whiteness was produced as the site, the unmarked place of the knowing subject.[53] This knowledge of race was projected onto dark bodies as racial knowledge (whose detailing, inventory, classification, and translation was the focus of folklore and anthropology), and ultimately was the operation through which racialized power was able to pass itself off as unmarked and without racial identity. Through its very claim to invisibility, whiteness functioned as the subject to a black other, a subject that guaranteed both the omnipotence of its own identity and simultaneously disavowed the humanity of blackness, a disavowal that necessarily takes the form of color blindness and racial neutrality. This is a disavowal that need not speak its own name, need not be embodied, and need not fix its location, because these have been secured through its racially marked other.

What does this historic production of whiteness as invisibility have to do with new technologies, identities, and black soundings? Everything, in the sense that the same cultural logic identified by Cruz as necessary for the production of a specific kind of modern subject is at work, I think, in discourses about new technologies and identities as neutral and beyond identity. The cultural moves that Cruz identifies as subject work in the nineteenth century, I want to call identity work in the late twentieth and early twenty-first centuries.

The terms of this work with the respect to new technologies are explicit in composer George Lewis's account of his experience in creating a computer program based on the core elements of the African American music tradition. Lewis, a second-generation member of the landmark Chicago musical collective Association for the Advancement of Creative Musicians, is a trombonist, composer, and scholar.[54] One of his fellow Chicagoans, composer and saxophonist Steve Coleman, describes Lewis as a mentor and a pioneer of computer music:

> George is a pioneer in creating computer programs that capture the experiences of working improvisational musicians. He has also been able to use his software as a tool to explore the way improvisers think and communicate with each other on stage. George first demonstrated some aspects of his Voyager software to me in the mid 1970s. This was a true inspiration and an accomplishment that I did not believe was possible at the time.[55]

Using "Voyager," his original computer program, as the basis of an extended case report, Lewis reflects on his encounter with the computer's operating system as he attempted to program improvisational music from the African American musical tradition.[56] In a brilliant meditation, "Too Many Notes: Computers, Complexity, and Culture in Voyager," Lewis considers the interface between computers and users, the capacity to program (and reproduce) elements of an explicitly African music and cultural tradition, as well as the potential of the computer (as an improvising machine) to function as a sound-production machine, and as a member of a performance ensemble. To realize these objectives, Lewis had to program the computer in such a way that it had to be aware of and respond to inputs and changes generated from outside it.[57] These demands also meant that Lewis had to program the computer to function as a generator of sound and to function autonomously within contingent and indeterminate performance conditions, all the while remaining open to mutuality and dialogic exchange. Tall orders to say the least, but, as Lewis suggests, all of these requirements are based on conventions and practices long established in the African American musical and cultural traditions and ways of making music.

So part of the challenge Lewis faced was to codify, translate, and then formally reproduce the structuring logic and organizing principles of the African American musical tradition—a kind of identity work if you will. In addition to dialogue and improvisation, Lewis notes that the African American musical tradition depends on rhythm (especially rhythmic complexity and contrasts); the aesthetics of multidominance ("the multiple use of textures, design patterns or shapes"); the establishment of "one's own sound" or voice; improvisation; shared and nonhierarchical musical process rather than centralized authority; continuous awareness and responsiveness.[58]

Lewis protégé and colleague, saxophonist Steve Coleman, also developed a computer program, called Rameses (after his interest in ancient Egyptian mythology), with the express purpose of bringing together many of his musical, spiritual, and philosophical ideas. Of his earliest forays into computer technology and music Coleman recalls, "I decided to try and develop some of my own ideas on computers so I started to learn how to program. This involved learning about the structure of computers and microprocessors and buying programming books to learn how to build sub-routines and how to construct flow charts."[59] As his skills and knowledge increased, Coleman began to "structure some basic interactive functions. These included programming the software to listen to chords played by a musician and then to create improvised melodies inside of these chords as they were being played. Rhythmically, melodically, and harmonically the program utilizes ideas that I have been working on for years in my own saxophone playing and compositionally with my band."[60]

In pursuit of an African American performance sensibility, Lewis sought to register the vitality of the music through more than mere formal composition. Indeed for Lewis, the real vibrancy of the music lies in the dialogic qualities of exchange that happen in performance. So, for example, in programming the computer to improvise and interact with other inputs, Lewis sought more than the computational capacity for randomness. He wanted to do more than simply program the computer to respond to a set of predetermined options or default positions.[61] Here is Lewis's conception of the project: "I conceive of a performance of Voyager as multiple parallel streams of music generation, emanating from both the computers and humans—a nonhierarchical improvisational, subject-subject model of discourse, rather than a stimulus/response setup."[62] By stressing the dialogic and nonhierarchical nature of interaction and improvisation, Lewis conceives of identity well beyond the narrow confines of identity as claims about rights, origins, or essential characteristics.

Steve Coleman offers equally insightful accounts of how his own program, Rameses, structures and reproduces qualities of an African American cultural sensibility:

> There is no predetermined music programmed into Rameses. . . . The software creates everything in real time (i.e., instantaneously) and is constantly improvising all of its parts. So it never repeats the music it creates. Each time Rameses plays, we are hearing the music for the first time; as a result the musicians do not know what it will create. We only know the general stylistic areas that it will create in and the compositional parameters. . . . Rameses interacts with the musicians in the following ways in real-time (it does not need to know what the musicians will do in advance). . . . It can listen to and follow the tempo of the musicians using "beat tracking" routines. . . . Rameses can listen to the improvisations played by musicians and respond by playing chords that are the result of its analysis of the improvised melodies. . . . It can listen to chords played by the musicians and simultaneously improvise melodies based on the chords. . . . It can create its own harmonic progression based on a system derived from the Kemetic Decans (ancient Egyptian interpretation of groups of stars in the sky).[63]

Steve Coleman's musical and spiritual universe is formed in an African-based cosmology that includes traditions, soundings, practices, deities, mythologies, and circuits from the black Atlantic world. Moreover, for Coleman the aesthetic and genre edges of this black cosmic imagination are fluid, and thus include hip-hop, computer technologies, and related cultural practices, Egyptian mysticism, funk, rhythm and blues, be-bop, different drumming traditions from around the world, comic books, science fiction. As with Lewis's Voyager, Coleman's quest with Rameses is to decode and then recode the very logic of a machine that comes technologically finished and complete.

In their attempts to codify and reproduce the core elements of an African American musical tradition, Lewis and Coleman confronted the cultural logic of an identity (whiteness) hiding or embedded in the structure of the machine. They had to deal with an identity that disavows its very existence with claims to neutrality and invisibility. In the face of the cultural authority and tradition of equally powerful practices, what is exposed is a discourse of identity that operates through disavowal and the power to pass itself off as beyond history. This is a move which Lewis clearly rejects:

> Musical computer programs, like any texts, are not "objective" or "universal," but instead represent the particular ideas of their creators. As notions

about the nature and function of music become *embedded into the struc-ture of soft-ware based musical systems and compositions,* interactions with these systems tend to reveal characteristics of the community of thought and culture that produced them. Thus it would be useful . . . to examine the implications of the experience of programming and perform-ing with Voyager as a kind of computer music making embodying African American cultural practice.[64]

Like Kolko and Bailey, Lewis recognizes the crucial role of what he calls "the community of thought"—in this case, the West, whiteness, and masculinity (and their attendant authority)—for structuring the terms of engagement with the new digital technologies. Whether presented as discourses about access, endless consumer possibility, or the utopian vision of finally escaping identity, this "community of thought" is not at all neutral, even though it is conceived, presented, or represented as such.

Where, as Cruz shows, blackness was important in the nineteenth century for the production of new subjects (subjects who could claim invisibility in a decidedly racial discourse), with the emergence of the new digital age in late modernity, identity, race, and gender are perhaps the last discursive sites of encounter and struggle for the hegemony of the modern universal subject. Allegedly beyond identity, this is the sub-ject through which power works by constructing a kind of racial knowl-edge whose hallmarks are invisibility, disaggregation, flexibility, and flu-idity (rather than discrete boundaries, aggregation, stability, fixity, and coherence) and whose identity, to the extent that it exists at all, is secured through its other.[65]

The insights offered by Lewis and Coleman, based on their experi-ences as programmers and composers, are instructive for the point I want to stress both about the community of interests embedded in tech-nologies and the crucial role of black composers for exposing those interests. By their examples, they show us where different cultural log-ics and interests are congealed and represented as natural.

But these critical insights also pose a thorny problem, one that relates to the business of equating or assigning to the "community of interests" a kind of cultural and racial specificity—or identity, if you will. How is Lewis able to pull this off? On what basis is he (and by extension, of course, am I) able to locate or assign identities—West, white, male—to the logics and procedures that represent themselves as neutral, invisible, and beyond identity? Lewis and Coleman both appreciate the produc-tive possibility of identity not as something from which one seeks escape—as was the case in the crisis of Cruz's nineteenth-century subjects who wanted to escape ethnicity, class, and other old-world ties of identity. Since Lewis recognizes the centrality of identity from the outset, his objective is never to rid Voyager or the music it generates of its cultural location; rather it is to make explicit, to stress those qualities of tradition and practice in which his music is located. Like Lewis, Steve Coleman is explicit about some of the cultural influences that bear on his music and his approach to programming. "Rameses," he notes,

> helps me to explore other methods for expressing these ideas so I also use it as an educational tool. Many of the ideas that I have today are difficult to realize using traditional methods so I have chosen to use the software as a research tool to create musical models for these ideas. In doing so, I hoped to see how some of the conceptual material that I imagine might sound when worked out by musicians. These ideas include working with astronomical/astrological and mystical ideas influenced by my study of ancient Egyptian cosmogony to create music.[66]

For me, the value of Lewis's achievement with Voyager and Coleman's accomplishment with Rameses is that they question the claims to the neutrality of digital technology by locating these technologies in history and culture by exposing the traces of the conditions of their production. They both show through their programming, composition, and performance that new information technologies are permeated with identities, interests, and politics. George Lewis put the matter this way: "If there is to be serious talk about 'our' identity as humans, those identities are continually conditioned and reinscribed through processes of interactivity, where negotiation, difference, partial perspective—and, in the case of music, sonic signaling enter the picture."[67] African Americans and members of the black diasporic formations throughout the world have confronted and deconstructed all sorts of claims to the innocence of various technologies of representation, regulation, and repression. In the process, they have made and remade their cultural and social world, in this case by asserting black humanity through black soundings.

KNOW-MOTION

San Francisco Bay Area composer and performance artist Pamela Z is a major figure, and one of the few African American women in the Bay Area experimental-music scene. A 2002 interview feature in the journal *Musicworks* introduces her to readers this way:

> San Francisco electrodiva Pamela Z has been consistently performing and composing since 1984. She created a body of work that has earned her the

coveted CalArts Alpert Award, a commission for the Bang on A Can All-stars, and frequent appearances in international new music festivals. In performance, she creates layered works combining operatic and extended vocal techniques with a battery of digital delays, found percussion objects, and sampled sounds triggered with a MIDI controller called the BodySynth™ which allows her to manipulate sound with physical gestures.[68]

I turn to Pamela Z's work to complicate my claims about the relationship between identity (broadly conceived) and technology, in large part because her approach to performance and composition illustrates the interface between digitally based technologies and the body. This interface includes the raced, gendered, and performing body as a field of signification in the context of motion and sound. By her own admission Pamela Z rejects thinking about musical production in terms of conventional assumptions about race, bodies, gender, even genre and audiences, and as such she challenges preconceived notions about identity, technology, and new music. Consider this description of her performance from Yale's *Theater Magazine*:

> In her most recent piece, "Gaijin," she blends live and sampled vocals, texts, and sounds into a lush polyphonic weave. Voices on multiple tracks reflect on the mysteries and disorientation of being an outsider, while, center stage, Pamela Z stands with quiet assurance at a microphone console, building and inhabiting a lonely character (who generates and absorbs the sound around her). Waving her wrists, she triggers humorously chirpy samples from elementary Japanese-language lesson tapes, while an endless loop of basic phonetics underscores her painful estrangement. Although the piece relies on digital delay technology, the human voice resonates in and above the soundscape with grace and haunting clarity.[69]

It is instructive, then, to consider Pamela Z's work in and thinking about music as a site within which to think through the relationship between identity and new technology.

While she is clearly aware of her identity as a black woman, the issue of racial identity is not at the forefront of her self-conception as an artist.[70] This makes sense, given her own social formation (she grew up in a mixed-race family and community), her wide cultural and artistic interests, and her musical training. So, where Steve Coleman and George Lewis's political, aesthetic, and experience of racial identity was formed and sustained in largely black urban communities, Pamela Z's racial identity was formed in a very different milieu. Musically, she records her early formation and influences this way:

> The influences I was clearly aware of were European avant-garde, and European and American pop music. . . . British invasion rock as a kid,

and in the 70s I was a Joni Mitchell head. I started listening to classical music in high school. As a music major in college, I was singing opera and art song, but I wasn't totally absorbed in that culture. I was always making my own music, and I was lucky to have one of the only teachers on faculty that permitted me to sing in clubs at night. I went through some confusion when I left school because I couldn't figure out how to combine all these vocal styles. I eventually became interested in punk and new wave, and through that discovered some avant-garde artist and electronic music people who were combining styles and collaborating across genre lines.[71]

Indeed, in her interview with me about the salience of identity for her work, and how she views herself in terms of identity, gender, social class, and the ontological world of the body, gender seems far more salient to her than race alone. On the other hand, as with Lewis and Coleman (whose work, politics, and worldview are informed by their location in and attempts to codify the fundamental elements of African American musical culture), for Pamela Z also live performance and the interaction between performer and audience are paramount. One might say that the issue of racial identity seems meaningful to the degree that, as she perceptively notes, it gets at questions of corporeality and the power of cultural assumptions to organize, classify, and assign value and meaning of music on the basis of race and gender.

In this respect, Pamela Z has some very interesting things to say about visibility in relationship to the power of racial discourse to shape the meaning of sound. In the case of new music, she contends that the visual can and often does takes precedence over sound; as she put it, "when people can see you they hear something else." It is this logic— one that identifies, categorizes, and assigns value—which produces the meaning of sound based largely on the preconceived relationship between race and sound. In the realm of new technology and music, blacks (including the South Asian populations in England and the United States) and the soundings they generate (especially those that utilize various new technologies) are discursively and culturally confined by critics, journalists, curators, and audiences to the realm of dance and club music, ostensibly evaluating the music according to how people who make the music look.

Pamela Z reports that, in her experience, there is the view among some curators and programmers that a common racial background is the basis for shared interest, similar work (if not ways of working), and, from the angle of programming, shared thematic possibilities.[72] Despite these concerns, Pamela Z does count among her compositions and performance pieces work that is specifically about the politics of identity. These are mostly pieces that explore the idea of foreignness and the role of speech and language in identity.

Pamela Z's observation, "when people can see you they hear something else," also seems useful for making sense of gender-based assumptions about appropriate instruments, musical genres, and bodies of work and musical activity. In other words, if racially marked bodies are assumed to produce certain kinds of sounds, then it is also true that certain kinds of gendered bodies are expected to produce certain sounds, performance styles/contexts, compositional competencies, and instrumental virtuosity. According to Pamela Z, this means that women are expected to be visible with the voice, their presumed area of competence. She says, "It seems that people's expectation of the kinds of tools an artist would use are somewhat separated along gender lines. . . . The tool that women seem to be expected to excel in using is the human voice. And when we do excel in that we get recognition for it . . . the message seems to be 'if you want recognition for what you do, you need to stick with the tools you are expected to use.'"[73] Men, on the other hand, are associated with composition, programming, and control over technology,

> Sometimes even men who are great improvisers and who feel quite at home making loud, bizarre, even shocking sounds in public when using some kind of external tool (a saxophone, a percussion instrument, a piece of sheet metal), become shy and uncomfortable when asked to experiment with their voices. Perhaps the external instrument is like armor or a shield between them and the audience, so using it to produce strange or unusual sounds may feel less awkward than making a sound that comes directly out of one's face. . . . I don't mean to over-generalize. There are many men who are quite happy using their voices and bodies in performance, and there are many women who are not. But in a general way, women in our culture are not only socialized to feel more comfortable baring themselves in that way, but people are socialized to feel more comfortable accepting it from women.[74]

Once again, the insight on offer seems to be that role assignments and expectations with respect to technologies, performance styles, instruments, and compositions are profoundly raced and gendered. Pamela Z's work is very much about breaking these kinds of stereotypes and unsettling the assumptions on which they are based. The emphasis on embodiment and performance is one way she addresses these issues. "It's interesting" she notes on her Web site, that I find myself thinking so much about these issues now. In the past, I have never really been very focused on the sociopolitical issues around gender and making art. I always went about tinkering with whatever was needed in order to do the things I wanted to do. I never remember personally having had any concern about the ability to do something technical having any connection to gender, and I don't remember feeling self-conscious about being the only woman among people doing the kinds of things I was interested in. But then of course, I was the same person who had to have it pointed out to me by others that I was the only Black person at a function or in an organization. I never really thought about these kinds of things much. Naïve as that may have been, I didn't even notice.[75]

Naive or not, Pamela Z did begin to notice that women artists that she spoke with were increasingly feeling isolated and intimidated in the male world of computers and electronics. "I spoke with a surprising number of women," she confesses,

who said that they had taken audio engineering courses and had felt intimidated by the men in the class, and even had felt pushed out of the way in situations where many were vying for hands-on time on the equipment. It seemed like a lot of their problems stemmed from a combination of unequal treatment by instructors, classmates, fellow musicians, etc., and their own lack of confidence in their own abilities to tackle the tasks at hand. This experience caused me to slowly become convinced that I needed to offer a workshop for women.[76]

In her own work, Pamela Z combines the insights gained from her experience as a woman in a largely male (and white) world with her love of electronic and experimental music. "I don't think that one can really divide tools into categories of feminine and masculine," she says.

Throughout history in various cultures, both men and women have always played a variety of instruments, though some cultures have placed limitations on who could do what. . . . But, if there is anything to the Yin and Yang of using the voice vs. using an external instrument, then the type of elecroacoustic music that combines vocal practice with electronics might be viewed as a way of exerting both feminine and masculine qualities in the performer. This type of work was pioneered by women and continues to be female-dominated, could be seen as a modern day extension of the age-old practice of singing while accompanying oneself on an acoustic instrument. All of the various women and men who do this probably arrived at this way of working from a variety of different paths. In my case, the practice of combining my voice with live processing and sampled sounds was a direct descendant of singing while playing a guitar. As I began to develop more facility with using digital processors to create layers of sound in live performance, songs on which I used the guitar began to disappear from my repertoire.[77]

Given her deep immersion in the world of computer and digital technology, especially in all aspects of her everyday life, it is little surprise that technology is so central to her work as a composer, performance artist, and modern person. The depth of her knowledge of and relationship to these new technologies is evident in this passage, which I quote at length:

> I am often asked how recent changes in technology have affected my art. It is difficult for anyone to be alive today in this culture and not be in some way touched by the sudden upsurge of computers and digital technology, and in this regard I am no exception. Not only has this technology had a major effect on my work as composer/performer, but it has infiltrated practically every aspect of my life. I compose music on the computer. I use digital sound processors and MIDI (Musical Instrument Digital Interface) equipment in live performance. I record, edit, and construct sound works using digital sound editing software and hardware in the computer and then use peripheral devices with my computer to burn CDs of those works so they can be heard by others. I use musical notation software to create scores when I compose works intended to communicate with others through email and to make others aware of my work through maintaining a website. And I use the computer to teach others to use digital audio and other software. I use the computer to do my books, manage my promotional materials, and to keep track of colleagues, venues, services, and members of the press. The list of computer-centered activity in my life seems endless. I haven't yet found a way to cook in the computer, but if left to my own devices, I'm, afraid that I might. . . . The computer is a tool and I have a very strong relationship with my tools.[78]

As immersed and knowledgeable as she is about the tools of her art, she remains skeptical and critical of the utopian (often male) celebration of technology, particularly in relationship to creativity.

> Of course, tools alone do not make great art . . . as an artist, it is always important for me to be concerned about what work I am actually making with this tool. It frustrates me to see a world so seduced by new technologies that many have forgotten to be concerned about output. We suddenly see a superabundance of works being created by people who are clearly more interested in what software they have mastered than they are in the value of what they are making with it. One hears endless jokes about content as sort of an afterthought in a project. . . . There have always been people who believe that having a great tool will make them great artists or magically result in the creation of great art . . . having a new tool can certainly inspire great work from someone who has the potential to make it. Hopefully, a good side effect of this rush to embrace new technology is the opening up of some new artists who perhaps never realized that they had that potential.[79]

Along with her embrace of the new technologies and her realization of its limits and possibilities is the actual business of how Pamela Z incorporates these elements into her work as a composer and performer. For Pamela Z, live performance is a primary means of direct engagement and interaction with her audience, an active attempt to, as she puts it, "get her face out of the computer," thereby challenging the masculine definition and stereotypic representation of new music and technological mastery. Performance and the relationship to the audience that it establishes are central to her work as a composer and to her use of computer technologies. Where Coleman and Lewis program, even install the computer as a member of a live performance ensemble, Pamela Z's approach is what I might call deeply embodied; that is the actual physical experience of the technology and its various uses are central to the total aural, sonic, and visual experience.

For a sense of her thinking about the relationship between performance, composition, and the computer technologies, consider these reflections from her about her work (all quotes are taken from her Web site; all added emphasis is mine):

> I learned during this period of time (the mid 1980s) that *performance itself was a discipline*, and that *I was as much a performer as I was a musician.*
>
> In the past several years I have been creating recorded work using digital editing software on my Mac. As I gained skill with non-destructive editing programs such as Digidesign's SoundDesigner and Pro Tools, I began working in new ways. I began making sculpted sound collages with small bits of layered text and found sounds. My first hard disc recording works were informed by live work I do with digital delay loops, but I quickly started making more complex and varied structures working with smaller bits of sound and altering samples.
>
> As a composer/performer, my choice of tools (instrumentation) is often determined by my own capabilities as a solo performer. I began using the BodySynth™ several years ago when I wanted to introduce pre-sampled sounds into my live works . . . this instrument which uses electrode sensors to measure the electrical impulses generated by the performer's muscles, allowed me to *use physical gestures to trigger samples and manipulate various sound parameters.* . . . I was able to introduce traffic noise, text samples, and sounds literally from my kitchen sink into my performance works. *The introduction of the instrument changed the way I was composing.*
>
> With the dramatic changes that came about in my music due to the use of this new tool, my hands and my *body were freed up for gesture and movement*, and I became more focused on the performance aspect of my work. I came to see the sound I was making, and my physical behavior while making it as an integrated whole.

Pamela Z's negotiation of new technologies, identity, and music comes together around her conception of the technology as a tool, as a means of organizing, heightening, and extending the musical experience. This emphasis on the circuit and relationship of sound, vision, and corporeality organized through digital technologies is crucial to my argument about identity because it offers yet another illustration of the centrality of *music* as a crucial meeting place for the encounter between identity and technology. Just as she does not settle easily for fixed racial identities, Pamela Z also questions conventional notions about the gendering of music and new digital technologies. In other words, by integrating performance and composition, technology and bodies, and multiple notions of identity in her work Pamela Z troubles each of these terms and imagines how they might be combined in different ways.

## CONCLUSION

With the Afrofuturists we see how new technologies enable black cultural workers to imagine black Atlantic cultures and histories differently. In the case of composers like George Lewis and Steve Coleman, we see the importance of the African American musical practices as critical tools for ferreting out specific identities embedded within technologies and, once exposed, for showing us how technologies can be used to expand and reimagine previously unimaginable connections. For example, Steve Coleman, ever on the lookout for opportunities to expand his musical, spiritual, and cultural resources, looks to cultural influences from traditional, vernacular, and popular practices around the world. Likewise, because of Pamela Z's careful exploration of the relationship between technology, sound, vision, and body through her performances, she literally shows us how to hear and see differently.

The artists, critics, and scholars that I have considered here offer cultural models of how black Atlantic cultures continue to unsettle and reimagine, negotiate, and inscribe in sound, social worlds of their own making. New digital and information technologies are resources for this process of unmaking and making social worlds through music. While access to these technologies is certainly shaped by race and social-class dynamics and inequalities, this needn't necessarily translate into pronouncements about the lack of will, imagination, or capacity of black people with respect to these tools and resources. The capacity to unmake and remake their social world through the appropriation and application of the black imaginary to all sorts of technologies is, of course, inscribed in the histories of popular black music cultures and practices from Trinidad and Tobago, Jamaica, the American South, Brazil, the South Bronx, to Brixton and Detroit. Like other technologies before them—the phonograph, radio, electronic amplification, the LP, and the magnetic tape—the latest digitally based technologies enter the social and cultural fields already deeply inscribed in habits, practices, assumptions, and identities, and marked by relations of power. Nevertheless, the cultural practices and visions of the social world that they help articulate are compelling evidence, I believe, that black people are neither technologically illiterate nor incapable of managing and employing these new tools productively.

# Conclusion

*Cultural Moves*

I'd like to end where I began: by reconsidering the distance between Edith Bunker's declaration, in *All in the Family,* of black progress on television, Regina's demand, in *I'll Fly Away*, for recognition, and the notable influence of black cultural practices on America's (and increasingly the world's) commercial image culture. When they do appear, televisual images of blackness seem to work overtime to shore up the representation of contemporary American society as racially and culturally diverse. The contemporary arrival to which *All in the Family*'s Edith Bunker refers, and the visibility and recognition that *I'll Fly Away*'s Regina eventually achieves, are considerably different from the cultural ends to which blackness was used in the production of the American nation as white and pure in a film like *Birth of a Nation* (which was also about fashioning the nation out of difference). Or are they?

Leaving this provocation to the side for the moment, lots of examples of black televisual visibility operating in the service of the nation (as racially and ethnically diverse) come to mind: In the immediate aftermath of the tragedy of 9/11, think of the spectacular televisual images of R&B artist R. Kelly performing his hit song "I Believe I Can Fly," against the backdrop of quickly edited shots of (mostly white) American sports excellence at the opening ceremony of the 2000 Winter Olympics. Picture the television images of Condoleezza Rice, the highest-ranking black woman in the president's administration and his National Security Advisor; or Colin Powell, the African American gen-

eral and secretary of state, making the American case for war against
Iraq in the Bush White House and at the United Nations Security Council. Think, finally, of the historic significance of the television broadcast
of African American actors Sidney Poitier, Denzel Washington, and
actress Halle Berry accepting Oscars for lifetime achievement and best
performances at the 2002 Academy Award ceremony.

These and similar "representations" of black achievement do recognize and effectively make visible black presence and accomplishment in
the national culture. But they are no guarantors of progressive projects
for racial justice. Indeed, these representations of black people can just
as easily be used to support political projects that deny any specific
claim or warrant on the part of black folk to experiencing disproportionately the effects of social injustice, economic inequality, racism, and
so on. As state and national campaigns for "color blindness" and
against affirmative action indicate, black visibility is often the basis for
claims to racial equality, the elimination of social and economic injustice, and the arrival of the time for racial invisibility. So, liberals use
media representation of black achievement (rather than images of, say,
criminality) to persuade constituents of the importance of diversity,
while conservatives use the same representations to celebrate the virtues
of color blindness and individual achievement. This state of affairs
expresses the contested nature of representation, and shows why representation remains an important site of cultural politics.

I want to ponder this question now because I want to trouble the
investment, overinvestment really, on the part of African American cultural producers, media activists, and scholars in representation as "the"
productive site of cultural politics. This overinvestment animates my
generally hopeful assessment, in chapter 1, of an ascendant black cultural formation and its purported impact on the American national
identity and imagination. There, I measured the political impact and
social meaning of the cultural moves, first against histories of black
exclusion, denial, and invisibility by American cultural institutions, and
second in terms of new possibilities for black cultural production that
get us beyond strategies of securing institutional and representational
spaces and defending black rights to be in those spaces.

In chapter 1 I pointed to theater, cinema, literature, and African American studies as examples of cultural strategies in which securing space
ensured black cultural recognition and legitimacy. Specifically, Wynton
Marsalis and the Lincoln Center jazz program provided an example of
how a canonical project could be used strategically to install jazz as a

form of black expressive culture in one of the nation's dominant cultural institutions. As I suggest throughout the chapter, there are other notable instances in which the strategic move to establish institutional space produced effective results. In a twenty-year period (1980–2000), canon makers in jazz, African American literature, cinema, theater, and African American studies enjoyed some success in canonizing and then installing programs in key public and national organizations. For example, although they converge in their formulations (owing to a network of experts and cultural advocates), organizations like Lincoln Center for the Performing Arts, the Smithsonian Institution, and public television recognize "specific" notions of jazz, ensuring their version of the music a place in the public imagination. With a stellar record of black cultural achievement in the United States, black folk have worked tirelessly to construct, advocate, install, and secure black influences in America's national cultural institutions.

No doubt, these efforts represent important struggles over representation. With important interventions into the debates and polemics about the relationship among culture, identity, history, politics, and representation in what we have come to understand as the cultural politics of representation, the discourse of black cultural politics shifted rather decisively and, in my view, productively away from preoccupations with positive and negative images, questions of representational accuracy, stereotypic exaggeration, and the bounded conceptions of the nation. Black-diaspora critics and audiences knew better and were more sophisticated. Within America and beyond, black representations from hip-hop to cinema were no longer preoccupied with neutralizing or escaping the controlling and judging gaze of whites. Conversations, references, historical memories, and cultural practices were at once too local and too widely dispersed to worry about what whites in America thought.

The crucial work of displacing the narrow framework of reversals or positive/negative images was occasioned by cultural and historical developments in critical race discourse, cinema, globalization, and culture. Prompted by analytic shifts occasioned by the use of critical concepts like diaspora and hybridity; the poetics of place; critiques of nationalism, the nation, and the state as objects of political struggle and social movements; and the circulation of black representation across new configurations of territory and space, preoccupations with positive and negative representations in television, cinema, and the arts seemed excessively local, protectionist, and exclusive. The politics of representation necessarily required an analytic and political shift to registers sensitive enough to detect and grapple with black similarity *and* difference(s), local *and* national concerns, popular *and* expert knowledge.

Effectively inscribed in the approach to cultural analysis and politics, the cultural politics of difference and representation helped to illuminate the limits of nationalism, racial and gender essentialism, and different claims on identity rooted in isolation, disconnection, and uniqueness, rather than new social relations and connections that are enabled by the new technical means of representation, articulation, and circulation. Cultural politics were so much more complicated than questions of positive and negative images.

Along with thinking differently about categories like race, gender, sexuality, identity, and nation, I believe that representation is now fair game for critical interrogation. That is, representation itself should be critically scrutinized, especially when it is coupled with critiques of *cultural politics* (as appeals to state and corporate power, correct and accurate representation, and some appropriate number of representations) and *the nation* (as a racially pluralistic, bounded, stable, geo-political entity whose legitimacy is secured through representations of the nation as family, land, and tradition). In this formulation of the cultural politics of representation, proliferations of black representations of the sort that I indicated at the beginning of this chapter help to reinforce existing ideas and relations of power that organize the nation rather than disturb or critque them.

My desire is less for an end to the politics of representation than the search for a different logic of representation and politics that imagines and represents forms of belonging, association, and practice capable of accounting for multiple and shifting notions of connectivity and identifications. Instead of merely affirming already complete or finished notions of black subjects, points of connection, and sites of circulation, in *Cultural Moves* I show how the practices, countermemories and alternative imaginations of a range of black cultural producers contest such notions and can serve as the basis of imagining different possibilities for constructing notions of black subjects and their relation to dominant conceptions of nation, community, and belonging.

That is, I believe that we need to critically scrutinize cultural projects like continuing struggles for cultural visibility, recognition, and inclusion in the national media, especially commercial "network" television.

Politically and historically, my argument is that the cultural politics of recognition rooted in the presumed discursive stability of black cultural representation, which relies on the continuing salience of mod-

ernist regimes of race and visibility, has given way to new cultural logics and technologies. We are approaching the limit of cultural politics
that aim primarily for cultural visibility and institutional recognition.
Prompted by the new information technologies, developments in genetic
engineering, the centrality of commercial popular culture, and its relationship to different global projects and enactments of new cultural politics of difference, we face the need for a different kind of cultural politics. As important to these circumstances are debates in black arts and
letters about blackness as a cultural discourse, exchanges in the social
sciences and policy circles about the actual social conditions of black
people, and conversations in technology and media studies about the
global circulation of information (including new storage, representational, networking capacities). This book asks whether or not identity
and representation remain productive sites of struggle, sources of critique, and affirmation. We know that quests for identity and representation can ensure a measure of recognition in the national culture, but
can such quests continue to ensure the measure of black cultural authority and legitimacy necessary to effectively challenge the order of things?

The intersection of black cultural politics, music, and new information technologies is, I believe, one of the cultural arenas where black cultural practice and cultural politics has most productively challenged and
moved beyond cultural politics of representation based almost entirely
on identity, recognition, and visibility. As I've shown, black composers
and performers are engaged in some of the most innovative cultural
practices in art and technology, and many do so with the aim of imagining subjects differently, imagining blackness differently, and using
blackness as the basis for imagining technology differently.

The chapters on art, television, and cultural politics of difference
focused on practices that critique preoccupations with recognition, representativeness, and black chauvinism. These chapters looked simultaneously outward and inward—out toward media studies and cultural
studies to show how these discourses productively grapple with difference, its impact, burdens, and responsibility, and possibility as these
concern black cultural practices; and inward to critique the orthodoxies
and strains of African American studies, nationalism, and black cultural
politics that manage and regulate the unruliness of media, new aesthetic
possibilities, and different generational visions. The artwork of Kara
Walker, the film documentaries of Marlon Riggs, Isaac Julian, and
Thomas Allen Harris, Clyde Taylor's critical study of aesthetics, and the
music of experimentalists and the jazz left announce but move beyond

the limited formulations of the role of visual culture, commercial culture, and media cultures in black politics of representation.

Artists and critics like Steve Coleman and George Lewis hold strong views about the state of black music and culture. In their work, these artists struggle to make a living room, as Abbey Lincoln says it, for new black imaginations. For a generation of fine artists and filmmakers, composers, musicians, and cultural critics, getting beyond black identities forged in injury, shame, and nationalist projects that limit the expression and possibility of blackness is of paramount importance. For others, like the programmers, code breakers, and data thieves who call themselves Afrofuturists, renegotiating and rethinking the terms of visibility, institutional status, and legitimation are required so that new futures might be conjured and imagined.

In *The History of Bourgeois Perception*, Donald Lowe is concerned with social and cultural technologies and their role in structuring perception (especially in relationship to the senses.[1] He writes, "The communication media in each period . . . emphasize different senses or combinations of them, to support a different hierarchical organization of sensing. And changes in the culture of communications media ultimately leads to changes in the hierarchy of sensing."[2] For my purposes, this formulation is helpful for thinking about black cultural visibility and institutional recognition, and the shifting historical, theoretical, and technological conditions that I have been describing.

Donald Lowe's appreciation of a different hierarchy of sensing, one which accompanies shifts in media, is suggestive, for my argument, about the limits of struggles for cultural representation that aim largely to install and protect identities. There is no doubt but that cultural politics that aim to ensure visibility and secure recognition are powerful (and necessary) responses to centuries of exclusion and abjection directed at blacks. But in shifting conditions of global, technological, and cultural transformations, they are also limited. Limited, that is, because the conditions of possibility—the cultural politics of difference, diaspora as a category of identity, globalization—that gave rise to struggles over representation have shifted, with new forms of global networking and connectivity, digitality, and information storage and retrieval. Though pitched partly as a clever marketing strategy, I think that Thelma Goldman's attempts to query the critical status of the cultural politics of blackness, based on the hegemony and coherence of black representation and recognition, is suggestive.[3]

A similarly productive strategy for locating the edges of the politics of representation is in play in the work of the jazz left: George Lewis (whose queries are as much about the presumed primacy of whiteness and its epistemological status owing to vision as they are about blackness); Kara Walker (whose queries go to the presumed black ownership and therefore protectionisms around slavery); and Pamela Z (whose work manages to incorporate vision into experimental music, while moving beyond a politics of representation by differently combining sound, bodies, gender, performance, and vision). The work of these artists unsettles the conventional commitment to cultural politics aimed at securing institutional space and visibility in mainstream cultural institutions. As we've seen in the case of the jazz left, musicians also engage in activities devoted to education, cultivating new audiences, and extending the tradition; they simply take place in commercial circuits and so-called popular social spaces that are largely invisible and of less value to cultural critics, gate keepers, and canon makers in dominant cultural institutions. By necessity these artists on the jazz left have had to cultivate new strategies and approaches to their practice. In other words, by making black abjection, assumptions about visibility, and sameness the critical locus of new practices, critiques, and imagination Kara Walker, Steve Coleman, George Lewis, the Afrofuturists, Thelma Goldman, Greg Tate, Paul Miller, and Pamela Z (among so many others) force a reckoning with the limits of cultural moves tethered to modern desires and politics.

These examples indicate some of the terms and contours where significant shifts in cultural politics are occurring. The examples suggest that as important as identity rooted in visibility and recognition is, these terms are no longer the primary basis upon which selves—black and otherwise—can be legally, culturally, and social constituted. This is not to say that they are no longer important or salient, but to suggest that we have reached the limits of such formulations and the politics that aim to secure, install, and protect these particular notions of self, nation, and community.

That we have reached the limit of a perception of black selves and black cultural politics organized around a monolithic, coherent, visible identity and conception of blackness is the chief basis of an argument for rethinking television, and especially the actual and imagined space of the networks, as the primary site of struggles for black visibility and recognition. Since it helps to constitute and circulate the representation and meaning of the nation, television in many ways is the perfect medium for black petitions for redress and recognition. Issues of recognition and visibility (and periodically difference and diversity) are central to television's very reason for being, so it remains a major cultural and social place where the entanglements of identity, race, nation, belonging, and recognition are played out.[4]

I want to jettison the implicit assumption that television, especially the network, is the premier site in which the nation is constituted and reflected. I take issue most with the politics of media activism driven by the seasonal inventory of black representation and the assumptions about recognition, visibility, and the nation on which it rests. Again, prompted by the example of George Lewis, I propose that we look critically at these political and cultural assumptions, the desires on which they are built, and the practices they produce. I want to advocate for more critical scholarship to query the production and salience of these presumed sites of black cultural politics, the forms of activity (and activism), and the structural conditions that shape the relationship between the television apparatus, the nation, blackness, and representation.

It is extremely difficult to demonstrate that we are at the limits of cultural politics of a certain sort in the face of race and ethnicity as a continuing source of abjection, marginalization, and oppression throughout the world. Historically, America's national culture has been grudgingly receptive to black visibility, while it has embraced, mimicked, even celebrated black soundings. Black cultural productions, as it were, proliferated in sound while certain forms and expressions of black visibility, especially in media and communication, remained confined and undeveloped. Because of such sobering reminders, the cultural (and I think political) significance of examples like those offered by Kara Walker, Steve Coleman, members of the jazz left, George Lewis, Pamela Z, and the Afrofuturists are very much worth considering for the ways that they show us how to go on, how to think differently, and how do cultural politics differently.

In *Cultural Moves* I have tried to think seriously about the kinds of cultural politics that have proved to be productive, lasting, and significant for contemporary life, while I have explored the limits of these politics, especially for what these limits tell us about contemporary black cultural and intellectual life in the context of a new hierarchy of the senses. Recognizing these limits, I have been in search for a way of moving beyond the constraints of existing commitments, formulations, and practices of cultural politics. By looking to alternative spaces and different practices and historical encounters (e.g., popular music, the interface with new technologies, and cultural discourses of blackness), we have only just begun to scratch the surface, to identify paths that might be pursued to think black cultural politics differently. Think them differently, that is, in the terms that recognize and appreciate the sensibilities and necessities ushered in by this shift in the hierarchy of the senses and the media through which those senses and our politics are structured and practiced. These are the reasons for my focus in the last section of the book on sight and sound, information and technology, identity and politics.

The artists, critics, and musicians I looked to in *Cultural Moves* have appreciated for some time now that we have exceeded the limits of cultural visibility and institutional recognition as the sole guarantor of black subjectivity and humanity. Pamela Z, George Lewis, Steve Coleman, and other experimentalists sonically represent and perform a new kind of perceptual capacity to imagine blackness. Together with the visual artists, they are changing the perceptual field in which blackness is understood and enacted.

# Notes

INTRODUCTION

1. For examples of such debates in the art world, see Holland Cotter, "Beyond Multiculturalism, Freedom?" *New York Times,* 29 July 2001; Michael Kimmelman, "A Black World of Ins and Outs," *New York Times,* 26 April 2002; Ian Parker, "Golden Touch," *New Yorker,* 14 January 2002, 44–49; Deborah Solomon, "The Downtowning of Uptown" *New York Times,* 19 August 2001.

2. Musical collectives like the Association for the Advancement of Creative Musicians, the Black Artist Group, and M-BASE are notable examples.

3. I accept the view that the meanings and significance of cultural representation are largely (though by no means exclusively) and actively produced in discourse (including aesthetic judgments about the veracity, quality, or value of a given representation or practice).

4. This movement of representations of blackness is of course animated by audience receptions that include desire and dread, veneration and loathing.

5. Eric Porter, *What Is This Thing Called Jazz? African American Musicians as Artists, Critics, and Activists* (Berkeley: University of California Press, 2002), is excellent on this point.

6. James Carey, "A Cultural Approach to Communication," in his *Culture as Communication: Essays on Media and Society* (Boston: Unwin Hyman, 1989), 13–36.

7. Frederic Jameson, *Postmodernism; or, The Cultural Logic of Late Capitalism* (Durham, N.C.: Duke University Press, 1991).

8. Tommy Lott, "Kara Walker Speaks: A Public Conversation on Racism, Art, and Politics with Tommy Lott," *Black Renaissance* 3, no. 1 (Fall 2000): 69–91.

9. See Cotter, "Beyond Multiculturalism, Freedom?"; Kimmelman, "A Black World"; Parker, "Golden Touch"; Solomon, "The Downtowning of Uptown."

10. Tamar Jacoby, "Adjust Your Sets," *New Republic*, 24 January 2000, www.tnr.com/archive/012400/jacoby012400.html (accessed 21 June 2001); and Tamar Jacoby, "Color Blind: The African American Absence in High Tech," *New Republic*, 29 March 1999, www.tnr.com/archive/0399/032999/jacoby032999.html (accessed 21 June 2001).

11. Jacoby, "Adjust Your Sets."

12. Robert W. McChesney, *Rich Media, Poor Democracy: Communication Politics in Dubious Times* (New York: New Press, 1999); Dan Schiller, *Digital Capitalism: Networking the Global Market System* (Cambridge, Mass.: MIT Press, 2000); Kevin Robins and Frank Webster, *The Times of the Technoculture: From the Information Society to the Virtual Life* (New York: Routledge, 1999).

13. Andrew Ross, *Real Love: In Pursuit of Cultural Justice* (New York: New York University Press, 1998).

14. Schiller, *Digital Capitalism;* Robins and Webster, *Times of the Technoculture.*

## CHAPTER 1. THE NEW CONDITIONS OF
## BLACK CULTURAL PRODUCTION

1. Raymond Williams, *The Sociology of Culture* (New York: Schocken Books, 1982).

2. Among the most contentious issues surrounding the exhibition were the representations of black masculinity, the appointment of Thelma Goldman as the show's curator, her selection of participating artists, its corporate underwriting, and its staging by a nationally recognized arts institution like the Whitney Museum.

3. Richard Powell, *Black Art and Culture in the 20th Century* (New York: Thames and Hudson, 1997); Clyde Taylor *The Mask of Art: Breaking the Aesthetic Contract* (Bloomington: Indiana University Press, 1998).

4. Stuart Hall, "New Ethnicities," in *Stuart Hall: Critical Dialogues in Cultural Studies,* ed. David Morley and Kuan-Hsing Chen (New York: Routledge, 1989), 441–50; Brian Phillip Harper, *Are We Not Men? Masculine Anxiety and the Problem of African-American Identity* (Oxford: Oxford University Press, 1996); Kobena Mercer, *Welcome to the Jungle: New Positions in Black Cultural Politics* (London: Routledge, 1994).

5. Paul Gilroy, *The Black Atlantic: Modernity and Double Consciousness* (Cambridge, Mass.: Harvard University Press, 1993).

6. Ibid.; George Lipsitz, *Dangerous Crossroads: Popular Music, Postmodernism, and the Poetics of Place* (London: Verso, 1994).

7. Dick Hebdige, *Cut 'n' Mix: Culture, Identity, and Caribbean Music* (London: Methuen, 1987).

8. Edward Guerrero, *Framing Blackness: The African American Image in Film* (Philadelphia: Temple University Press, 1993); S. Craig Watkins, *Representing: Hip-Hop Culture and the Production of Black Cinema* (Chicago: University of Chicago Press, 1998).

9. And such contributions are celebrated and legitimated through commendations like the awarding of the 1993 Nobel Prize in literature to Toni Morrison and the publication (under the general editorship of Henry Louis Gates, Jr.) of the *Norton Anthology of African American Literature* (1997).

10. George Wolf's tenure at the Public Theater, Wynton Marsalis's leadership of the jazz program at Lincoln Center, and Henry Louis Gates, Jr.'s, appointment to revive the Department of African and African American Studies at Harvard University are only three of the most visible and controversial examples.

11. Michael Denning, *The Cultural Front: The Laboring of American Culture in the Twentieth Century* (London: Verso, 1997).

12. Ibid.

13. The concept of cultural formation is anticipated by if not applicable to two earlier historical moments: the Harlem Renaissance in the 1920s and the Black Arts Movement in the 1960s. Harold Cruse's important book *The Crisis of the Negro Intellectual* (New York: Morrow, 1967) offers a negative, but no less critical, example of why these recent cultural moves might be productively characterized by a term like cultural formation. Indeed, for Cruse the failure of the Harlem Renaissance as a cultural movement was the absence of a viable institutional and economic infrastructure (to defend the interests of black artists and intellectuals and that might serve as the basis to seize and hold institutional space). Accordingly there was too little organizational stability, institutional legitimacy, and economic autonomy with which to shield these movements from the predictable shifts of interests, economic support, and connection to material experiences of working-class blacks. Unable to sustain themselves financially, to maintain autonomy socially, and to root themselves in the day-to-day experiences of those for whom they sought to speak and represent, according to Cruse these moments of cultural possibility simply withered.

14. Richard Merelman, *Representing Black Culture: Racial Conflict and Cultural Politics in the United States* (New York: Routledge, 1995).

15. Robin D. G. Kelley, *Yo Mama's Disfunktional! Fighting the Culture Wars in Urban America* (Boston: Beacon Press, 1997).

16. Herman Gray, *Watching Race: Television and the Struggle for Blackness* (Minneapolis: University of Minnesota Press, 1995).

17. Angela D. Dillard, "Multicultural Conservativism: What It Is, Why It Matters," *Chronicle of Higher Education*, 2 March 2001, B7–10.

18. Darnell Hunt, *O.J.: Fact and Fiction* (Cambridge: Cambridge University Press, 1999).

19. Watkins, *Representing.*

20. Ibid.

21. Stuart Hall, "What Is This 'Black' in Black Popular Culture?" in *Black Popular Culture: A Project by Michele Wallace*, ed. Gina Dent, 21–37 (Seattle: Bay Press, 1992).

22. John T. Caldwell, "Televisual Politics: Negotiating Race in the L.A. Rebellion," in *Living Color: Race and Television in the United States*, ed. Sasha Torres, 161–95 (Durham, N.C.: Duke University Press, 1998); John Fiske, *Media Matters: Everyday Culture and Political Change* (Minneapolis: Univer-

sity of Minnesota Press, 1994); Dick Hebdige, *Hiding in the Light: On Images and Things* (London: Routledge, 1998).

23. Mike Davis, *City of Quartz: Excavating the Future in Los Angeles* (London: Verso, 1992).

24. Jimmie Reeves and Richard Campbell, *Cracked Coverage: Television News, the Anti-Cocaine Crusade, and the Reagan Legacy* (Durham, N.C.: Duke University Press, 1994); Gray, *Watching Race*; Kelley, *Yo Mama's Disfunktional*; Watkins, *Representing*.

25. Judith Stacey, *Rethinking Family Values: In the Name of the Family* (New York: Beacon Press, 1996); Harper, *Are We Not Men?*

26. Roderick Ferguson, *Aberrations in Black: Toward a Queer of Color Critique* (Minneapolis: University of Minnesota Press, 2003).

27. Ibid.

28. Cornel West, one of the members of Harvard's celebrated dream team, was involved in a dispute with Harvard University president Lawrence Sommers over West's research and political activity. The dispute eventually led to the breakup of the academic dream team at Harvard, when West accepted a faculty position at Princeton University. While it has not has created the same reverberations at Lincoln Center, Marsalis ended his long association with Columbia Records. For more, see David Hajdu, "Wynton's Blues," *Atlantic Monthly*, March 2003, 43–58.

29. Michael Berube, "Public Academy," *New Yorker*, 9 January 1995, 73–80.

30. For a somewhat more critical discussion of the emerging new black intellectuals, see Adolph Reed, "What Are the Drums Saying, Booker? The Current Crisis of the Black Intellectual," *Village Voice*, 11 April 1995, 35.

31. Jack E. White, "The Beauty of Black Art," *Time*, October 10, 1994, 66

32. Throughout much of the 1990s neoconservatives developed and sustained a strong ideological, political, and intellectual presence in public discourse and the media. Through talk radio, television talk shows, think tanks, and private foundations the neoconservative ideologues flooded the public imagination with their particular brand of ideas. This culminated of course in the explicit branding of Fox News as the ideological mouthpiece of the neoconservative cause.

33. Anne du Cille, *Skin Trade* (Cambridge, Mass.: Harvard University Press, 1996).

34. Paul Gilroy, "After the Love Has Gone: Bio-Politics and Etho-Politics in the Black Public Sphere," *Public Culture* 7, no. 1 (1994): 49–77.

35. Cornell West articulates a similar view of the dangers of market values and cautions about the dangers of black popular culture defined solely in terms of these values; Cornel West, *Race Matters* (Boston: Beacon Press, 1993).

36. Avery Gordon, *Ghostly Matters: Haunting and the Sociological Imagination* (Minneapolis: University of Minnesota Press, 1997).

37. Gilroy, *The Black Atlantic*.

38. Lipsitz, *Dangerous Crossroads*.

CHAPTER 2. JAZZ TRADITION, INSTITUTIONAL FORMATION, AND
CULTURAL PRACTICE

My thanks to the following friends, colleagues, and students who generously
encouraged, read, and commented on various drafts of this chapter: Dwight
Andrews, Leonard Brown, Russell Ellis, Stephen Feld, Janet Francendese, Rosa
Linda Fregoso, Lisa Guererro, Saidiya Hartman, Robin D. G. Kelley, Elizabeth
Long, Tommy Lott, Bill Lowe, Ronald Redono, David Scott, Sterling Stuckey,
Lisa Thompson, Robert Thompson, David Wellman, Deborah Woo, and
Richard Yarborough. Special thanks also to my research assistant, Cindy Lui,
who helped me track down press accounts of Marsalis and the Lincoln Center
program.

1. On these and similar themes, see Bernard Gendron, "Moldy Figs and
Modernists: Jazz at War (1942–46)," in *Jazz among the Discourses*, ed. Krin
Gabbard (Durham, N.C.: Duke University Press, 1995) 31–57; Steven Elworth,
"Jazz in Crisis, 1948–1958: Ideology and Representation," in *Jazz among the
Discourses*, ed. Krin Gabbard (Durham, N.C.: Duke University Press, 1995),
57–76.

2. "Jazz: A Special Section," *New York Times Magazine*, 25 June 1995,
29–40; Gene Santoro, "All That Jazz," *Nation*, 8 January 1996, 34–36; Peter
Watrous, "Old Jazz Is Out, New Jazz Is Older," *New York Times*, 31 March
1994; Linda Williams, "A Young Musician Trumpets a Revival of Traditional
Jazz," *Wall Street Journal*, 24 September 1986.

3. Richard Guilliatt, "The Young Lions Roar," *Los Angeles Times*, 13 September 1992.

4. Jervis Anderson, "Medium Cool," *New Yorker*, 12 December 1994,
69–83; Richard Guilliat, "Eminence Jazz," *San Jose Mercury News*, 11 June
1993; "Jazz: A Special Section," *New York Times Magazine*; Gene Santoro,
"Young Man with a Horn," *Nation*, 1 March 1993, 280–84; Williams, "A
Young Musician."

5. Alex Ross, "Asking Some Good, Hard Truths about Music," *New York
Times*, 12 November 1995.

6. For more recent developments in Marsalis's career see, David Hajdu,
"Wynton's Blues," *Atlantic Monthly*, March 2003, 43–58.

7. Other notable examples of the effective use of similar strategies in important cultural sites include highly visible figures in theater, film, and African
American studies.

8. Frank Conroy, "Stop Nit Picking a Genius," *New York Times Magazine*,
25 June 1995, 28–31, 48, 54, 70; Wynton Marsalis, "What Jazz Is—and Isn't,"
editorial, *New York Times*, 31 July 1988; Wynton Marsalis, *Sweet Swing Blues
on the Road* (New York: W. W. Norton, 1994).

9. Tony Scherman, "What Is Jazz?" *American Heritage*, October 1995,
66 ff.

10. Ibid.

11. Ibid.

12. Ibid.; quotations are from various places in the article.

13. Ibid.

14. Ibid.; my emphasis.

15. Marsalis, "What Jazz Is," 24.

16. Marsalis, *Sweet Swing Blues on the Road,* 141.

17. Marsalis, "What Jazz Is" and *Sweet Swing Blues on the Road.*

18. Scherman, "What Is Jazz?" 66 ff.

19. Quoted in Williams, "A Young Musician," 1.

20. James A. Liska, "Wynton and Branford: A Common Understanding," *Down Beat,* February 1994, 42 ff.; my emphasis.

21. Ibid.; my emphasis.

22. Marsalis, "What Jazz Is," 21; my emphasis.

23. Ibid.; my emphasis.

24. Ibid.; my emphasis.

25. Ibid.

26. Williams, "A Young Musician," 1.

27. Ibid.; my emphasis.

28. Marsalis, "What Jazz Is," 21.

29. Stanley Crouch is an essayist and jazz critic and Albert Murray is a novelist, biographer, and jazz writer.

30. Terry Treachout, "The Color of Jazz," *Commentary,* September 1995, 50 ff.; my emphasis.

31. Ibid.; Crouch serves as artistic advisor to Marsalis in the jazz program at Lincoln Center.

32. Ibid.; my emphasis.

33. Ibid.; my emphasis.

34. Scherman, "What Is Jazz?" 66 ff.; my emphasis.

35. Marsalis, *Sweet Swing Blues on the Road,* 142–43.

36. Watrous, "Old Jazz Is Out," C11.

37. Marsalis, "What Jazz Is," 24; my emphasis.

38. For more on this, see Santoro, "All That Jazz," 34; Ross, "Asking Some Good, Hard Truths," J3; Watrous, "Old Jazz Is Out."

39. See Santoro, "All That Jazz"; Peter Watrous, "Is There a Mid-Life Crisis at the JVC Festival?" *New York Times,* Arts and Leisure Section, 8 July 1995, 13.

40. Santoro, "All That Jazz."

41. Ibid.; Starbucks also owns a West Coast chain of upscale music retailers, Hear Music.

42. Williams, "A Young Musician."

43. George Lipsitz, *Dangerous Crossroads: Popular Music, Postmodernism, and the Poetics of Place* (London: Verso, 1994); Santoro, "All That Jazz."

44. See Krin Gabbard, ed., *Jazz among the Discourses* (Durham, N.C.: Duke University Press, 1995); Santoro, "All That Jazz."

45. For example, Nathaniel Mackey, "Other: From Noun to Verb," in *Jazz among the Discourses,* ed. Krin Gabbard (Durham, N.C.: Duke University Press, 1995), 76–100; Santoro, "Young Man with a Horn"; Watrous, "Old Jazz Is Out."

46. Mackey, "Other: From Noun to Verb."

47. Patrick Brantlinger, *Bread and Circuses: Theories of Mass Culture and Social Decay* (Ithaca, N.Y.: Cornell University Press, 1983); Max Horkheimer and Theodor Adorno, "The Culture Industry: Enlightenment as Mass Deception," in *Dialectic of Enlightenment*, ed. Max Horkheimer and Theodor Adorno, trans. John Cumming (New York: Seabury Press, 1944; reprint, 1972), 120–67.

48. For more on how these operations work in jazz and rock, see Santoro, "All That Jazz"; Williams, "A Young Musician"; Robert Wasler, *Running with the Devil: Power, Gender, and Madness in Heavy Metal Music* (Hanover, N.H.: University Press of New England, 1993).

49. Robin D. G. Kelley, "The Riddle of the Zoot Suit: Malcolm Little and Black Cultural Politics during World War II," in *Race Rebels: Culture, Politics, and the Black Working Class*, ed. Robin D. G. Kelley (New York: Free Press, 1994), 35–55.

50. Mackey, "Other: From Noun to Verb."

51. Krin Gabbard, "Ken Burns's 'Jazz': Beautiful Music, but Missing a Beat," *Chronicle of Higher Education*, 15 December 2000, B18–19; see also Ben Ratliff, "Fixing, for Now, the Image of Jazz," *New York Times*, 7 January 2001, sec. 2, 32–33; and "A Roundtable on Ken Burns's *Jazz*," moderated by Geoffrey Jacques, *Journal of Popular Music Studies* 13, no. 2 (Fall 2001): 207–27.

52. See Gabbard, *Jazz among the Discourses.*

CHAPTER 3. THE JAZZ LEFT

1. Craig LaBan, "The Whole History of Jazz, according to Lincoln Center," master's thesis, Columbia School of Journalism, 1994; Eric Porter, *What Is This Thing Called Jazz? African American Musicians as Artists, Critics, and Activists* (Berkeley: University of California Press, 2002); George Lewis, "Experimental Music in Black and White: The AACM in New York, 1970–1985," *Current Musicology* 71–73 (Spring 2001–2): 100–158; see also chapter 1 in this volume; Don Byron, quoted in interview with Josh Kun, photocopy possessed by author; see also, Peter Watrous, "Remember Mickey Katz? No? Well, Just Listen to This," *New York Times*, 19 January 1990, C1, C24; and Jeremy Wolff, "A 'Cat' from the Bronx Makes His Mark on Klezmer," *Wall Street Journal*, 19 September 1991, A12.

2. George Lewis, for example, insists that the genre category "jazz" is much too narrow and limiting a description of the contemporary practices of black creative music. For Lewis jazz continues to enforce and limit the aesthetic and creative boundaries available to black musicians; Lewis, "Experimental Music in Black and White."

3. In his account of the history of the Association for the Advancement of Creative Musicians, George Lewis is especially attentive to the discursive practices and affects of journalists and critics. See Lewis, "Experimental Music in Black and White."

4. Scott DeVeaux, *The Birth of Bebop: A Social and Musical History* (Berkeley: University of California Press, 1997); Preston Love, *A Thousand Honey*

*Creeks Later: My Life in Music from Basie to Motown and Beyond* (Hanover, N.H.: University Press of New England, 1997); Robert Gordon, *Can't Be Satisfied: The Life and Times of Muddy Waters* (Boston: Little, Brown, 2002); Horace Tapscott, *Songs of the Unsung: The Musical and Social Journey of Horace Tapscott*, ed. Steven Isoardi (Durham, N.C.: Duke University Press, 2001); Fred Wesley, *Hit Me, Fred: Recollections of a Sideman* (Durham, N.C.: Duke University Press, 2002); Count Basie and Albert Murray, *Good Morning Blues: The Autobiography of Count Basie* (New York: Da Capo Press, 1985; reprint, 1995); Sherrie Tucker, *Swing Shift: "All Girl" Bands of the 1940s* (Durham, N.C.: Duke University Press, 2000); Quincy Jones, *Q: The Autobiography of Quincy Jones* (New York: Doubleday, 2001).

5. Robin D. G. Kelley, "We Are Not What We Seem: The Politics and Pleasures of Community," in *Race Rebels: Culture, Politics, and the Black Working Class*, ed. Robin D. G. Kelley (New York: Free Press, 1994), 161–83; and "The Riddle of the Zoot Suit: Malcolm Little and Black Cultural Politics during World War II," in *Race Rebels: Culture, Politics, and the Black Working Class*, ed. Robin D. G. Kelley (New York: Free Press, 1994), 35–55; Love, *Thousand Honey Creeks Later*; Duke Ellington, *Music Is My Mistress* (New York: Da Capo Press, 1973); Albert Murray, *Stomping The Blues* (New York: McGraw-Hill, 1976).

6. Porter, *What Is This Thing Called Jazz?*; John F. Szwed, *Space Is the Place: The Lives and Times of Sun Ra* (New York: Pantheon Books, 1997); Tommy Lee Lott, "The 1960s Avant-Garde Movement in Jazz," *Social Identities* 7, no. 2 (2001): 1–11; Tapscott, *Songs of the Unsung*; Lewis, "Experimental Music in Black and White"; Ronald Radano, *New Musical Figuration: Anthony Braxton's Cultural Critique* (Chicago: University of Chicago Press, 1993).

7. For more on these specific ideas, see Krin Gabbard, ed., *Jazz among the Discourses* (Durham, N.C.: Duke University Press, 1995); Lewis, "Experimental Music in Black and White"; Tapscott, *Songs of the Unsung*.

8. For more about the impact of rules and procedure on artworks, see Howard Becker, *Art Worlds* (Berkeley: University of California Press, 1982); Paul Lopes, *The Rise of a Jazz Art World* (Cambridge: Cambridge University Press, 2002).

9. Trumpeter Lester Bowie suggests that the relationship between jazz and the popular music of his formative period was very much the same as those of his mentors and those who came before him. In other words popular music has always been an important source in the standard jazz repertoire. Quoted in LeBan, "The Whole History of Jazz."

10. The question of ownership and representation is one of the central tensions characterizing much of the press coverage about the (controversial) Lincoln Center program and the Ken Burns documentary for PBS.

11. See, for example, Diana Crane, ed. *The Sociology of Culture: Emerging Theoretical Perspectives*, (Oxford: Blackwell Publishers, 1994), including the introduction; Lopes, *The Rise of a Jazz Art World*.

12. A middle generation of musicians is very important to the jazz left. Among these I would include David Murray, Julius Hemphill, Leroy Jenkins, Henry Threadgill. Many of this generation of musicians were formed in the con-

text of musical collectives in the 1960s and 1970s in organizations like Black Artist Group (BAG) in St. Louis and the Association for the Advancement of Creative Musicians (AACM) in Chicago. George Lipsitz, "Like a Weed in a Vacant Lot: The Black Artist Group in St. Louis," in *Decomposition: Post Disciplinary Performance*, ed. Sue-Ellen Case, P. Brett, and S. L. Foster (Bloomington: Indiana University Press, 2000), 51–61.

13. Kevin Fellez, "Between Rock and a Jazz Place: Intercultural Interchange in Fusion Musicking" (Ph.D. diss., History of Consciousness Program, University of California, Santa Cruz, 2004).

14. George Lewis, "Improvised Music after 1950: Afrological and Eurological Perspectives," *Black Music Research Journal* 16 (1996): 91–122.

15. Steve Dollar, "The Lightening Rod." *Down Beat*, February 1996, 26.

16. Ibid.

17. John Litweiler, "Thank You! Ornette!" *Down Beat*, January 1992, 31.

18. For more on Harmolodics, Inc., see Vivien Goldman, "Harmolodic Harlem," *Village Voice*, 3 September 1996, 41, 44.

19. Gene Santoro, "Dancing in Your Head," *Nation*, 12 August 1991, 199 ff.

20. Ibid.

21. Ibid.

22. Robert Walser, "Deep Jazz: Notes on Interiority, Race and Criticism," in *Inventing the Psychological: Toward a Cultural History of Emotional Life in America*, ed. Joel Pfister and Nancy Schnog (New Haven, Conn.: Yale University Press, 1997), 271–96.

23. For more on the AACM, see Porter, *What Is This Thing Called Jazz?* and Lewis, "Experimental Music in Black and White."

24. As I noted earlier this political, organizational, and cultural approach or project to was also practiced with great effect in Los Angeles with Horace Tapscott, St. Louis with BAG, Greenwich Village with RivBea Studios with Sam Rivers. Indeed, I would contend that one of the structural conditions of possibility that made such locally based organizational experiments possible was the presence of committee high school bands and band teachers who remained connected to local communities and trained successive generations of aspiring musicians. In addition to places like Kansas City, Detroit, and Chicago (DuSable High School), some of these formidable teachers are located in places like Washington, D.C., Houston, New Orleans, and Berkeley, among others.

25. John Corbett, "Early AE(C)," *Down Beat*, June 1994, 49; Lewis, "Experimental Music in Black and White."

26. Lott, "The 1960s Avant-Garde Movement in Jazz"; Lewis, "Experimental Music in Black and White"; Porter, *What Is This Thing Called Jazz?*

27. I would note in this respect that it is more than a bit ironic, how the concept of tradition functions rather more rigidly and fixedly in the context of the nationalist based politics of the period—notably black power and various incarnations of pan-Africanism. Musically of course, for many of the musicians and culture workers, the concept of tradition as fixed and unerring is rather more limiting and conservative.

28. For more on the avant-garde, see Lott, "The 1960s Avant-Garde Movement in Jazz"; Porter, *What Is This Thing Called Jazz?*

29. John Corbett, "The Music's Still Happenin'," *Down Beat,* December 1990, 61, 66.

30. Ibid.

31. Ibid.; see also Lewis, "Experimental Music in Black and White," and "Improvised Music after 1950."

32. Howard Mandel, "From Chicago, Deep in the Art of Jazz," *Washington Post,* 23 September 1984.

33. Robert Palmer, "20th Anniversary for an Unusual Jazz Ensemble," *New York Times,* 14 April 1985.

34. Quoted in Mandel, "From Chicago, Deep in the Art of Jazz," H12.

35. Quoted in ibid.

36. Quoted in ibid.

37. Litweiler, "Thank You! Ornette!" 31.

38. Quoted in Peter Watrous, "Brooklyn Academy Finds Room for Outsiders of Jazz," *New York Times,* 12 October 1995; my emphasis.

39. Ibid.; my emphasis.

40. Wynton Marsalis has been duly celebrated for a similar musical dexterity and mastery, having won Grammys in both the jazz and the classical categories as well as a Pulitzer Prize for composition.

41. Jeremy Wolff, "A 'Cat' from the Bronx Makes His Mark on Klezmer," *Wall Street Journal,* September 19, 1991, A12.

42. Ibid; Byron also includes running commentaries about the critics, the press, and racial discourse in his recorded work.

43. Politics are never far from Byron's music, expressed most directly in the titles of his compositions and recording sessions. In his music Byron has dealt with topics ranging from the Tuskegee Experiments and affirmative action to the marginalization of Jodi Al-Fyad, father of Princess Diana's boyfriend.

44. Don Byron, quoted in interview with Josh Kun, unpublished ms., n.d.

45. Errol T. Louis, "Jazz Makes a New Sound with Soul, Pop, and Computers; Brooklyn Musical Collective: Macro-Basic Array of Structured Extemporizations," *Smithsonian,* October 1989, 176; Lewis, "Experimental Music in Black and White."

46. Quoted in Kevin Whitehead, "Jazz Rebels: Lester Bowie and Greg Osby," *Down Beat,* August 1993, 17.

47. Ibid.; my emphasis.

48. Ibid.

49. Porter, *What Is This Thing Called Jazz?*

50. Whitehead, "Jazz Rebels," 20; my emphasis.

51. Louis, "Jazz Makes a New Sound," 176 ff.

52. This information is from the Coleman Web site, www.m-base.com, which contains essays, biographical information, discographies, and booking information.

53. Steve Coleman Web site (accessed 15 May 1998).

54. Ibid.

55. Interview with Vjay Iyer, M-BASE Web page; Vijay Iyer, "Steve Coleman, M-Base, and Musical Collectivism," M-Base Web site (accessed May 1998).

56. Ibid.

57. Most notable among these are Greg Osby and Cassandra Wilson.

58. At least one of these residencies was financially supported by the Lilla Wallace Reader's Digest Fund for Audience Development. Dan Ouellette, "Tree of Jazz Grown in Brooklyn Reaches Bay Area," *San Francisco Chronicle*, 27 July 1996; Ben Ratliff, "A Jazz Guerrilla Blows Back in, Spreading Ideas," *New York Times*, 18 August 2002.

59. Derk Richardson, "Outward Bound," *San Francisco Bay Guardian*, 4–10 September 1996; Ouellette, "Tree of Jazz." See Lewis, "Experimental Music in Black and White," on BAG and AACM; Lipsitz, "Like a Weed in a Vacant Lot," on BAG; Tapscott, *Songs of the Unsung*, on UGMAA in Los Angeles.

60. Richardson, "Outward Bound," 40.

61. Ibid.

62. Ibid.

63. For a comparison of the state of jazz at another New York cultural institution, Carnegie Hall, see Robin Pogrebin, "New Director at Carnegie Eliminates Its Jazz Band." *New York Times*, 17 January 2002.

64. See Lewis, "Experimental Music in Black and White," for a very useful discussion of the limits of black identities produced around the politics of strict boundaries and genres, and the role of the AACM in complicating notions of blackness.

65. With structural changes in the music business, especially with respect to touring, the tensions over the relationship of jazz to popular music, transformations in the racial patterns of consumption and the availability of black venues, it is perhaps doubly ironic that the road and the street continue to be sources of inspiration and new possibilities, even as the actual road and street become harder to negotiate as sources of work and sustained cultural practice.

66. For an interesting account of developments in Marsalis's own career see David Hajdu, "Wynton's Blues," *Atlantic Monthly*, March 2003, 43–58.

67. Porter, *What Is This Thing Called Jazz?*; Gabbard, *Jazz among the Discourses*; Nathaniel Mackey, "Other: From Noun to Verb," in Gabbard, *Jazz among the Discourses*; DeVeaux, *The Birth of Bebop*; Fellez, "Between Rock and a Jazz Place."

68. Tucker, *Swing Shift*; DeVeaux, *The Birth of Bebop*; Gabbard, *Jazz among the Discourses*; Porter, *What Is This Thing Called Jazz?*; Lewis, "Experimental Music in Black and White."

69. One could easily count as a measure of this mainstreaming the number of television commercials and programs as well as Hollywood films that use jazz for their sound tracks.

70. See, for example, Stuart Hall, "What Is This 'Black' in Black Popular Culture?" in *Black Popular Culture: A Project by Michele Wallace*, ed. Gina Dent (Seattle: Bay Press, 1992), 21–37.

## CHAPTER 4. WHERE HAVE ALL THE BLACK SHOWS GONE?

A different version of this chapter appeared as "Cultural Identity and American Television in the Post-Network, Post–Civil Rights Era," and was originally published as "Black Representation in the Post-Network, Post–Civil Rights World of Global Media," in *Ethnic Minorities and the Media: Changing Cultural Boundaries,* ed. Simon Cottle (Buckingham, Eng.: Open University Press, 2000).

1. Herman Gray, *Watching Race: Television and the Struggle for Blackness* (Minneapolis: University of Minnesota Press, 1995).

2. John T. Caldwell, "Convergence Television: Aggregating Form and Re-Purposing Content in the Culture of Conglomeration," in *Television after TV,* ed. Lynn Spigel (Durham, N.C.: Duke University Press, forthcoming).

3. Bambi L. Haggins, "Why 'Beulah' and 'Andy' Still Play Today: Minstrelsy in the New Millennium," *Emergences: Journal for the Study of Media and Composite Cultures* 11, no. 2 (2001): 189–99; Kristal Brent Zook, *Color by Fox: The Fox Network and the Revolution in Black Television* (New York: Oxford University Press, 1999).

4. Gray, *Watching Race*; S. Craig Watkins, *Representing: Hip-Hop Culture and the Production of Black Cinema* (Chicago: University of Chicago Press, 1998); Kristal Brent Zook, "How I Became the Prince of a Town Called Bel Air: Nationalist Desire in Black Television" (Ph.D. diss., University of California, Santa Cruz, 1994).

5. James Sterngold, "A Racial Divide Widens on Network TV," *New York Times,* 29 December 1998.

6. Burrough and Masters, "Cable Guys"; Byran Burrough and Kim Masters, "Hollywood's Fading Charms," *Economist,* 22 March 1997, 81–89.

7. Edmund L. Andrews, "Congress Votes to Reshape Communications Industry, Ending a Four-Year Struggle," *New York Times,* 2 February 1996.

8. Robert W. McChesney, *Rich Media, Poor Democracy: Communication Politics in Dubious Times* (New York: New Press, 1999).

9. Ibid.

10. Ken Auletta, "American Keiretsu," *New Yorker,* 20 October 1997, 225–28.

11. See Susan G. Davis, *Spectacular Nature: Corporate Culture and the Sea Experience* (Berkeley: University of California Press, 1997).

12. Auletta, "American Keiretsu."

13. It was evident as early as the spring of 1997 when the networks announced their fall season, the same season that I wrote the original draft of this chapter.

14. This is a telling observation, since by the 2001 season ABC began to enjoy considerable success with the Damon Wayans vehicle, *My Wife and Kids.* See Haggins, "Why 'Beulah' and 'Andy' Still Play Today,"

15. Victoria E. Johnson, "Welcome Home? CBS, PAX-TV and 'Heartland' Values in a Neo-Network Era," *The Velvet Light Trap: A Critical Journal of Film and Television* 46 (2000): 40–56; John T. Caldwell, *Televisuality: Style, Crisis, and Authority in American Television* (New Brunswick, N.J.: Rutgers University Press, 1995).

16. Rupert Murdock's Fox Network is the obvious example here.

17. Todd Gitlin, *Inside Prime Time* (New York: Pantheon Books, 1983); Johnson, "Welcome Home?"

18. The success of MTV's *The Osbournes* and reality failures like *The Chair* make the point about the volatility of this environment.

19. Bill Carter, "A Wiley Upstart That Did a Lot of Things Right," *New York Times Magazine,* 4 January 1998.

20. This skepticism is not specific to black-oriented television programming, but is true more generally of television programming regardless of genre, audience, or schedule. The force of this logic seems to impact black-oriented programming more directly, since there is so little programming to begin with and the shows that do make it to the network schedules are pressured to produce the requisite ratings in a very short time frame.

21. See George Lipsitz, *Dangerous Crossroads: Popular Music, Postmodernism, and the Poetics of Place* (London: Verso, 1994). Using hip-hop as the primary site for the production of a black public sphere, in a book that has generated more polemic than insight, Todd Boyd argues that, on matters of politics, style, and popular culture, the new black public sphere also represents a generational divide and expresses a profound rupture with the period of civil rights, which defined so much of black cultural and political identity. See Todd Boyd, *The New H.N.I.C. (Head Niggas in Charge): The Death of Civil Rights and the Reign of Hip-Hop* (New York: New York University Press, 2002).

22. Sterngold, "A Racial Divide."

23. Though the range of difference within a given market niche will perhaps be reduced, the proliferation of niches—the five-hundred-channel model touted for digital television—could mean more programming outlets for black film, video, and television makers. (The hegemony of corporate control of television means that even with the proliferation of channels and new delivery systems, this proliferation may well mean that these five-hundred-plus channels will look more alike than different.)

24. Both BET and Univision began as small, specialized cable networks and were subsequently purchased by major media companies—Viacom in the case of BET and General Electric in the case of Univision.

25. In an ironic illustration of my point here, I came across a story about similar concerns in a local English language newspaper published in Mexico City, while working on this chapter in San Miguel de Allende, Mexico (David Bauder, "Latina Heroine Wins Over US Toddlers," *The News* [Mexico City], 15 July 2001).

CHAPTER 5. TELEVISION AND THE POLITICS OF DIFFERENCE

Thanks to Lynn Spigel, Jan Olessen, Michael Curtin for comments on earlier drafts of this chapter. Parts of this chapter appeared as my "Desiring the Network and Network Desire," *Critical Studies in Mass Communication* 18, no. 1 (2001): 103–8.

1. George Lipsitz, "The Meaning of Memory: Family, Class, and Ethnicity in Early American Network Television," in *Time Passages: Collective Memory and American Popular Culture,* by George Lipsitz (Minneapolis: University of Minnesota Press, 1990), 39–77; Lynn Spigel, "The Suburban Home Companion:

Television and the Neighborhood Ideal in Postwar America," in *Welcome to the Dreamhouse: Popular Media and Postwar Suburbs*, by Lynn Spigel (Durham, N.C.: Duke University Press, 2001), 31–59; Spigel, *Make Room for TV: Television and the Family Ideal in Postwar America* (University of Chicago Press, 1992); William Boddy, *Fifties Television: The Industry and Its Critics* (Urbana: University of Illinois Press, 1990); Michael Curtin, *Redeeming the Wasteland: Television Documentary and Cold War Politics* (New Brunswick, N.J.: Rutgers University Press, 1995); Mark Williams, "Entertaining 'Difference': Strains of Orientalism in Early Los Angeles Television," in *Living Color: Race and Television in the United States*, ed. Sasha Torres (Durham, N.C.: Duke University Press, 1998), 12–34; Pamela Wilson, "Confronting the 'Indian Problem': Media Discourses of Race, Ethnicity, Nation, and Empire in 1950s America," in *Living Color*, ed. Sasha Torres, 35–61; Victoria E. Johnson, "Citizen Welk: Bubbles, Blue Hair and Middle America," in *The Revolution Wasn't Televised: Sixties Television and Social Conflict*, ed. Lynn Spigel and Michael Curtin (New York: Routledge, 1997), 265–85; Darrell Y. Hamamoto, "White Christian Nation," in *Monitored Peril: Asian Americans and the Politics of TV Representation*, by Darrell Y. Hamamoto (Minneapolis: University of Minnesota Press, 1994), 1–31.

2. Spigel, *Welcome to the Dreamhouse*.

3. Ien Ang, *Living Room Wars: Rethinking Media Audiences for a Postmodern World* (New York: Routledge, 1996).

4. For more on the role of television in the production of this identity, see Boddy, *Fifties Television*; Michael Curtin, *Redeeming the Wasteland: Television Documentary and Cold War Politics* (New Brunswick, N.J.: Rutgers University Press, 1995); Spigel, *Welcome to the Dreamhouse*.

5. Ang, *Living Room Wars*.

6. Bambi L. Haggins, "Why 'Beulah' and 'Andy' Still Play Today: Minstrelsy in the New Millennium," in *Globalization, Convergence, Identity: Ethnic Notions and National Identity*, ed. John T. Caldwell and Bambi L. Haggins, special issue, pt. 2, *Emergences: Journal for the Study of Media and Composite Cultures* 11, no. 2 (2001): 189–99.

7. Brian Lowery, Elizabeth Jensen, and Greg Braxton, "Networks Decide Diversity Doesn't Pay," *Los Angeles Times*, 30 July 1999; my emphasis.

8. Ang, *Living Room Wars*; Todd Gitlin, *Inside Prime Time* (New York: Pantheon Books, 1983); Eileen Meehan, "Why We Don't Count: The Commodity Audience," in *The Logics of Television: Essays in Cultural Criticism*, ed. Patricia Mellencamp (Bloomington: Indiana University Press, 1990), 117–37.

9. Lowery, Jensen, and Braxton, "Networks Decide Diversity Doesn't Pay"; my emphasis.

10. Ibid.

11. For an interesting discussion of this issue, see Joshua Gamson, "Diversity Follies," *American Prospect* 11, no. 4 (2000); available from www.americanprospect.org.

12. Lowery, Jensen, and Braxton, "Networks Decide Diversity Doesn't Pay"; my emphasis.

13. Ibid.; my emphasis; see also Haggins, "Why 'Beulah' and 'Andy' Still Play Today."

14. For more on this topic, see Tamar Jacoby, "Adjust Your Sets" *New Republic*, 24 January 2000, www.tnr.com/archive/012400/jacoby012400.html (accessed 21 June 2001).

15. Lowery, Jensen, and Braxton, "Networks Decide Diversity Doesn't Pay"; my emphasis.

16. In January 2000 both NBC and ABC announced major settlements with the NAACP that would ensure programs to promote diversity both on camera and in employment practices. "ABC Agrees to Deal on Minorities," *San Francisco Chronicle*, 8 January 2000.

17. Johnson, "Citizen Welk"; Spigel, *Welcome to the Dreamhouse*.

18. Raymond Williams, *Television: Technology and Cultural Form* (New York: Schocken Books, 1974).

19. John Hartley, *The Uses of Television* (New York: Routledge, 1999).

20. The following works examine the way that television's programming content (Newcomb) and industrial structure (Boddy) worked to produce the feeling of national identification and belonging: Boddy, *Fifties Television*; Horace Newcomb, "From Old Frontier to New Frontier," in *The Revolution Wasn't Televised: Sixties Television and Social Conflict*, ed. Lynn Spigel and Michael Curtin (New York: Routledge, 1997), 287–305.

21. Spigel, *Welcome to the Dreamhouse*. In an especially rich line of argument, Sasha Torres suggest that television's news coverage of blacks in this period was far more generous. As she shows, this coverage is less a matter of altruism than the need for television as an emerging medium and genre to establish its legitimacy as a news discourse. Similarly, television provided the movement with the opportunity and the stage to establish its moral claims to social justice and full participation in the nation. In her view, this complex relationship resulted in a television-produced image of a nation struggling with issues of racial difference as the basis of inequality and injustice. See Sasha Torres, *Black, White, and in Color: Television and Black Civil Rights* (Princeton, N.J.: Princeton University Press, 2003), 13–36.

22. Curtin, *Redeeming the Wasteland*; See also Michael Curtin, "Dynasty in Drag: Imagining Global TV," in *The Revolution Wasn't Televised: Sixties Television and Social Conflict*, ed. Lynn Spigel and Michael Curtin (New York: Routledge, 1997), 245–65.

23. See Boddy, *Fifties Television*; Mark Alvey, "The Independents: Rethinking the Television Studio System," in *The Revolution Wasn't Televised: Sixties Television and Social Conflict*, ed. Lynn Spigel and Michael Curtin (New York: Routledge, 1997), 139–61.

24. Hartley, *The Uses of Television*; Spigel, *Make Room for TV*; Spigel, "The Suburban Home Companion: Television and the Neighborhood Ideal in Postwar America," in *Welcome to the Dreamhouse*, 31–60.

25. Anna McCarthy, *Ambient Television: Visual Culture and Public Space* (Durham, N.C.: Duke University Press, 2000).

26. Spigel, *Make Room for TV*.

27. Williams, *Television*.

28. For a fuller discussion of this articulation, see Alvey, "The Independents"; Johnson, "Citizen Welk."

29. Lipsitz, "The Meaning of Memory"; Spigel, *Welcome to the Dreamhouse.*

30. Hartley, *The Uses of Television*; Lipsitz, "The Meaning of Memory"; Spigel, *Make Room for TV*; Spigel, "Outer Space and Inner Cities: African American Responses to NASA," in *Welcome to the Dreamhouse*, 141–85.

31. Spigel, *Make Room for TV.*

32. John Hartley also pays careful attention to the cultural and industrial operations and assumptions by which television viewing was located and organized as a gendered domestic experience; Hartley, *The Uses of Television.*

33. For a discussion of television's relationship to representations of Native Americans and Asian Americans, see Wilson, "Confronting the 'Indian Problem'"; Hamamoto, "White Christian Nation."

34. Torres, *Black, White, and in Color.*

35. Stuart Hall, "What Is This 'Black' in Black Popular Culture?" in *Black Popular Culture: A Project by Michele Wallace,* ed. Gina Dent (Seattle: Bay Press, 1992), 21–37; Cornel West, "The New Cultural Politics of Difference," in *Out There: Marginalizations and Contemporary Cultures,* ed. Russell Ferguson et al. (Cambridge, Mass.: MIT Press, 1990), 19–39.

36. Lipsitz, "The Meaning of Memory"; George Lipsitz, "Law and Order: Civil Rights Laws and White Privilege," in *The Possessive Investment in Whiteness: How White People Profit from Identity Politics,* by George Lipsitz (Philadelphia: Temple University Press, 1998), 24–46.

37. See Melvin L. Oliver and Thomas M. Shapiro, *Black Wealth/White Wealth: A New Perspective on Racial Inequality* (New York: Routledge, 1995); Spigel, "Outer Space and Inner Cities."

38. Marlon T. Riggs, *Color Adjustment,* film (San Francisco: California Newsreel, 1991); Spigel, *Welcome to the Dreamhouse.*

39. For more on the turn to relevance in television, see Gitlin, *Inside Prime Time.*

40. Sarah Binet-Weiser argues that the racial politics of visibility involve making racial difference visible while not disturbing the logic around which the dominant (racial) center holds. See Sarah Binet-Weiser, *The Most Beautiful Girl in the World* (Berkeley: University of California Press, 1999). See also Haggins, "Why 'Beulah' and 'Andy' Still Play Today."

41. Herman Gray, *Watching Race: Television and the Struggle for Blackness* (Minneapolis: University of Minnesota Press, 1995).

42. See Robert M. Entman and Andrew Rojecki, *The Black Image in the White Mind* (Chicago: University of Chicago Press, 2000).

43. As Lynn Spigel points out, the possible exception to this situation is television news, especially in times of crisis (personal communication, October 1999).

44. On the idea of neo-networks see Curtin, "Dynasty in Drag"; John T. Caldwell, "The Business of New Media," in *The New Media Handbook,* ed. Dan Harries (London: BFI Publishing, 2002); John T. Caldwell, "Convergence Television: Aggregating Form and Re-Purposing Content in the Culture of Conglomeration," in *Television after TV,* ed. Lynn Spigel (Durham, N.C.: Duke University Press, 2004).

45. Caldwell, "Convergence Television."

46. James Hay, "Unaided Virtues: The Neoliberalization of the Domestic Sphere," *Television and New Media* 1, no. 1 (2000): 53–73.

47. Caldwell, "The Business of New Media" and "Convergence Television."

48. See McCarthy, *Ambient Television.*

49. Ibid.; Michael Curtin, "Feminine Desire in the Age of Satellite Television," *Journal of Communication* (Spring 1999): 55; Caldwell, "The Business of New Media" and "Convergence Television."

50. Hartley, *The Uses of Television.*

51. Caldwell, "Convergence Television."

52. Caldwell, "The Business of New Media" and "Convergence Television"; Anna Everett and John T. Caldwell, eds., *Theories and Practices of Digitextuality* (New York: Routledge, 2003).

53. Curtin, "Feminine Desire in the Age of Satellite Television," and Curtin, "Gatekeeping in the Neo-Network Era," in *Advocacy Groups and the Entertainment Industry,* senior ed. Michael Susman (Westport, Conn.: Praeger, 2000); John T. Caldwell, *Televisuality: Style, Crisis, and Authority in American Television* (New Brunswick, N.J.: Rutgers University Press, 1995); Caldwell, "Convergence Television."

54. John T. Caldwell and Bambi L. Haggins, eds., *Globalization, Convergence, Identity: Ethnic Notions and National Identity,* special issue, pt. 2, *Emergences: Journal for the Study of Media and Composite Cultures* 11, no. 2 (November 2001); L. S. Kim and Gilberto Moises Blasini, "The Performance of Multicultural Identity in US Network Television: Shiny, Happy Popstars (Holding Hands)," in *Globalization, Convergence, Identity,* ed. Caldwell and Haggins, 287–309; Caldwell, "Convergence Television."

55. See, for example, Lawrence Levine, *The Opening of the American Mind: Canons, Culture, and History* (Boston: Beacon Press, 1996); Judith Stacey, *In the Name of the Family: Rethinking Family Values in the Postmodern Age* (Boston: Beacon Press, 1996); and Maurita Sturkin, *Tangled Memories: The Vietnam War, the AIDS Epidemic, and the Politics of Remembering* (Berkeley: University of California Press, 1997).

56. For John Hartley this active engagement indicates what he calls do-it-yourself citizenship crafted from the knowledge produced by television. See Hartley, *The Uses of Television.*

57. Kim and Blasini, "The Performance of Multicultural Identity."

58. Robert Goldman and Stephen Papson, *Sign Wars: The Cluttered Landscape of Advertising* (New York: Guilford Press, 1999); S. Craig Watkins, *Representing: Hip-Hop Culture and the Production of Black Cinema* (Chicago: University of Chicago Press, 1998).

59. Lipsitz, *The Possessive Investment in Whiteness;* see also Entman and Rojecki, *The Black Image.*

60. Gray, *Watching Race;* Robin D. G. Kelley, *Yo Mama's Disfunktional! Fighting the Culture Wars in Urban America* (Boston: Beacon Press, 1997); Watkins, *Representing.*

61. Caldwell, "Convergence Television."

62. Jacoby, "Adjust Your Sets"; Entman and Rojecki, *The Black Image.*

63. Thanks to Michael Curtin for his discussion and clarification on this point. Thanks also to Lynn Spigel for insisting on the distinction, in this case, between television news and television entertainment.

64. Ang, *Living Room Wars*, 172.

65. Ibid., 174.

66. Robin R. Means Coleman, *African American Viewers and the Black Situation Comedy* (New York: Garland Publishing, 2000).

67. Ang, *Living Room Wars*, 179.

68. Darnell Hunt's empirically based work on race and media is very suggestive in the area of what he calls raced ways of seeing and the assumptions about nation, justice, fairness that are articulated by race. See Darnell Hunt, *Screening the Los Angeles "Riots": Race, Seeing, and Resistance* (Cambridge: Cambridge University Press, 1997), and *O.J.: Fact and Fiction* (Cambridge: Cambridge University Press, 1999). See also Entman and Rojecki, *The Black Image.*

69. Kim and Blasini, "The Performance of Multicultural Identity"; Caldwell and Haggins, *Globalization, Convergence, Identity,* special issue, pt. 2, of *Emergences.*

70. Ang, *Living Room Wars*, 144.


CHAPTER 6. DIFFERENT DREAMS, DREAMS OF DIFFERENCE

1. Clyde Taylor, *The Mask of Art: Breaking the Aesthetic Contract* (Bloomington: Indiana University Press, 1998).

2. "Crystal palaces" are prestigious cultural institutions that authorize and legitimate Western aesthetics; the reference is Taylor's and is taken from Ralph Elison's *Invisible Man* (1952; reprint, New York: Vintage Books, 1972).

3. Angharad N. Valdivia, ed., *Feminism, Multiculturalism, and the Media: Global Diversities* (Thousand Oaks, Calif.: Sage Publications, 1995); and Gregg Barak, ed., *Media, Process, and the Social Construction of Crime: Studies in Newsmaking Criminology* (New York: Garland Publishing, 1994).

4. Taylor, *The Mask of Art.*

5. Gregg Barak, "Reflexive Newsmaking and Representation," *Critical Studies in Mass Communication* 16, no. 4 (December 1999): 480.


CHAPTER 7. CULTURAL POLITICS AS OUTRAGE(OUS)

1. Herman Gray, *Watching Race: Television and the Struggle for Blackness* (University of Minnesota Press, 1995).

2. See for instance the controversy over British painter Chris Ofili's painting *The Holy Virgin Mary,* which appeared in Sensation 2000 at the Brooklyn Museum. For more on Ofili see Jonathan Jones, "Paradise Reclaimed," *Guardian,* 15 June 2002; see also the exhibition catalogue for *Freestyle,* presented by the Studio Museum of Harlem and curated by Thelma Goldman: *Freestyle Exhibition* (New York: Studio Museum of Harlem, April 28–June 24, 2001).

3. For more on the use of similar strategies to represent blackness, see Goldman, *Freestyle.*

4. Goldman, introduction to ibid., 14–15.

5. Paul Gilroy, *Small Acts: Thoughts on the Politics of Black Culture* (London: Serpent's Tail Press, 1993), 104.

6. Kobena Mercer, *Welcome to the Jungle: New Positions in Black Cultural Politics* (London: Routledge, 1994), 239.

7. Ibid.

8. See, for example, films that deal with diasporic memories of the mise-en-scène of slavery, including *Sankofa, Quilimbo, and Roots.*

9. David Theo Goldberg, *Racist Culture: Philosophy and the Politics of Meaning* (Cambridge, Mass.: Blackwell, 1993); George Lipsitz, *The Possessive Investment in Whiteness: How White People Profit from Identity Politics* (Philadelphia: Temple University Press, 1998); and Ann Laura Stoller, *Race and the Education of Desire* (New York: Routledge, 1995).

10. Clyde Taylor, *The Mask of Art: Breaking the Aesthetic Contract* (Bloomington: Indiana University Press, 1998).

11. Kara Walker, "Upon My Many Masters: An Outline," in *San Francisco Museum of Modern Art Exhibition Catalogue* (San Francisco: San Francisco Museum of Modern Art, 1997).

12. For interesting examples, see Goldman, *Freestyle.*

13. Mercer, *Welcome to the Jungle,* 203–4.

14. Renaissance Society at the University of Chicago Newsletter (Chicago: Renaissance Society at the University of Chicago, 1997), 2. See also: Tommy Lee Lott, "Kara Walker Speaks: A Public Conversation on Racism, Art, and Politics with Tommy Lott," *Black Renaissance/Renaissance Noire* 3, no. 1 (Fall 2000): 69–93; Walker, "Upon My Many Masters"; Lawrence Rinder, interview with Kara Walker, in *Kara Walker: No Mere Words,* exhibition program notes, exhibited 3 April–15 May 1999 (Oakland: California College of Arts and Crafts and the Capp Street Project, 1999), 46–47; David Coleman, "Pretty and on the Outside," *George* (June–July 1996): 117–18.

15. Another example from literature that deploys a similar strategy of outrageousness that provoked far less public reaction is *Negrophobia: An Urban Parable* (New York: St. Martin's Press, 1992), by Darius James. In the novel James unleashes a sustained barrage of stereotypes, twisted fantasies, and horrifying images. The sheer force and density of this onslaught renders these images inert by the book's end. Organized as a screenplay in the form of a novel, midway through one gets the sense that the desired aesthetic and political effect is to make us see and engage with these twisted images for just what they are. Other artists whose work is deliberately unsettling if not shocking include Carrie Mae Weems, George Wolf, Gary Simmons, Robert Colescott, Adrian Piper, and Glenn Ligon.

16. Thelma Golden, *Black Male: Representations of Masculinity in Contemporary American Art* (New York: Whitney Museum of American Art, 1994), 24.

CHAPTER 8. IS (CYBER) SPACE THE PLACE?

1. See Kevin Robins and Frank Webster, *The Times of the Technoculture: From the Information Society to the Virtual Life* (New York: Routledge, 1999).

2. James Carey, *Communication as Culture: Essays on Media and Society* (Boston: Unwin Hyman, 1989), 9.

3. In addition to being very old tales, for Gil Rodman these responses are also problematic because they are fundamentally binary and thus offer no possibility for thinking about these issues outside of the binary logic on which they depend. See Gilbert B. Rodman, "The Net Effect: The Public's Fear and the Public Sphere," in *Virtual Publics: Policy and Community in an Electronic Age*, ed. Beth E. Kolko (New York: Columbia University Press, 2000), 9–48.

4. Arjun Appaduri, *Modernity at Large: Cultural Dimensions of Globalization* (Minneapolis: University of Minnesota Press, 1996); Dan Schiller, *Digital Capitalism: Networking the Global Market System* (Cambridge, Mass.: MIT Press, 2000); Manuel Castells, *The Rise of the Network Society*, vol. 1 (Cambridge, Mass.: Blackwell Publishers, 1996).

5. About this twin logic, see Michael Curtin, "Feminine Desire in the Age of Satellite Television," *Journal of Communication* (Spring 1999): 55; and Michael Curtin, "Gatekeeping in the Neo-Network Era," in *Advocacy Groups and Prime Time Television*, senior ed. Michael Susman (Westport, Conn.: Praeger, 2000); John T. Caldwell, "The Business of New Media," in *The New Media Handbook*, ed. Dan Harries (London: BFI Publishing, 2002).

6. John Fiske, *Media Matters: Everyday Culture and Political Change* (Minneapolis: University of Minnesota Press, 1994), 239; also Dan Schiller, *Digital Capitalism: Networking the Global Market System* (Cambridge, Mass.: MIT Press, 2000).

7. Allucquere R. Stone, *The War of Desire and Technology at the Close of the Mechanical Age* (Cambridge, Mass.: MIT Press, 1995), 169; see also Carey, *Communication as Culture.*

8. Fiske, *Media Matters*, 250; also Schiller, *Digital Capitalism*; Robins and Webster, *The Times of the Technoculture.*

9. Raymond Williams, *Marxism and Literature* (Oxford: Oxford University Press, 1977).

10. Fiske, *Media Matters*; Williams, *Marxism and Literature.*

11. Fiske, *Media Matters*, 237.

12. Carey, *Communication as Culture*, 195.

13. Perhaps the most explicit conception of new technology as natural is one that aligns the capacities for information transfer, rapid market transactions, and consumer access to business and commercial interests; George Lewis, "Singing the Alternative Interactivity Blues," *Front* 7, no. 2 (1995): 18–22; reprinted in *Grantmakers in the Arts* 8, no. 1 (Spring 1997).

14. Schiller, *Digital Capitalism.*

15. Fiske, *Media Matters*, 239.

16. Ibid.

17. Stuart Hall, "What Is This 'Black' in Black Popular Culture?" in *Black Popular Culture: A Project by Michele Wallace*, ed. Gina Dent (Seattle: Bay Press, 1992), 21–37; Cornel West, "The New Cultural Politics of Difference," in *Out There: Marginalizations and Contemporary Cultures*, ed. Russell Ferguson et al. (Cambridge, Mass.: MIT Press, 1990), 19–39.

18. Hall, "What Is This 'Black' in Black Popular Culture?"

19. See Ken Auletta, "American Keiretsu," *New Yorker*, 20 and 27 October 1997, 225–28; "The Big Ten," *Nation*, 14 January 2002, 27; Robert W. McChesney, "The Media System Goes Global," in *Rich Media Poor Democracy: Communication Politics in Dubious Times*, by Robert W. McChesney (New York: New Press, 1999), 78–118.

20. William J. Mitchell, *City of Bits: Space, Place, and the Infobahn* (Cambridge, Mass.: MIT University Press, 1996), 170–71.

21. For an interesting history of technology and culture including, for example, questions of embodiment and gender, see Katherine Hayles, *How We Become Post Human: Virtual Bodies in Cybernetics, Literature, and Information* (Chicago: University of Chicago Press, 1999).

22. See, for example, Naomi Klein, *No Logo: Taking Aim at the Brand Bullies* (New York: Picador, 2000); Eddie Yuen, George Katsiaficas, and Daniel Burton Rose, eds., *The Battle of Seattle: The New Challenge to Capitalist Globalization* (New York: Soft Skull Press, 2001).

23. Donald A. Schon, Bish Sanyal, and William J. Mitchell, eds., *High Technology and Low Income Communities: Prospects for the Positive Use of Advanced Information Technology* (Cambridge, Mass.: MIT Press, 1999).

24. Fiske, *Media Matters*; see also Mike Davis, *City of Quartz: Excavating the Future in Los Angeles* (London: Verso, 1992); Robert Gooding-Williams, ed., *Reading Rodney King, Reading Urban Uprisings* (New York: Routledge, 1993); Constance Penley and Andrew Ross, eds., *Technoculture* (Minneapolis: University of Minnesota Press, 1991); John T. Caldwell, "Televisual Politics: Negotiating Race in the L.A. Rebellion," in *Living Color: Race and Television in the United States*, ed. Sasha Torres (Durham, N.C.: Duke University Press, 1998), 161–95.

25. Fiske, *Media Matters*, esp. chap. 5; James Lull, *Media, Communication, Culture: A Global Approach* (New York: Columbia University Press, 1995); Susan O'Donnell and Guillermo Delgado, "Using the Internet to Strengthen the Indigenous Nations of the Americas," *Media Development* 42, no. 3 (1995): 36–39.

26. On this, see Hayles, *How We Become Post Human*; Mitchell, *City of Bits*; Mark Poster, *The Mode of Information: Poststructuralism and Social Context* (Chicago: University of Chicago Press, 1990).

27. Beth E. Kolko, Lisa Nakamura, and Gilbert B, Rodman, eds., *Race in Cyberspace* (New York: Routledge, 2000).

28. Hall, "What Is This 'Black' in Black Popular Culture?"; George Lipsitz, *Dangerous Crossroads: Popular Music, Postmodernism, and the Poetics of Place* (London: Verso, 1994); Lisa Lowe and David Lloyd, eds., *The Politics of Culture in the Shadow of Capital* (Durham, N.C.: Duke University Press, 1997); Lull, *Media, Communication, Culture*; Robin D. G. Kelley, *Yo Mama's Dysfunktional! Fighting the Culture Wars in Urban America* (Boston: Beacon Press, 1997).

29. Lisa Lowe, *Immigrant Acts: On Asian American Cultural Politics* (Durham, N.C.: Duke University Press, 1996).

30. Though I would still claim that in the case of modern black diasporic formations in the West there remains much critical work to be done.

31. Lull, *Media, Communication, Culture*, 113–59.

32. See Lipsitz, *Dangerous Crossroads*; Lowe and Lloyd, *The Politics of Culture in the Shadow of Capital*; Lull, *Media, Communication, Culture*.

33. On this point the insights of James Hays, Bruce Robins and Frank Webster, John Caldwell, and David Morley are especially interesting. Each writer critiques the equation of market, technology, and access to commodities with democracy and freedom; each writer also considers the new technologies in relationship to older modernist forms of representation like cinema and television, and especially the ways that electronic technologies transform spatial relations, in particular within the domestic sphere. See Robins and Webster, *The Times of the Technoculture*; James Hay, "Unaided Virtues: The Neoliberalization of the Domestic Sphere," *Television and New Media* 1, no. 1 (2000): 53–73; John T. Caldwell, "Theorizing the Digital Landrush," introduction to *Electronic Media and Technoculture*, ed. John T. Caldwell (New Brunswick, N.J.: Rutgers University Press, 2000), 1–31; David Morley, *Home Territories: Media, Mobility, and Identity* (London: Routledge, 2000).

34. Bill Nichols considers Benjamin's observations on the impact of mechanical reproduction on art as a beginning for thinking about issues of culture, representation, and the digital revolution: Bill Nichols, "The Work of Culture in the Age of Cybernetic Systems," in *Electronic Media and Technoculture*, ed. Caldwell, 90–114. At the same time, as the velocity and volume of these cultural forms and products increase, all kinds of people and communities are available and accessible to each other both inside and out of the structuring logic that others have been trying to expose and interrogate.

35. Caldwell, *Electronic Media and Technoculture*.

36. Andrew Ross, "Jobs in Cyberspace," in *Real Love: In Pursuit of Cultural Justice*, by Andrew Ross (New York: New York University Press, 1998), 7–34; Schiller, *Digital Capitalism*; McChesney, "The Media System Goes Global"; Robins and Webster, *The Times of the Technoculture*.

37. Guillermo Delgado and Marc Becker, "Latin America: The Internet and Indigenous Texts," *Cultural Survival Quarterly*, 21, no. 4 (31 January 1998): 23–28; O'Donnell and Delgado, "Using the Internet."

38. Robins and Webster, *The Times of the Technoculture*; Morley, *Home Territories*.

39. Yuen, Katsiaficas, and Rose, *The Battle of Seattle*.

40. Stone, *The War of Desire and Technology*, 168.

CHAPTER 9. MUSIC, IDENTITY, AND NEW TECHNOLOGY

1. In addition to being the title of one of Sun Ra's most famous recordings, *Space Is the Place* is also the title of a recent Sun Ra biography: see John F. Szwed, *Space Is the Place: The Lives and Times of Sun Ra* (New York: Pantheon Books, 1997). Graham Locke also has an excellent discussion of Sun Ra's conception and use of (outer) space as the basis of his own philosophy of life (particularly as it relates to racial injustice) and artistic performance: Graham Lock, *Blutopia: Visions of the Future and Revisions of the Past in the Works of Sun Ra, Duke Ellington, and Anthony Braxton* (Durham, N.C.: Duke University

Press, 1999). For an interesting take on the implications of Sun Ra, outer space, and black cultural politics, see Lynn Spigel, "Outer Space and Inner Cities: African American Responses to NASA," in *Welcome to the Dreamhouse: Popular Media and Postwar Suburbs*, by Lynn Spigel (Durham, N.C.: Duke University Press, 2001), 141–85; and Michael C. Pounds, *Race in Space: The Representation of Ethnicity in "Star Trek" and "Star Trek: The Next Generation"* (Lanham, Md.: Scarecrow Press, 1999).

2. In proposing such an assessment, I am especially mindful of the fact that such enactments critique as well as reinscribe some old notions about identity and technology. My position is not that encounters between blackness and identity are inherently oppositional and resistant, as some enthusiasts might have it. Rather, it is that such encounters organize, bring together, and express relations, histories, and circumstances that themselves are bound up with relations of power and struggles whose outcomes cannot be known in advance and whose politics are not contained in the sound itself.

3. George Lipsitz, *Dangerous Crossroads: Popular Music, Postmodernism, and the Poetics of Place* (London: Verso, 1994).

4. Black music cultures have always negotiated with, borrowed from, and been transformed by cultural practices located near and far from them. One impact of these encounters is, of course, that they have complicated notions of blackness.

5. See chapter 7 on Kara Walker. See also, Holland Cotter, "Beyond Multiculturalism, Freedom?" *New York Times*, 29 July 2001; Michael Kimmelman, "A Black World of Ins and Outs," *New York Times*, 26 April 2002; Ian Parker "Golden Touch," *New Yorker*, 14 January 2002, 44–49; Deborah Solomon, "The Downtowning of Uptown," *New York Times*, 19 August 2001.

6. Mark Anthony Neal, *Soul Babies: Black Popular Culture and the Post-Soul Aesthetic* (New York: Routledge, 2000); Keith Negus, *Music, Genres, and Corporate Cultures* (London: Routledge, 1999); Nabeel Zuberi, "Black Whole Styles: Sounds, Technology, and Diaspora Aesthetics," in *Sounds English: Transnational Popular Music*, by Nabeel Zuberi (Urbana: University of Illinois Press, 2001), 131–80; Ronald Radano and Phillip V. Bohlman, *Music and the Racial Imagination* (Chicago: University of Chicago Press, 2000); Georgina Born and David Hesmondhalgh, "On Difference, Representation, and Appropriation in Music," introduction to *Western Music and Its Others: Difference, Representation, and Appropriation in Music*, ed. Georgina Born and David Hesmondhalgh (Berkeley: University of California Press, 2000), 1–58; John Hutnyk, "Authenticity or Cultural Politics," in *Critique of Exotica Music, Politics, and the Culture Industry*, by John Hutnyk (London: Pluto Press, 2000), 114–37; Robert Walser, "Deep Jazz: Notes on Interiority, Race and Criticism," in *Inventing the Psychological: Toward a Cultural History of Emotional Life in America*, ed. Joel Pfister and Nancy Schnog (New Haven, Conn.: Yale University Press, 1997), 271–96.

7. Is it the case, then, that the encounter between black soundings and the new digital technologies releases blackness from the burden of representation? Alternatively, is it the case that twenty-first-century digital technologies and the capacities that they produce make race in general and blackness in particular

more important, because of the novel ways and sites in which blackness can be imagined?

8. Paul Gilroy, "After the Love Has Gone: Bio-Politics and Etho-Politics in the Black Public Sphere," *Public Culture* 7, no. 1 (1994): 49–77; Zuberi, "Black Whole Styles."

9. Some of the generally recognized elements that define black music's Atlantic encounter with technology in the early-twenty-first-century Atlantic world looks (or more appropriately sounds) something like this: The *scenes:* the Caribbean, the United States, and the United Kingdom are the major spatial sites of musical travel and encounter. *Musics:* reggae, dub, rhythm and blues, disco, fusion jazz, zuk, soka, and related black diasporic musics (Bangra in England, chutney soka in Trinidad-Tobago, fleeting gestures toward calypso in the Caribbean, and European—English, German and French—electronic soundings) are combined in such a way that they extend blackness beyond literal geographical territory. *Significant figures:* Grand Master Flash, Africa Bambata, Herbie Hancock, Lee Scratch Perry, Sun Ra, George Clinton. *Debates:* the loss of the public sphere, the privatization and deskilling of black music production, the salience of race, nation, identity for the production, performance, and meaning of (diaspora) blackness in the twenty-first century. And, as importantly, the relevance of critical cultural theory to identifying and judging the cultural politics performed by these imaginative musical encounters and the subjects that are produced in the process. See Ben Williams, "Black Street Technology: Detroit Techno and the Information Age," in *Technicolor: Race, Technology, and Everyday Life*, ed. Alondra Nelson, Thuy Linh N. Tu, and Alicia Headlam Himes (New York: New York University Press, 2001), 154–76; Gayatri Gopinath, "Bombay, U.K., Yuba City: Bangra Music and the Engendering of Diaspora," *Diaspora* 4, no. 3 (1995): 303–22; Zuberi, "Black Whole Styles"; Erik Davis, "Roots and Wires: Polyrhythmic Cyberspace and Black Electronic," *Erik Davis' Figments and Inklings* Web site, www.techgnosis.com/cyberconf.html (accessed 31 January 2002); and Davis, "Dub, Scratch, and the Black Star: Lee Perry on the Mix," *Erik Davis' Figments and Inklings* Web site, www.techgnosis.com/dub.html (accessed 31 January 2002).

10. Gayle Wald, "'I Want It That Way': Teenybopper Music and the Girling of Boy Bands" (forthcoming book chapter).

11. Kevin Kelly, "Where Music Will Be Coming From," *New York Times Magazine*, 17 March 2002, 29–31; *Wired* music issue, May 2002.

12. My thanks to Josh Kun for explaining the details of this process.

13. Kodwo Eshun, *More Brilliant Than the Sun: Adventures in Sonic Fiction* (London: Quartet, 1998).

14. DJ Spooky, AKA, That Subliminal Kid Web site, www.djspooky.com (accessed 11 January 2002).

15. Simon Frith, *Performing Rites* (Cambridge, Mass.: Harvard University Press, 1996); Josh Kun, "Against Easy Listening: Audiotropic Readings and Transnational Soundings," in *Everynight Life: Culture and Dance in Latin/o America*, ed. Celeste Fraser Delgado and Jose Esteban Muñoz (Durham, N.C.: Duke University Press, 1997), 288–309.

16. Kevin Robins and Frank Webster, *The Times of the Technoculture: From the Information Society to the Virtual Life* (New York: Routledge, 1999); David Morley and Kevin Robins, *Spaces of Identity: Global Media, Electronic Landscapes, and Cultural Boundaries* (London: Routledge, 1995).

17. Robins and Webster, *The Times of the Technoculture*; Morley and Robbins, *Spaces of Identity*; Dan Schiller, *Digital Capitalism: Networking the Global Market System* (Cambridge, Mass.: MIT Press, 2000).

18. Tamar Jacoby, "Color Blind: The African American Absence in High Tech," *New Republic*, 29 March 1999, www.tnr.com/archive/0399/032999/ jacoby032999.html, (accessed 21 June 2001); Thomas Novak and Donna L. Hoffman "Bridging the Digital Divide: The Impact of Race on Computer Access and Internet Use," *Project 2000 Vanderbilt University* Web site, 1998, www.2000.ogsm.vanderbiltuniversity.edu (accessed 26 June 2000); Anthony Walton, "Technology versus African Americans," *Atlantic Monthly*, January 1999, www.atlantic.com (accessed 6 June 2001); University of Southern California and Massachusetts Institute of Technology, Race in Digital Space: A National Conference on Race and New Media Technologies, Web site, cms.mit.edu/race/press.html (accessed 6 June 2001); Leonce Gaither, "Is the Web Too Cool for Blacks?" *Salon*, www.salon.com/June97/21st/1001970605 .html (accessed 6 June 2001).

19. Cameron Bailey, "Virtual Skin: Articulating Race in Cyberspace," in *Immersed in Technology: Art in Virtual Environments*, ed. Mary Anne Moser and Douglas MacLeod (Cambridge, Mass.: MIT Press, 1996), 29–49; Beth E. Kolko, Lisa Nakamura, and Gilbert B, Rodman, *Race in Cyberspace* (New York: Routledge, 2000); Walton, "Technology versus African Americans"; see also chapter 8 in this volume on identity and technology.

20. As an explicit instance of racing, Asians and South Asians are stereotyped as almost always fully presented and represented as technologically competent and thus never in need of support for access and greater representation in the high-tech world.

21. Walton, "Technology versus African Americans."

22. Ibid., 4.

23. Given the already congealed corporate structure and control, trade and exchange policies, economies of scale, and corporate investment, it seems reasonable to conclude that the basic nature of participation in the Internet is as consumers. That is, the global and capitalist structure of new technologies, for purposes of considering issues of access, participation, and social relations, is, as it were, complete and finished as a political, social, and cultural matter.

24. Walton, "Technology versus African Americans."

25. Kolko, Nakamura, and Rodman, *Race in Cyberspace*; Alondra Nelson, "Braving the New World: Race and Technology: Afrofuturism: Beyond the Digital Divide," in *Race and Public Policy*, ed. Makani N. Themba (Oakland: Applied Research Center, 2000), 37–40; Kali Tal, "The Unbearable Whiteness of Being: African American Critical Theory and Cyberculture," Kali Tal Web site, 1996, www.freshmonsters.com/kalital/Text/Articles/whiteness.html (accessed 6 June 2001); Alondra Nelson, Thuy Linh N. Tu, and Alicia Headlam Himes, eds.,

*Technicolor: Race, Technology, and Everyday Life* (New York: New York University Press, 2001); also William J. Mitchell, *City of Bits: Space, Place, and the Infobahn* (Cambridge, Mass.: MIT Press, 1996).

26. Walton, "Technology versus African Americans."

27. Naomi Klein, *No Logo: Taking Aim at the Brand Bullies* (New York: Picador, 2000); Robert Goldman and Stephen Papson, *Nike Culture: The Sign of the Swoosh* (London: Sage Publications, 1996).

28. Walton, "Technology versus African Americans."

29. Gaither, "Is the Web Too Cool for Blacks?"

30. Ibid.

31. Ibid.

32. Schiller, *Digital Capitalism*; Robins and Webster, *The Times of the Technoculture*; Manuel Castells, *The Rise of the Network Society*, vol. 1 (Cambridge, Mass.: Blackwell Publishers, 1996.).

33. Beth E. Kolko, "Erasing @Race: Going White in the (Inter)Face," in *Race in Cyberspace*, ed. Beth E. Kolko, Lisa Nakamura, and Gilbert Rodman (New York: Routledge, 2000), 213–32.

34. Bailey, "Virtual Skin." Of course the American suburbs were raced and classed spaces from their very inception. Melvin L. Oliver and Thomas M. Shapiro, *Black Wealth/White Wealth: A New Perspective on Racial Inequality* (New York: Routledge, 1995); Lynn Spigel, "The Suburban Home Companion: Television and the Neighborhood Ideal in Postwar America," in *Welcome to the Dreamhouse: Popular Media and Postwar Suburbs,* by Lynn Spigel (Durham, N.C.: Duke University Press, 2001), 31–59; and Spigel, "Outer Space and Inner Cities."

35. Kolko, "Erasing @race"; my emphasis.

36. Kolko, Nakamura, and Rodman, *Race in Cyberspace,* 10.

37. The politics and effects of such efforts is a related, though not immediate question at this point.

38. Kolko, Nakamoura, and Rodman, *Race in Cyberspace,* 4–5.

39. John Akrumpha, "The Last Angel of History," *First Run/Icarus Films* (Brooklyn, N.Y.), 1996, www.frif.com/new97/the_last_.html (accessed August 2003).

40. The figure of the black musician as scientist was cultivated and performed masterfully by the late trumpeter Lester Bowie, as a founding member of the Art Ensemble of Chicago. Bowie frequently appeared in performance dressed in a white lab coat. See Eric Porter, *What Is This Thing Called Jazz? African American Musicians as Artists, Critics, and Activists* (Berkeley: University of California Press, 2002).

41. Perusing the World Wide Web in search of black-based technology Web sites is an interesting experience. Grouped together and linked up in a virtual pastiche of genres, performances, focuses, and politics are a host of djs, technology geeks, small entrepreneurs and business organizations, civil rights organizations, college courses, and reading lists. Titles like Black Futurists, Black Geeks, and Net Noir collect chat rooms and people together to form a resource for like-minded explorers of the Web. All manner of manifestos, position papers, conference proceedings, and services (postings, listings, announcements,

and links) are routine fare on such Web pages. For more on these Web communities, see www.blackvoices.com; www.blackgeeks.net; www.geocities.com/wallstreet/floor/8647/blackweb.html.

42. The point needs to be made, as well, that for all of its radical possibilities of ruptures and reconfiguring identity, blackness still meets digital technologies on the social ground and cultural meaning of identity and technology. The subsequent critique, as powerful and compelling as it is, still comes after both have been configured and deployed into a social, cultural, and political field.

43. Kun, "Against Easy Listening." My thanks to April Henderson at UCSC, whose dissertation research was on hip-hop in Samoa and the Pacific Islands. Henderson's work has been helpful in thinking through terms and forms of travel, as well as the limits of conventional categories like diaspora, dwelling, travel, and so on, with respect to hip-hop and popular music in general.

44. For more on the influence of black soundings on black diasporic practices, see Davis, "Dub, Scratch, and the Black Star Lee Perry."

45. On the question of the stimulus/response model of interaction between computers and humans, see George Lewis, "Singing the Alternative Interactivity Blues," *Front* 7, no. 2 (1995): 18–22; reprinted in *Grantmakers in the Arts* 8, no. 1 (Spring 1997).

46. Steve Coleman, interview with Herman Gray, 1 and 8 April 2001; Pamela Z, interview with Herman Gray, 19 September 2001.

47. Grandmaster Flash, interview with Terry Gross, National Public Radio's *Fresh Air*, 8 July 2002.

48. Gerald Marzoratti, "All by Himself," *New York Times Magazine*, 17 March 2002, 32–37, 68–70; Ethan Smith, "Organization Moby," *Wired*, May 2002, 89–94.

49. Derrick May, "The Screamers," *Wired*, May 2002, 108; my emphasis.

50. Methodologically, musicians talking about their practice and the kinds of meaningful categories that inform and organize their practice is crucial and bears on theoretical formulations and conceptual categories, as I was reminded in an interview with performance artist and composer Pamela Z. I approached her with what was weak and premature notion of what I thought of as black identity, and her response—that gender rather than race was a more salient identity for her—was significant, for it quickly reminded me that as a cultural matter at the level of everyday life, blackness is never as total and complete an identity as one might think. Similarly for composer George Lewis, technologies are always embedded in and structured by power relations of aesthetic value, race, and gender. For Lewis, the new digital technologies congeal materially and fix discursively the terms, practices, and structures through which identities are produced and maintained. The challenge for composers like Lewis and Pamela Z is to expose and then recode or reprogram technologies so that different traditions, experiences, encounters, and identities can proliferate.

51. Jon Cruz, *Culture on the Margins: The Black Spiritual and the Rise of American Cultural Interpretation* (Princeton, N.J.: Princeton University Press, 1999); Radano and Bohlman, *Music and the Racial Imagination*; Born and Hesmondhalgh, "On Difference"; Walser, "Deep Jazz"; Olly Wilson, "Black Music

as an Art Form," in *The Jazz Cadence of American Culture*, ed. Robert G.. O'Meally, 82–101 (New York: Columbia University Press, 1998).

52. Cruz, *Culture on the Margins*.

53. Ibid.

54. George Lewis, "Experimental Music in Black and White: The AACM in New York, 1970–1985," *Current Musicology* 71–73 (Spring 2001–2): 100–158. For more on the AACM, see Porter, *What Is This Thing Called Jazz?*; Ronald Radano, *New Music Figuration: Anthony Braxton's Cultural Critique* (Chicago: University of Chicago Press, 1993).

55. Quote taken from program notes to *Tempo*, Berkeley Festival of Contemporary Performance, University of California, Berkeley School Of Music, 1–9 July 2001.

56. Lewis's desire was to create a composition involving both computers and real musicians performing together in real time within black performance traditions. Along with his mentor, Muhal Richard Abrams, Lewis is one of the most prolific and articulate proponents of computer-based music. His impressive curriculum vitae is full of commissions, performances, residences, awards, compositions, and recordings from over twenty years of experience in the field.

57. George Lewis, "Too Many Notes: Computers, Complexity, and Culture in Voyager," *Leonardo Music Journal* 10 (2000): 33–39.

58. Quotes from ibid., 33. Note that on this point, Lewis not only spoke to the computer like a brother (which is to say like a member of the band), but he wanted to ensure that the computer is capable of producing its own sound. Drawing from the recognition of the importance of a distinctive sound, a personality, as part of the African American musical tradition, Lewis notes that "part of the task of constructing Voyager consisted of providing the program with its own sound"; ibid., 33; Wilson, "Black Music as an Art Form."

59. Quote taken from program notes to *Tempo*.

60. Ibid.

61. In his estimation, while this kind of programming capacity is represented to consumers and users as interactive, according to Lewis it is not. Lewis, "Singing the Alternative Interactivity Blues."

62. Lewis, "Too Many Notes," 34.

63. Quote taken from program notes to *Tempo*.

64. Lewis, "Too Many Notes," 33; my emphasis.

65. Thanks to Rosa Linda Fregoso and Barbara Barnes for helping me to think more carefully about this point.

66. Quote taken from program notes to *Tempo*.

67. Lewis, "Too Many Notes," 39.

68. Kathy Kennedy, "A Few Facets of Pamela Z," *Musicworks: Explorations in Sound* 76 (2000), Pamela Z Web site, www.pamelaz.com (accessed July 2002).

69. Tom Sellar, "Parts of Speech," *Theater Magazine*, Winter 2000, 59–66.

70. Unless otherwise indicated all references to Pamela Z reported in this section are taken from a telephone interview that I conducted with her on 19 September 2001; quoted materials are also taken from materials that appear on her Web site, www.pamelaz.com.

71. Kennedy, "A Few Facets of Pamela Z."

72. As an example, in her interview with me, she pointed to the case of a curator (at an art center where she was in residence) who suggested an African American theme for the resident group of composers, based quite simply on the fact that all of the artists were composers, performers, and black. For Pamela Z, this presumed commonality seemed terribly superficial and had very little to do with the actual work or interests of the resident group.

73. Pamela Z Web site (accessed 3 September 2001).

74. Ibid.

75. Ibid.

76. Ibid.

77. Ibid.

78. Ibid.

79. Ibid.

CONCLUSION

1. Donald Lowe, *The History of Bourgeois Perception* (Chicago: University of Chicago Press, 1982).

2. Ibid., 7.

3. Thelma Goldman, introduction to *Freestyle Exhibition* (New York: Studio Museum of Harlem, April 28–June 24, 2001).

4. David Morley, *Home Territories: Media, Mobility, and Identity* (London: Routledge, 2000).

# Bibliography

"ABC Agrees to Deal on Minorities." *San Francisco Chronicle*, 8 January 2000.

Akrumpha, John. "The Last Angel of History." *First Run/Icarus Films* (Brooklyn, N.Y.), 1996, www.frif.com/new97/the_last_.html (accessed August 2003).

Alexander, Clifford. "The Networks' Empty Promises." *New York Times*, 18 August 1999.

Alvey, Mark. "The Independents: Rethinking the Television Studio System." In *The Revolution Wasn't Televised: Sixties Television and Social Conflict*, ed. Lynn Spigel and Michael Curtin, 139–61. New York: Routledge, 1997.

Anderson, Jervis. "Medium Cool." *New Yorker*, 12 December 1994, 69–83.

Andrews, Edmund L. "Congress Votes to Reshape Communications Industry, Ending a Four-Year Struggle." *New York Times*, 2 February 1996.

Ang, Ien. *Living Room Wars: Rethinking Media Audiences for a Postmodern World*. New York: Routledge, 1996.

Appaduri, Arjun. *Modernity at Large: Cultural Dimensions of Globalization*. Minneapolis: University of Minnesota Press, 1996.

Auletta, Ken. "American Keiretsu." *New Yorker*, 20 and 27 October 1997, 225–28.

Bailey, Cameron. "Virtual Skin: Articulating Race in Cyberspace." In *Immersed in Technology: Art in Virtual Environments*, ed. Mary Anne Moser and Douglas MacLeod, 29–49. Cambridge, Mass.: MIT Press, 1996.

Baker, Dave. "Strictly Jazz." *Oakland Tribune*, 15 December 1994.

Barak, Gregg. "Reflexive Newsmaking and Representation." *Critical Studies in Mass Communication* 16, no. 4 (December 1999): 480

———, ed. *Media, Process, and the Social Construction of Crime: Studies in Newsmaking Criminology*. New York: Garland Publishing, 1994.

Basie, Count, and Albert Murray. *Good Morning Blues: The Autobiography of Count Basie*. New York: Da Capo Press, 1985. Reprint, 1995.

Bauder, David. "Latina Heroine Wins Over US Toddlers." *The News* (Mexico City), 15 July 2001.

Becker, Howard. *Art Worlds*. Berkeley: University of California Press, 1982.

Berube, Michael. "Public Academy." *New Yorker*, 9 January 1995, 73–80.

"The Big Ten." *Nation*, 14 January 2002, 27.

Binet-Weiser, Sarah. *The Most Beautiful Girl in the World*. Berkeley: University of California Press, 1999.

Boddy, William. *Fifties Television: The Industry and Its Critics*. Urbana: University of Illinois Press, 1990.

"Boot Up the Television Set." *Economist*, 28 June–14 July 1997, 73–75.

Born, Georgina, and David Hesmondhalgh. "On Difference, Representation, and Appropriation in Music." Introduction to *Western Music and Its Others: Difference, Representation, and Appropriation in Music*, ed. Georgina Born and David Hesmondhalgh, 1–58. Berkeley: University of California Press, 2000.

Boyd, Todd. *Am I Black Enough for You?* Bloomington: Indiana University Press, 1997.

———. *The New H.N.I.C. (Head Niggas in Charge): The Death of Civil Rights and the Reign of Hip-Hop*. New York: New York University Press, 2002.

Boynton, Robert. "The New Intellectuals." *Atlantic Monthly*, March 1995, 53.

———. "Out of Africa and Back." *New York Times*, 14 April 2002, 36–38.

Brantlinger, Patrick. *Bread and Circuses: Theories of Mass Culture and Social Decay*. Ithaca, N.Y.: Cornell University Press, 1983.

Braxton, Greg. "Director Diversity Seen as Lacking." *Los Angeles Times (Orange County Edition)* 30 January 2002.

———. "NAACP Raises Possibility of Boycott." *Los Angeles Times*, 16 August 2001.

Burns, Ken. *Jazz*. Walpole, N.H.: Florentine Films, 2001.

Burrough, Byran, and Kim Masters. "Cable Guys." *Vanity Fair*, January 1997, 76–79, 126–31.

———. "Hollywood's Fading Charms." *Economist*, 22 March 1997, 81–89.

Caldwell, John T. "The Business of New Media." In *The New Media Handbook*, ed. Dan Harries. London: BFI Publishing, 2002.

———. "Convergence Television: Aggregating Form and Re-Purposing Content in the Culture of Conglomeration." In *Television after TV*, ed. Lynn Spigel. Durham, N.C.: Duke University Press, 2004.

———. "Televisual Politics: Negotiating Race in the L.A. Rebellion." In *In Living Color: Race and Television in the United States*, ed. Sasha Torres, 161–95. Durham, N.C.: Duke University Press, 1998.

———. *Televisuality: Style, Crisis, and Authority in American Television*. New Brunswick, N.J.: Rutgers University Press, 1995.

———. "Theorizing the Digital Landrush." Introduction to *Electronic Media and Technoculture*, ed. John T. Caldwell, 1–31. New Brunswick, N.J.: Rutgers University Press, 2000.

———, ed. *Electronic Media and Technoculture*. New Brunswick, N.J.: Rutgers University Press, 2000.

Caldwell, John T., and Bambi L. Haggins, eds. Special issue, pt. 2. *Globalization, Convergence, Identity: Ethnic Notions and National Identity*. Emer-

*gences: Journal for the Study of Media and Composite Cultures* 11, no. 2 (November 2001).

Calmore, John O. "Critical Race Theory, Archie Shepp, and Fire Music: Securing an Authentic Intellectual Life in a Multicultural World." In *Critical Race Theory: The Key Writings That Formed the Movement*, ed. Kimberlé Crenshaw, Neil Gotanda, Gary Peller, and Kendall Thomas, 315–29. New York: New Press, 1995.

Carey, James. *Communication as Culture: Essays on Media and Society*. Boston: Unwin Hyman, 1989.

———. "A Cultural Approach to Communication." In *Communication as Culture: Essays on Media and Society*, by James Carey, 13–36. Boston: Unwin Hyman, 1989.

Carman, John. "The New Prime-Time Schedule." *San Francisco Chronicle and Examiner*, 14 September 1997.

Carter, Bill. "Broadcast Networks Come Back Strong: An Old Medium Holds New Luster for Buyers." *New York Times*, 2 August 1995.

———. "A Wiley Upstart That Did a Lot of Things Right." *New York Times Magazine*, 4 January 1998, 1, 34.

Castells, Manuel. *The Rise of the Network Society*. Vol. 1. Cambridge, Mass.: Blackwell, 1996.

Coleman, David. "Pretty and on the Outside." *George* (June–July 1996): 117–18.

Coleman, Robin R. Means. *African American Viewers and the Black Situation Comedy*. New York: Garland Publishing, 2000.

Coleman, Steve. Interviews by Herman Gray. Telephone interview, September 1997. In-person interview, Berkeley, 1 and 8 April 2001.

———. "Steve Coleman, M-Base, and Musical Collectivism." Interview by Vijay Iyer. Steve Coleman Web site, n.d., www.m-base.com (accessed 15 May 1998).

Conroy, Frank. "Stop Nit Picking a Genius." *New York Times Magazine*, 25 June 1995, 28–31, 48, 54, 70.

Corbett, John. "Anthony Braxton: Of Science and Sinatra." *Down Beat*, April 1994, 28–32.

———. "The Art Ensemble, 1967/68." *Down Beat*, June 1994, 49.

———. John Corbet, "Early AE(C)." *Down Beat*, June 1994.

———. "The Music's Still Happenin'." *Down Beat*, December 1990, 61, 66.

Cotter, Holland. "Beyond Multiculturalism, Freedom?" *New York Times*, 29 July 2001.

Cottle, Simon, ed. *Ethnic Minorities and the Media: Changing Cultural Boundaries*. Buckingham, Eng.: Open University Press, 2000.

Crane Diana. "The Challenge of the Sociology of Culture to Sociology as a Discipline." Introduction to *The Sociology of Culture: Emerging Theoretical Perspectives*, ed. Diana Crane, 1–19. Oxford: Blackwell, 1994.

———, ed. *The Sociology of Culture: Emerging Theoretical Perspectives*. Oxford: Blackwell, 1994.

Croteau, David, and William Hoynes. *The Business of Media: Corporate Media and the Public Interest*. Thousand Oaks, Calif.: Pine Forge Press, 2001.

Crouch, Stanley. *The All American Skin Game; or, The Decoy of Race*. New York: Pantheon Books, 1995.

Cruse, Harold. *The Crisis of the Negro Intellectual.* New York: Morrow, 1967.

Cruz, Jon. *Culture on the Margins: The Black Spiritual and the Rise of American Cultural Interpretation.* Princeton, N.J.: Princeton University Press, 1999.

Curtin, Michael. "Dynasty in Drag: Imagining Global TV." In *The Revolution Wasn't Televised: Sixties Television and Social Conflict,* ed. Lynn Spigel and Michael Curtin, 245–65. New York: Routledge, 1997.

———. "Feminine Desire in the Age of Satellite Television." *Journal of Communication* (Spring 1999): 55.

———. "Gatekeeping in the Neo-Network Era." In *Advocacy Groups and Prime Time Television,* senior ed. Michael Susman. Westport, Conn.: Praeger, 2000.

———. *Redeeming the Wasteland: Television Documentary and Cold War Politics.* New Brunswick, N.J.: Rutgers University Press, 1995.

Davis, Erik. "Dub, Scratch, and the Black Star: Lee Perry on the Mix." *Erik Davis' Figments and Inklings* Web site, www.techgnosis.com/dub.html (accessed 31 January 2002).

———. "Roots and Wires: Polyrhythmic Cyberspace and Black Electronic." *Erik Davis' Figments and Inklings* Web site, www.techgnosis.com/cyberconf.html (accessed 31 January 2002).

———. "Songs in the Key of F12." *Wired,* May 2002, 96–101.

Davis, Mike. *City of Quartz: Excavating the Future in Los Angeles.* London: Verso, 1992.

Davis, Miles, and Quincy Troupe. *Miles Davis: The Autobiography.* New York: Simon and Schuster, 1989.

Davis, Susan G. *Spectacular Nature: Corporate Culture and the Sea Experience.* Berkeley: University of California Press, 1997.

Delgado, Guillermo, and Marc Becker. "Latin America: The Internet and Indigenous Texts" *Cultural Survival Quarterly* 21, no. 4 (31 January 1998): 23–28.

Denning, Michael. *The Cultural Front: The Laboring of American Culture in the Twentieth Century.* London: Verso, 1997.

DeVeaux, Scott. *The Birth of Bebop: A Social and Musical History.* Berkeley: University of California Press, 1997.

Dilday, K. A. "A Black Drama Beats the Clichés, and the Odds." *New York Times,* 24 June 2001.

Dillard, Angela D. "Multicultural Conservativism: What It Is, Why It Matters." *Chronicle of Higher Education,* 2 March 2001, B7–10.

DiMaggio, Paul. "Cultural Entrepreneurship in Nineteenth-Century Boston: The Creation of an Organizational Base for High Culture in America." In *Rethinking Popular Culture: Contemporary Perspectives in Cultural Studies,* ed. Chandra Mukerji and Michael Schudson, 374–97. Berkeley: University of California Press, 1991.

DJ Spooky, AKA, That Subliminal Kid's Web site, www.djspooky.com (accessed 11 January 2002).

Dollar, Steve. "The Lightening Rod." *Down Beat,* February 1996, 26.

Du Cille, Anne. *Skin Trade.* Cambridge, Mass.: Harvard University Press, 1996.

Dyer, Richard. *White*. New York: Routledge, 1997.

Early, Gerald. "A Place of Our Own." *The New York Times*, 14 April 2002, 34, 35, 40.

Edwards, Jim. "Nice TV." *Brills Content* 4, no. 2 (2001): 88–94.

Elber, Lynn. "NAACP Renews Talk of Network Boycott." *San Francisco Chronicle*, 16 August 2001.

Elison, Ralph. *The Invisible Man*. 1952. Reprint, Vintage Books, 1972.

Ellington, Duke. *Music Is My Mistress*. New York: Da Capo Press, 1973.

Elworth, Steven. "Jazz in Crisis, 1948–1958: Ideology and Representation." In *Jazz among the Discourses*, ed. Krin Gabbard, 57–76. Durham, N.C.: Duke University Press, 1995.

Entman, Robert M., and Andrew Rojecki. *The Black Image in the White Mind*. Chicago: University of Chicago Press, 2000.

Eshun, Kodwo. *More Brilliant Than the Sun: Adventures in Sonic Fiction*. London: Quartet, 1998.

———. "Motion Capture." Cybernetic Culture Research Unit, n.d., www.ccru.demon.co.uk/swarm1/1_motion (accessed 11 January 2002).

Everett, Anna, and John T. Caldwell, eds. *Theories and Practices of Digitextuality*. New York: Routledge, 2003.

Fellez, Kevin. "Between Rock and a Jazz Place: Intercultural Interchange in Fusion Musicking." Ph.D. diss., History of Consciousness Program, University of California, Santa Cruz, 2004.

Ferguson, Roderick. *Aberrations in Black: Toward a Queer of Color Critique*. Minneapolis: University of Minnesota Press, 2003.

Fiske, John. *Media Matters: Everyday Culture and Political Change*. Minneapolis: University of Minnesota Press, 1994.

Flash, Grandmaster. Interview with Terry Gross. National Public Radio's *Fresh Air*, 8 July 2002.

Flores, Lisa, and Mark L. McPhail. "From Black and White to *Living Color*: A Dialogic Exposition into the Social (Re)Construction of Race, Gender, and Crime." *Critical Studies in Mass Communication* 14, no. 1 (March 1997): 106–22.

Frith, Simon. *Performing Rites*. Cambridge, Mass.: Harvard University Press, 1996.

Gabbard, Krin. "Ken Burns's *Jazz*: Beautiful Music, but Missing a Beat." *Chronicle of Higher Education*, 15 December 2000, B18–19.

———, ed. *Jazz among the Discourses*. Durham, N.C.: Duke University Press, 1995.

Gaither, Leonce. "Is the Web Too Cool for Blacks?" *Salon*, www.salon.com/June97/21st/1001970605.html (accessed 6 June 2001).

Gamson, Joshua. "Diversity Follies." *American Prospect* 11, no. 4 (2000). Available also from www.americanprospect.org.

Gates, Henry Louis, Jr., and Nellie Y. McKay, eds. *The Norton Anthology of African American Literature*. New York: W. W. Norton, 1996.

Gendron, Bernard. "Moldy Figs and Modernists: Jazz at War (1942–46)." In *Jazz among the Discourses*, ed. Krin Gabbard, 31–57. Durham, N.C.: Duke University Press, 1995.

Gilroy, Paul. *The Black Atlantic: Modernity and Double Consciousness.* Cambridge, Mass.: Harvard University Press, 1993.

———. "After the Love Has Gone: Bio-Politics and Etho-Politics in the Black Public Sphere." *Public Culture* 7, no. 1 (1994): 49–77.

———. *Against Race: Imagining Political Culture Beyond the Color Line.* Cambridge, Mass.: Harvard University Press, 2000.

———. *Small Acts: Thoughts on the Politics of Black Culture.* London: Serpent's Tail Press, 1993.

Giroux, Henry. "In Living Color: Black, Bruised, and Read All Over." In *Channel Surfing: Race Talk and the Destruction of Today's Youth,* by Henry Giroux, 137–73. New York: St. Martin's Press, 1997.

Gitlin, Todd. *Inside Prime Time.* New York: Pantheon Books, 1983.

Goldberg, David Theo. *The Racial State.* London: Blackwell, 2002.

———. *Racist Culture: Philosophy and the Politics of Meaning.* Cambridge, Mass.: Blackwell, 1993.

———. "Spatial Rhetorics: The Architecture of Conferencing." *Appendx: A Journal about Culture, Theory, and Praxis,* no. 3 (1996): 166–73.

———. "Whither West? The Making of a Public Intellectual." In *Racial Subjects: Writing on Race in America,* by David Theo Goldberg, 123–26. New York: Routledge, 1997.

Goldberg, David T., Michael Musheno, and Lisa Bower. *Between Law and Culture: Relocating Legal Studies.* Minneapolis: University of Minnesota Press, 2001.

Goldman, Robert, and Stephen Papson. *Nike Culture: The Sign of the Swoosh.* London: Sage Publications, 1996.

———. *Sign Wars: The Cluttered Landscape of Advertising.* New York: Guilford Press, 1999.

Goldman, Thelma. *Black Male: Representations of Masculinity in Contemporary American Art.* New York: Whitney Museum of American Art, 1994.

———, curator. *Freestyle Exhibition.* New York: Studio Museum of Harlem, April 28–June 24, 2001.

Goldman, Vivien. "Harmolodic Harlem." *Village Voice,* 3 September 1996, 41, 44.

Gooding-Williams, Robert, ed. *Reading Rodney King, Reading Urban Uprisings.* New York: Routledge, 1993.

Gopinath, Gayatri. "Bombay, U.K., Yuba City: Bangra Music and the Engendering of Diaspora." *Diaspora* 4, no. 3 (1995): 303–22.

Gordon, Avery. *Ghostly Matters: Haunting and the Sociological Imagination.* Minneapolis: University of Minnesota Press, 1997.

Gordon, Robert. *Can't Be Satisfied: The Life and Times of Muddy Waters.* Boston: Little, Brown, 2002.

Gray, Herman. "A Different Dream of Difference." *Critical Studies in Mass Communication* 18, no. 1 (2001): 103–8.

———. "Jazz Tradition, Institutional Formation, and Cultural Practice: The Canon and the Street as Frameworks for Oppositional Black Cultural Politics." In *From Sociology to Cultural Studies,* ed. Elizabeth Long, 351–73. London: Blackwell, 1997.

———. *Watching Race: Television and the Struggle for Blackness.* Minneapolis: University of Minnesota Press, 1995.

Guerrero, Edward. *Framing Blackness: The African American Image in Film.* Philadelphia: Temple University Press, 1993.

Guilliatt, Richard. "Eminence Jazz." *San Jose Mercury News,* 11 June 1993.

———. "The Young Lions Roar." *Los Angeles Times,* 13 September 1992.

Haggins, Bambi L. "Why 'Beulah' and 'Andy' Still Play Today: Minstrelsy in the New Millennium." *Emergences: Journal for the Study of Media and Composite Cultures* 11, no. 2 (2001): 189–99.

Hajdu, David. "Wynton's Blues." *Atlantic Monthly,* March 2003, 43–58.

Hall, Stuart. "New Ethnicities." In *Stuart Hall: Critical Dialogues in Cultural Studies,* ed. David Morley and Kuan-Hsing Chen, 441–50. New York: Routledge, 1989.

———. "What Is This 'Black' in Black Popular Culture?" In *Black Popular Culture: A Project by Michele Wallace,* ed. Gina Dent, 21–37. Seattle: Bay Press, 1992.

Hamamoto, Darrell Y. "White Christian Nation." In *Monitored Peril: Asian Americans and the Politics of TV Representation,* by Darrell Y. Hamamoto, 1–31. Minneapolis: University of Minnesota Press, 1994.

Harper, Brian Phillip. *Are We Not Men? Masculine Anxiety and the Problem of African-American Identity.* New York: Oxford University Press, 1996.

Hartley, John. *The Uses of Television.* New York: Routledge, 1999.

Hass, Nancy. "A TV Generation Is Seeing beyond Color." *New York Times,* 22 February 1998.

Hay, James. "Unaided Virtues: The Neoliberalization of the Domestic Sphere." *Television and New Media* 1, no. 1 (2000): 53–73.

Hayles, Katherine. *How We Become Post Human: Virtual Bodies in Cybernetics, Literature, and Information.* Chicago: University of Chicago Press, 1999.

Hebdige, Dick. *Cut 'n' Mix: Culture, Identity, and Caribbean Music.* London: Methuen, 1987.

———. *Hiding in the Light: On Images and Things.* London: Routledge, 1998.

Hinton, Milt. *Bass Lines: The Stories and Photographs of Milt Hinton.* Philadelphia: Temple University Press, 1988.

Horkheimer, Max, and Theodor Adorno. "The Culture Industry: Enlightenment as Mass Deception." In *Dialectic of Enlightenment,* ed. Max Horkheimer and Theodor Adorno, trans. John Cumming, 120–67. New York: Seabury Press, 1944. Reprint, 1972.

Hunt, Darnell. *O.J.: Fact and Fiction.* Cambridge: Cambridge University Press, 1999.

———. *Screening the Los Angeles "Riots": Race, Seeing, and Resistance.* Cambridge: Cambridge University Press, 1997.

Hutnyk, John. "Authenticity or Cultural Politics." In *Critique of Exotica Music, Politics, and the Culture Industry,* by John Hutnyk, 114–37. London: Pluto Press, 2000.

Iyer, Vijay. "Steve Coleman, M-Base, and Musical Collectivism." Steve Coleman Web site, 1996, www.cnmat.berkeley.edu/~vijay/toc.html (accessed September 1998).

Jacoby, Tamar. "Adjust Your Sets." *New Republic*, 24 January 2000, www.tnr.com/archive/012400/jacoby012400.html (accessed 21 June 2001).

————. "Color Blind: The African American Absence in High Tech." *New Republic*, 29 March 1999, www.tnr.com/archive/0399/032999/jacoby032999 .html (accessed 21 June 2001).

James, Darius. *Negrophobia: An Urban Parable*. New York: St. Martin's Press, 1992.

James, Meg. "Latino Networks Feel Underrated." *Los Angeles Times*, 25 March 2002.

Jameson, Frederic. *Postmodernism; or, The Cultural Logic of Late Capitalism*. Durham, N.C.: Duke University Press, 1991.

"Jazz: A Special Section." *New York Times Magazine*, 25 June 1995, 29–40.

Johnson, Victoria E. "Citizen Welk: Bubbles, Blue Hair and Middle America." In *The Revolution Wasn't Televised: Sixties Television and Social Conflict*, ed. Lynn Spigel and Michael Curtin, 265–85. New York: Routledge, 1997.

————. "Welcome Home? CBS, PAX-TV and 'Heartland' Values in a Neo-Network Era." *The Velvet Light Trap: A Critical Journal of Film and Television* 46 (2000): 40–56.

Jones, Jonathan. "Paradise Reclaimed." *Guardian*, 15 June 2002.

Jones, Quincy. *Q: The Autobiography of Quincy Jones*. New York: Doubleday, 2001.

Kelley, Robin D. G. "The Riddle of the Zoot Suit: Malcolm Little and Black Cultural Politics during World War II." In *Race Rebels: Culture, Politics, and the Black Working Class*, ed. Robin D. G. Kelley, 35–55. New York: Free Press, 1994.

————. "We Are Not What We Seem: The Politics and Pleasures of Community." In *Race Rebels: Culture, Politics, and the Black Working Class*, ed. Robin D. G. Kelley, 161–83. New York: Free Press, 1994.

————. *Yo Mama's Disfunktional! Fighting the Culture Wars in Urban America*. Boston: Beacon Press, 1997.

Kelly, Kevin. "Where Music Will Be Coming From." *New York Times Magazine*, 17 March 2002, 29–31.

Kennedy, Kathy. "A Few Facets of Pamela Z." *Musicworks: Explorations in Sound* 76 (2000). Available at *Pamela Z* Web site, www.pamelaz.com (accessed July 2002).

Kim, L. S., and Gilberto Moises Blasini. "The Performance of Multicultural Identity in US Network Television: Shiny, Happy Popstars (Holding Hands)." *Emergences: Journal for the Study of Media and Composite Cultures* 11, no. 2 (2001): 287–309.

Kimmelman, Michael. "A Black World of Ins and Outs." *New York Times*, 26 April 2002.

Klein, Naomi. *No Logo: Taking Aim at the Brand Bullies*. New York: Picador, 2000.

Kolko, Beth E. "Erasing @Race: Going White in the (Inter)Face." In *Race in Cyberspace*, ed. Beth E. Kolko, Lisa Nakamura, and Gilbert Rodman, 213–32. New York: Routledge, 2000.

Kolko, Beth E., Lisa Nakamura, and Gilbert B. Rodman, eds. *Race in Cyberspace*. New York: Routledge, 2000.

Kun, Josh. "Against Easy Listening: Audiotropic Readings and Transnational Soundings." In *Everynight Life: Culture and Dance in Latin/o America*, ed. Celeste Fraser Delgado and Jose Esteban Mu{nt}oz, 288–309. Durham, N.C.: Duke University Press, 1997.

———. Interview with Don Byron. Unpublished ms., n.d.

LeBan, Craig. *The Whole History of Jazz, According to Lincoln Center*. Unpublished manuscript, 1994.

Leeds, Jeff and Chuck Philips. "Soul Train's Creator Accuses MTV of Unfair Booking Rules." *Los Angeles Times*, 17 August 2001.

Levine, Lawrence. *The Opening of the American Mind: Canon, Culture, and History*. Boston: Beacon Press, 1996.

Lewis, George. "Experimental Music in Black and White: The AACM in New York, 1970–1985." *Current Musicology* 71–73 (Spring 2001–2): 100–158.

———. "Improvised Music after 1950: Afrological and Eurological Perspectives." *Black Music Research Journal* 16 (1996): 91–122.

———. "Singing the Alternative Interactivity Blues." *Front* 7, no. 2 (1995): 18–22. Reprinted in *Grantmakers in the Arts* 8, no. 1 (Spring 1997).

———. "Too Many Notes: Computers, Complexity, and Culture in Voyager." *Leonardo Music Journal* 10 (2000): 33–39.

Lewis, Michael. "Boom Box." *New York Times Magazine*, 13 August 2001, 36–42.

Lipsitz, George. *Dangerous Crossroads: Popular Music, Postmodernism, and the Poetics of Place*. London: Verso, 1994.

———. "Law and Order: Civil Rights Laws and White Privilege." In *The Possessive Investment in Whiteness: How White People Profit from Identity Politics*, by George Lipsitz, 24–46. Philadelphia: Temple University Press, 1998.

———. "Like a Weed in a Vacant Lot: The Black Artist Group in St. Louis." In *Decomposition: Post Disciplinary Performance*, ed. Sue-Ellen Case, P. Brett, and S. L. Foster, 51–61. Bloomington: Indiana University Press, 2000.

———. "The Meaning of Memory: Family, Class, and Ethnicity in Early American Network Television." In *Time Passages: Collective Memory and American Popular Culture*, by George Lipsitz, 39–77. Minneapolis: University of Minnesota Press, 1990.

———. *The Possessive Investment in Whiteness: How White People Profit from Identity Politics*. Philadelphia: Temple University Press, 1998.

Liska, James A. "Wynton and Branford: A Common Understanding." *Down Beat*, February 1994, 42–44.

Litweiler, John. "Thank You, Ornette!" *Down Beat*, January 1992, 31.

Lock, Graham. *Blutopia: Visions of the Future and Revisions of the Past in the Works of Sun Ra, Duke Ellington, and Anthony Braxton*. Durham, N.C.: Duke University Press, 1999.

Lopes, Paul. *The Rise of a Jazz Art World*. Cambridge: Cambridge University Press, 2002.

Lott, Eric. "Double V, Double-Time: Bebop's Politics of Style." In *Jazz among the Discourses*, ed. Krin Gabbard, 243–56. Durham, N.C.: Duke University Press, 1995.

Lott, Tommy Lee. "Kara Walker Speaks: A Public Conversation on Racism, Art, and Politics with Tommy Lott." *Black Renaissance/Renaissance Noire* 3, no. 1 (Fall 2000): 69–91.

———. "The 1960s Avant-Garde Movement in Jazz." *Social Identities* 7, no. 2 (2001): 1–11.

Louis, Errol T. "Jazz Makes a New Sound with Soul, Pop, and Computers; Brooklyn Musical Collective: Micro-Basic Array of Structured Extemporizations." *Smithsonian*, October 1989, 176.

Love, Preston. *A Thousand Honey Creeks Later: My Life in Music from Basie to Motown and Beyond*. Hanover, N.H.: University Press of New England, 1997.

Lowe, Donald. *The History of Bourgeois Perception*. Chicago: University of Chicago Press, 1982.

Lowe, Lisa. *Immigrant Acts: On Asian American Cultural Politics*. Durham, N.C.: Duke University Press, 1996.

Lowe, Lisa, and David Lloyd, eds. *The Politics of Culture in the Shadow of Capital*. Durham, N.C.: Duke University Press, 1997.

Lowery, Brian, Elizabeth Jensen, and Greg Braxton. "Networks Decide Diversity Doesn't Pay." *Los Angeles Times*, 30 July 1999.

Lull, James. *Media, Communication, Culture: A Global Approach*. New York: Columbia University Press, 1995.

Mackey, Nathaniel. "Other: From Noun to Verb." In *Jazz among the Discourses*, ed. Krin Gabbard, 76–100. Durham, N.C.: Duke University Press, 1995.

Mahon, Maureen. "Black Like This: Race, Generation, and Rock in the Post–Civil Rights Era." *American Ethnologist* 27, no. 2 (2002): 283–311.

Mandel, Howard. "From Chicago, Deep in the Art of Jazz." *Washington Post*, 23 September 1984.

Marsalis, Wynton. *Sweet Swing Blues on the Road*. New York: W. W. Norton, 1994.

———. "What Jazz Is—and Isn't." Editorial, *New York Times*, 31 July 1988.

Marzoratti, Gerald. "All by Himself." *New York Times Magazine*, 17 March 2002, 32–37, 68–70.

Masters, Kim. "Hollywood Vertigo." *Vanity Fair*, February 1997, 66–72.

May, Derrick. "The Screamers." *Wired*, May 2002, 108.

McCarthy, Anna. *Ambient Television: Visual Culture and Public Space*. Durham, N.C.: Duke University Press, 2000.

McChesney, Robert W. "The Media System Goes Global." In *Rich Media Poor Democracy: Communication Politics in Dubious Times*, by Robert W. McChesney, 78–118. New York: New Press, 1999.

———. *Rich Media, Poor Democracy: Communication Politics in Dubious Times*. New York: New Press, 1999.

Meehan, Eileen. "Why We Don't Count: The Commodity Audience." In *The Logics of Television: Essays in Cultural Criticism*, ed. Patricia Mellencamp, 117–37. Bloomington: Indiana University Press, 1990.

Mellencamp, Patricia, ed. *The Logics of Television: Essays in Cultural Criticism.* Bloomington: Indiana University Press, 1990.

Mercer, Kobena. *Welcome to the Jungle: New Positions in Black Cultural Politics.* London: Routledge, 1994.

Merelman, Richard. *Representing Black Culture: Racial Conflict and Cultural Politics in the United States.* New York: Routledge, 1995.

Miller, Paul D. "Deep Shit: A Conversation with Chris Ofili." DJ Spooky, AKA, That Subliminal Kid Web site, www.djspooky.com (accessed 11 January 2002).

Mitchell, William J. *City of Bits: Space, Place, and the Infobahn.* Cambridge, Mass.: MIT Press, 1996.

Morley, David. *Home Territories: Media, Mobility, and Identity.* London: Routledge, 2000.

Morley, David, and Kevin Robins. *Spaces of Identity: Global Media, Electronic Landscapes, and Cultural Boundaries.* London: Routledge, 1995.

Murray, Albert. *The Blue Devils of Nada: A Contemporary American Approach to Aesthetic Statement.* New York: Pantheon Books, 1996.

———. *Stomping the Blues.* New York: McGraw-Hill, 1976.

Music issue. *Wired,* May 2002.

*Musicworks* Web site, www.musicworks.ca (accessed 29 July 2002).

"NAACP Sees Scant Progress on TV." *New York Times,* 15 August 2001.

Neal, Mark Anthony. *Soul Babies: Black Popular Culture and the Post-Soul Aesthetic.* New York: Routledge, 2000.

———. *What the Music Said: Black Popular Music and Black Public Culture.* New York: Routledge, 1999.

Negus, Keith. *Music, Genres, and Corporate Cultures.* London: Routledge, 1999.

Nelson, Alondra. "Braving the New World: Race and Technology: Afrofuturism: Beyond the Digital Divide." In *Race and Public Policy,* ed. Makani N. Themba, 37–40. Oakland: Applied Research Center, 2000.

Nelson, Alondra, Thuy Linh N. Tu, and Alicia Headlam Himes, eds. *Technicolor: Race, Technology, and Everyday Life.* New York: New York University Press, 2001.

Newcomb, Horace. "From Old Frontier to New Frontier." In *The Revolution Wasn't Televised: Sixties Television and Social Conflict,* ed. Lynn Spigel and Michael Curtin, 287–305. New York: Routledge, 1997.

Nichols, Bill. "The Work of Culture in the Age of Cybernetic Systems." In *Electronic Media and Technoculture,* ed. John T. Caldwell, 90–114. New Brunswick, N.J.: Rutgers University Press, 2000.

Norris, Floyd. "Broadcast Networks Come Back Strong: Capital Cities and CBS Have Happy Investors." *New York Times,* 2 August 1995.

Novak, Thomas, and Donna L. Hoffman. "Bridging the Digital Divide: The Impact of Race on Computer Access and Internet Use." *Project 2000 Vanderbilt University* Web site, 1998, www.2000.ogsm.vanderbiltuniversity.edu (accessed 26 June 2000).

"Now What? The Dawn of the Post Network, Post Broadcast, Post Mass Television Age." *New York Times Magazine,* 20 September 1998, 53–107.

O'Donnell, Susan, and Guillermo Delgado. "Using the Internet to Strengthen the Indigenous Nations of the Americas." *Media Development* 42, no. 3 (1995): 36–39.

Oliver, Melvin L., and Thomas M. Shapiro. *Black Wealth/White Wealth: A New Perspective on Racial Inequality.* New York: Routledge, 1995.

O'Meally, Robert G., ed. *The Jazz Cadence of American Culture.* New York: Columbia University Press, 1998.

"Once More with Feeling." *Economist,* 12 April 1997, 64–65.

Ong, Aihwa. "Cultural Citizenship as Subject-Making: Immigrants Negotiate Racial and Cultural Boundaries in the United States." *Current Anthropology* 37, no. 5 (1996): 737–62.

Ouellette, Dan. "Tree of Jazz Grown in Brooklyn Reaches Bay Area." *San Francisco Chronicle,* 27 July 1996.

Palmer, Robert. "20th Anniversary for an Unusual Jazz Ensemble." *New York Times,* 14 April 1985.

Pamela Z Web site, www.pamelaz.com (accessed 3 September 2001).

Pareles, Jon. "Crisscrossing the Cultural Boundaries: Vernon Reid Likes Forging Unlikely Artistic Alliances." *New York Times,* 23 September 1998.

Parker, Ian. "Golden Touch." *New Yorker,* 14 January 2002, 44–49.

Penley, Constance, and Andrew Ross, eds. *Technoculture.* Minneapolis: University of Minnesota Press, 1991.

Pogrebin, Robin. "New Director at Carnegie Eliminates Its Jazz Band." *New York Times,* 17 January 2002.

———. "Toil and Trouble at the Public: A Debate over Whether George Wolfe's Institution Needs New Direction." *New York Times,* 18 October 2000.

Porter, Eric. *What Is This Thing Called Jazz? African American Musicians as Artists, Critics, and Activists.* Berkeley: University of California Press, 2002.

Poster, Mark. *The Mode of Information: Poststructuralism and Social Context.* Chicago: University of Chicago Press, 1990.

Pounds, Michael C. *Race in Space: The Representation of Ethnicity in "Star Trek" and "Star Trek: The Next Generation."* Lanham, Md.: Scarecrow Press, 1999.

Powell, Richard. *Black Art and Culture in the 20th Century.* New York: Thames and Hudson, 1997.

Prestianni, Sam. "What Wynton Doesn't Hear: Lester Bowie Explains." *San Francisco Weekly,* 11 September 1996, 27.

Radano, Ronald. *New Musical Figurations: Anthony Braxton's Cultural Critique.* Chicago: University of Chicago Press, 1993.

Radano, Ronald, and Phillip V. Bohlman. *Music and the Racial Imagination.* Chicago: University of Chicago Press, 2000.

Ratliff, Ben. "Fixing, for Now, the Image of Jazz." *New York Times,* 7 January 2001.

———. "A Jazz Guerrilla Blows Back in, Spreading Ideas." *New York Times,* 18 August 2002.

Reed, Adolph. "What Are the Drums Saying, Booker? The Current Crisis of the Black Intellectual." *Village Voice,* 11 April 1995, 35.

Reeves, Jimmie, and Richard Campbell. *Cracked Coverage: Television News, the Anti-Cocaine Crusade, and the Reagan Legacy.* Durham, N.C.: Duke University Press, 1994.

Renaissance Society at the University of Chicago, Newsletter. Chicago: Renaissance Society at the University of Chicago, 1997.

Richardson, Derk. "Outward Bound." *San Francisco Bay Guardian*, 4–10 September 1996.

Riggs, Marlon T. *Color Adjustment.* Film. San Francisco: California Newsreel, 1991.

Rinder, Lawrence. Interview with Kara Walker. In *Kara Walker: No Mere Words*, exhibition program notes, exhibited 3 April–15 May 1999, 46–47. Oakland: California College of Arts and Crafts and the Capp Street Project, 1999.

Robins, Kevin, and Frank Webster. *The Times of the Technoculture: From the Information Society to the Virtual Life.* New York: Routledge, 1999.

Rodman, Gilbert B. "The Net Effect: The Public's Fear and the Public Sphere." In *Virtual Publics: Policy and Community in an Electronic Age*, ed. Beth E. Kolko, 9–48. New York: Columbia University Press, 2000.

Roediquer, David R. *The Wages of Whiteness: Race and the Making of the American Working Class.* London: Verso, 1991.

Rogin, Michael. *Blackface, White Noise: Jewish Immigrants in the Hollywood Melting Pot.* Berkeley: University of California Press, 1996.

Ross, Alex. "Asking Some Good, Hard Truths about Music." *New York Times*, 12 November 1995.

Ross, Andrew. "Jobs in Cyberspace." In *Real Love: In Pursuit of Cultural Justice*, by Andrew Ross, 7–34. New York: New York University Press, 1998.

———. *Real Love: In Pursuit of Cultural Justice.* New York: New York University Press, 1998.

"A Roundtable on Ken Burns's *Jazz.*" Moderated by Geoffrey Jacques. *Journal of Popular Music Studies* 13, no. 2 (Fall 2001): 207–27.

Salamon, Julie. "An Evolving Vision in Black and White." *New York Times*, 1 February 2002.

Santoro, Gene. "All That Jazz." *Nation*, 8 January 1996, 34–36.

———. "The Avant-Garde." *Nation*, 13 April 1992, 497.

———. "Dancing in Your Head." *Nation*, 12 August 1991, 199–201.

———. "The World Saxophone Quartet: Building on a New Tradition." *Down Beat*, July 1989, 16–19.

———. "Young Man with a Horn." *Nation*, 1 March 1993, 280–84.

Sato, Art. Interview by Herman Gray. San Francisco, 21 April 1997.

Scherman, Tony. "What Is Jazz?" *American Heritage*, October 1995, 66–86.

Schiesel, Seth. "Where the Message is the Medium: For Disney's Eisner, the Business is Content, Not Conduits." *New York Times*, 2 July 2001.

Schiller, Dan. *Digital Capitalism: Networking the Global Market System.* Cambridge, Mass.: MIT Press, 2000.

Schon, Donald A., Bish Sanyal, and William J. Mitchell, eds. *High Technology and Low Income Communities: Prospects for the Positive Use of Advanced Information Technology.* Cambridge, Mass.: MIT Press, 1999.

Scott, Janny. "Who Gets to Tell a Black Story?" *New York Times,* 11 June 2000.

"Screen Actors Guild Employment Statistics Reveal Increase in Total TV/Theatrical Roles and Increases for All Minorities in 2000." Press release. Screen Actors Guild Web site, 2001, www.sag.org (accessed 16 August 2001).

Sellar, Tom. "Parts of Speech." *Theater Magazine,* Winter 2000, 59–66.

Smith, Ethan. "Organization Moby." *Wired,* May 2002, 89–94.

Smith, Joan. "Wynton Blows His Horn for Jazz." *San Francisco Examiner,* 18 December 1994.

Solomon, Deborah. "The Downtowning of Uptown." *New York Times,* 19 August 2001.

Spigel, Lynn. *Make Room for TV: Television and the Family Ideal in Postwar America.* Chicago: University of Chicago Press, 1992.

———. *Welcome to the Dreamhouse: Popular Media and Postwar Suburbs.* Durham, N.C.: Duke University Press, 2001.

———. "White Flight." In *The Revolution Wasn't Televised: Sixties Television and Social Conflict,* ed. Lynn Spigel and Michael Curtin, 47–72. New York: Routledge, 1997.

———, ed. *Television after TV.* Durham, N.C.: Duke University Press, forthcoming.

Sreenath, Srenivasan. "Newscasts in Tagalog and Songs in Gaelic." *New York Times,* 8 September 1997.

Stacey, Judith. *In the Name of the Family: Rethinking Family Values in the Postmodern Age.* Boston: Beacon Press, 1996.

Sterngold, James. "How Cable Captured the Mini Series and the High Ground." *New York Times Magazine,* 20 September 1998, 86–87.

———. "A Racial Divide Widens on Network TV." *New York Times,* 29 December 1998.

Stoller, Ann Laura. *Race and the Education of Desire.* New York: Routledge, 1995.

Stone, Allucquere R. *The War of Desire and Technology at the Close of the Mechanical Age.* Cambridge, Mass.: MIT Press, 1995.

Sturkin, Maurita. *Tangled Memories: The Vietnam War, the AIDS Epidemic, and the Politics of Remembering.* Berkeley: University of California Press, 1997.

"Survey: E-Entertainment." *Economist,* 7 October 2000, special section.

Sutter, Mary, and Laurel Wentz. "U.S. Conexiones." *Advertising Age,* 16 July 2001, 14.

Szwed, John F. *Space Is the Place: The Lives and Times of Sun Ra.* New York: Pantheon Books, 1997.

Tal, Kali. "The Unbearable Whiteness of Being: African American Critical Theory and Cyberculture." Kali Tal Web site, 1996, www.freshmonsters.com/kalital/Text/Articles/whiteness.html (accessed 6 June 2001).

Tapscott, Horace. *Songs of the Unsung: The Musical and Social Journey of Horace Tapscott.* Ed. Steven Isoardi. Durham, N.C.: Duke University Press, 2001.

Taylor, Clyde. *The Mask of Art: Breaking the Aesthetic Contract.* Bloomington: Indiana University Press, 1998.

"Ted Turner's Management Consultant." *Economist,* 22 March 1997, 96.

*Tempo.* Program notes, Berkeley Festival of Contemporary Performance, University of California, Berkeley School Of Music, 1–9 July 2001.

Torres, Sasha. *Black, White, and in Color: Television and Black Civil Rights.* Princeton, N.J.: Princeton University Press, 2003.

———, ed. *In Living Color: Race and Television in the United States.* Durham, N.C.: Duke University Press, 1998.

Treachout, Terry. "The Color of Jazz." *Commentary,* September 1995, 50–54.

"Trialogues along the Color Lines." *Critical Studies in Mass Communication* 16, no. 4 (1999): 478–88.

Tucker, Sherrie. *Swing Shift: "All Girl" Bands of the 1940s.* Durham, N.C.: Duke University Press, 2000.

University of Southern California and Massachusetts Institute of Technology. Race in Digital Space: A National Conference on Race and New Media Technologies. Web site, cms.mit.edu/race/press.html (accessed 6 June 2001).

Valdivia, Angharad N., ed. *Feminism, Multiculturalism, and the Media: Global Diversities.* Thousand Oaks, Calif.: Sage Publications, 1995.

Wald, Gayle. "'I Want It That Way': Teenybopper Music and the Girling of Boy Bands." Forthcoming book chapter.

Walker, Kara. "Upon My Many Masters: An Outline." In *San Francisco Museum of Modern Art Exhibition Catalogue.* San Francisco: San Francisco Museum of Modern Art, 1997.

Walser, Robert. "Deep Jazz: Notes on Interiority, Race, and Criticism." In *Inventing the Psychological: Toward a Cultural History of Emotional Life in America,* ed. Joel Pfister and Nancy Schnog, 271–96. New Haven, Conn.: Yale University Press, 1997.

———. *Running with the Devil: Power, Gender, and Madness in Heavy Metal Music.* Hanover, N.H.: University Press of New England, 1993.

Walton, Anthony. "Technology versus African Americans." *Atlantic Monthly,* January 1999. Available at www.atlantic.com (accessed 6 June 2001).

Watkins, S. Craig. *Representing: Hip-Hop Culture and the Production of Black Cinema.* Chicago: University of Chicago Press, 1998.

Watrous, Peter. "Brooklyn Academy Finds Room for Outsiders of Jazz." *New York Times,* 12 October 1995.

———. "Is There a Mid-Life Crisis at the JVC Festival?" *New York Times,* 8 July 1995.

———. "Old Jazz Is Out, New Jazz Is Older." *New York Times,* 31 March 1994.

———. "Remember Mickey Katz? No? Well, Just Listen to This." *New York Times,* 19 January 1990.

Wesley, Fred. *Hit Me, Fred: Recollections of a Sideman.* Durham, N.C.: Duke University Press, 2002.

West, Cornel. "The New Cultural Politics of Difference." In *Out There: Marginalizations and Contemporary Cultures,* ed. Russell Ferguson et al., 19–39. Cambridge, Mass.: MIT Press, 1990.

———. *Race Matters.* Boston: Beacon Press, 1993.

White, Jack E. "The Beauty of Black Art." *Time,* October 10, 1994, 66.

Whitehead, Kevin. "Jazz Rebels: Lester Bowie and Greg Osby." *Down Beat,* August 1993, 17.

Williams, Ben. "Black Street Technology: Detroit Techno and the Information Age." In *Technicolor: Race, Technology, and Everyday Life,* ed. Alondra Nelson, Thuy Linh N. Tu, and Alicia Headlam Himes, 154–76. New York: New York University Press, 2001.

Williams, Linda. "A Young Musician Trumpets a Revival of Traditional Jazz." *Wall Street Journal,* 24 September 1986.

Williams, Mark. "Entertaining 'Difference': Strains of Orientalism in Early Los Angeles Television." In *In Living Color: Race and Television in the United States,* ed. Sasha Torres, 12–34. Durham, N.C.: Duke University Press, 1998.

Williams, Raymond. *Marxism and Literature.* Oxford: Oxford University Press, 1977.

———. *The Sociology of Culture.* New York: Schocken Books, 1982.

———. *Television: Technology and Cultural Form.* New York: Schocken Books, 1974.

Wilson, Olly. "Black Music as an Art Form." In *The Jazz Cadence of American Culture,* ed. Robert G. O'Meally, 82–101. New York: Columbia University Press, 1998.

Wilson, Pamela. "Confronting the 'Indian Problem': Media Discourses of Race, Ethnicity, Nation, and Empire in 1950s America." In *In Living Color: Race and Television in the United States,* ed. Sasha Torres, 35–61. Durham, N.C.: Duke University Press, 1998.

Wolff, Jeremy. "A 'Cat' from the Bronx Makes His Mark on Klezmer." *Wall Street Journal,* 19 September 1991.

Yuen, Eddie, George Katsiaficas, and Daniel Burton Rose, eds. *The Battle of Seattle: The New Challenge to Capitalist Globalization.* New York: Soft Skull Press, 2001.

Z, Pamela. Interview by Herman Gray. Telephone interview, 19 September 2001.

———. "A Tool Is a Tool." In *Women in New Media (Web Site),* ed. Judy Malloy. Cambridge, Mass.: MIT Press, forthcoming. Available at Pamela Z Web site, www.pamelaz.com/tool.htm.

Zabor, Rafi, and Vic Garbarini. "Wynton vs. Herbie: The Purist and the Crossbreeder Duke It Out." *Musician,* March 1985, 52–64.

Zook, Kristal Brent. *Color by Fox: The Fox Network and the Revolution in Black Television.* New York: Oxford University Press, 1999.

———. "How I Became the Prince of a Town Called Bel Air: Nationalist Desire in Black Television." Ph.D. diss., University of California, Santa Cruz, 1994.

Zuberi, Nabeel. "Black Whole Styles: Sounds, Technology, and Diaspora Aesthetics." In *Sounds English: Transnational Popular Music,* by Nabeel Zuberi, 131–80. Urbana: University of Illinois Press, 2001.

# Index

| | |
|---|---|
| Compositor: | Sheridan Books, Inc. |
| Text: | 10/13 Sabon |
| Display: | Sabon |
| Printer and binder: | Sheridan Books, Inc. |